Corporate DNA

T0300481

Corporate DNA

Learning from Life

Ken Baskin

with original artwork by Ethan Geehr

Routledge
Taylor & Francis Group

LONDON AND NEW YORK

First published by Butterworth-Heinemann

This edition published 2011 by Routledge
2 Park Square, Milton Park, Abingdon, Oxon OX14 4RN
711 Third Avenue, New York, NY 10017, USA

Routledge is an imprint of the Taylor & Francis Group, an informa business

Library of Congress Cataloging-in-Publication Data

Baskin, Ken, 1947–
    Corporate DNA : learning from life / Ken Baskin with original artwork by Ethan Geehr.
        p.   cm.
    Includes bibliographical references and index.
    ISBN 0-7506-9844-6 (alk. paper)
    1. Management.   2. Organization.   3. Organizational learning.
    4. Paradigms (Social sciences)   5. Biological models.   I. Title.
    HD31.B369436   1998
    658—dc21   98-5770
                                                                              CIP

British Library Cataloguing-in-Publication Data

A catalogue record for this book is available from the British Library.

To my two fathers—
my dad, Milton Samuel Baskin, and
my intellectual father, Alfred Werner

Contents

Foreword

Ken Baskin offers us a wonderful opportunity: to explore the implications of living systems for the design and management of organizations in turbulent times. He presents a rich illustration of how we can learn from nature to create organizations that will adapt and evolve with change.

Forget about reengineering!

Focus on developing the corporate DNA that can encode the capacities for life and development throughout your enterprise.

These are some of the messages that Baskin brings to the modern manager. He encourages us to learn from the example of fast, flexible organizations, and to chart a powerful course toward our unknown future guided by the principles of transformation that shape patterns of survival in the natural world.

His arguments integrate and translate some of the latest insights from the natural sciences and new research on chaos and complexity into practical management strategies that can help any organization seeking to rethink its future. He helps to show us how we can begin to shed the mechanical models that are locking it into the past.

His analysis of how information can be used as a form of "corporate identity" and how an understanding of its "corporate nervous system" can be shaped to tap the advantages of both centralized and local intelligence are particularly provocative. Coupled with a lively analysis of how patterns of evolution spread over millions of years in nature yet are taking place at a breathless speed in businesses, such as in the computer and health care industries, Ken Baskin focuses our attention on a way of thinking that challenges us to see the ecology of organizational relationships in a new light.

It is difficult to hold onto old mechanical conceptions of organization in view of the challenges presented here. I recommend this book to anyone who wants to grasp the implications of current research on living systems and what this metaphor tells us about the nature and potential of our organizations. The mode of organic thinking that Ken Baskin develops will become increasingly important as we continue to cope with challenges of the chaotic environments that are part of our journey into the 21st century.

Gareth Morgan
Author, *Images of Organization*
Distinguished Research Professor
York University, Toronto
February 1998

Acknowledgments

When I started writing this book, I thought it would be a solitary task. Just me and my computer locked for hours every day in my office. Talk about your serious misconceptions. At every turn I've been surrounded by people who've given me more help and support than I could have imagined. It seems impossible to thank each one. However, I can't skip this opportunity to mention as many as I can remember.

First of all, I couldn't have completed this book without the support and help of my wife, Martha Aleo, whose readings of the manuscript consistently pushed me to be clearer and more specific. My son, Max, also helped by sharing his very different understanding of the distinctions between machines and living things. In addition, from the beginning I've drawn on the readings of Miles Kotay, on the intellectual nourishment of Gus Jaccaci, and on the insight and editing skills of Dr. Margaret King and Jamie O'Boyle.

Another set of readers has supported me and helped redirect my attention when needed throughout the process. They include, in no particular order, Carl Whisner, Aili Pogust, Art Shostack, Ed Paxton, Larry Lemasters, Suzanne Auckerman, Roger Lewin, Birute Regine, Gregory Bruce, Joe Coates, Carol LeFaivre Rochester, John Mahaffie, Tom McNamee, Preston Ringo, Eric Spieler, Bob Yovovich, Josh Rosenthal, John Adams, Meryl Bralower, Kate Huston, Helen Harte, Steve Piersanti, and Dick Watson. I hope any others I may have overlooked won't feel slighted.

Beyond that, I want to thank the whole cast of characters who helped me in my efforts at gathering information on prototype organic corporations. At The Ritz-Carlton, they included Lauren Klein and Pat Mene. Hal Rosenbluth and Keami Lewis were also generous with their time at Rosenbluth Travel. At 3M, Lauren Sutton, Dominic Tallarico, and Geoff Nicholson provided examples that proved invaluable to demonstrating my ideas. I'd also like to extend my thanks to Georg Bauer, Doug Rozman, and Bruce Lee at Mercedes-Benz Credit Corporation.

I appreciated the time Mark Sasscer and the others, who preferred not to be mentioned by name, took to talk about the culture change at Bell Atlantic. I'm deeply indebted, too, to Tom Petzinger, Jr., who led me to use the Mercedes-Benz Credit Corporation as a model for organic transformation, then offered both support and critical readings of much of the manuscript. Finally, he introduced me to Curt Lindberg at VHA, Inc. Lindberg, in turn, helped me to make connections with Mary Ann Keyes and Debbie Zastocki, who gave me important insights into how bureaucracies can transform themselves; Linda Rausch, Jim Dwyer, Linda Dewolf, and Owen McNally, who helped me understand the power of community-based health care to transform communities; and Kelly Breazeale, Jim Roberts, and Mark Levine, who, along with Lindberg, widened my understanding of the transformation in health care markets.

Finally, I want to thank Karen Speerstra for her support while I was writing this book, and Roger Main, who never let me forget why I was writing it.

INTRODUCTION

The Einstein Dilemma

Thus, the task is not so much to see what no one yet has seen, but to think what nobody yet has thought about that which everybody sees.
—Schopenhauer

On a muggy night in August 1992, I stood on a runway at Memphis International Airport, in awe of the spectacle swirling around me. At Federal Express, they call it their "nightly miracle." Like most nights, on this one the company took over the Memphis International Airport from 11 P.M. to 5 A.M. Company jets start flying in at 11:30 P.M. The work force of 5,000 would unload a million packages, sort them over more than 200 miles of conveyor belts, and reload them. By 3:30 A.M. the jets would be in the air, delivering the packages we'd receive that day.

Outside the hangars, people swarmed, rushing simultaneously in every direction, either driving one of 7,000 vehicles that ferry packages to be sorted and reloaded, or racing on foot to some destination only they seemed to know. In the hangar where FedExers sorted packages, our boxes, cylinders, and oversized envelopes cascaded down conveyor belts. Every once in a while, a mechanical arm would bat one down a chute to another belt, apparently at random. All along the route, FedExers stood with their ubiquitous bar-code scanners to ensure the company would deliver our packages on time. And they do deliver the packages on time, about 98 percent of the time.

How, I wondered, do they do it? People were moving too fast for over-the-shoulder supervision. Not only that. Most of the 5,000 performing the nightly miracle were part-timers, many of them students from Memphis State University—no different from any of the students that CEOs love to curse as ill-prepared and undertrained for the jobs their companies offer. Yet every night, they come together as an integrated team and perform their miracle.

All of a sudden, the spectacle brought to mind another delivery system—our own circulatory system, with red blood cells rushing from

1

the heart to the lungs to pick up oxygen, back to the heart, and then out to the farthest parts of the body. Federal Express, it seemed to me, was doing something similar. It had integrated these 5,000 part-timers into its corporate body. But how?

As I toured company facilities later that day, an answer to my question formed: Federal Express could integrate 100,000 people into a single corporate body by using information much the way our own bodies do. That is, the company made sure that its people, like all the cells in our bodies, knew their jobs inside out, understood the purposes of the body as a whole, and had access to information about any procedure they wanted to know about. Federal Express had created a corporate equivalent of DNA on which its people could draw to do their jobs flawlessly without supervision and had distributed it as universally as DNA is distributed in our bodies.

This idea of a corporate body with its own DNA was a revelation to me. I had worked for bureaucracies, where people were treated as replaceable parts in a corporate machine. Most managers seemed to believe their people had little need to know anything beyond the standard operating procedures for their jobs. Now it seemed possible to run organizations in a very different way.

That, I realized, was what business writers meant when they discussed an organic model of organization. I'd come across the term about a year before as I worked on a paper about bureaucracy as a "mechanical model" for a corporate executive. An organic model seemed the logical alternative to a mechanical one. But in all my reading I couldn't find anyone to explain how an organic model would translate living things into organizations modeled on them.

Then on my visit to Federal Express, it became clear: Managers can run their organizations according to the design principles that make living systems successful. That is, they can run their organizations *as if those organizations were living things*. Intuitively, it seemed right. After all, to survive, living things must continually learn from and adapt to their environments. In today's increasingly turbulent markets, that's what corporations must do to survive. Where better to figure out how to become a learning organization than from living things, which must learn to survive?

This is hardly a revolutionary idea. In 1961, two British academics, Tom Burns and G. M. Stalker, published *The Management of Innovation*. In that book, they studied several Scottish electronics firms and identified two systems of management, the mechanistic and the organic. They concluded that mechanistic management systems are preferable for relatively stable market conditions and that organic systems work better in conditions of change. In 1961, they could say that neither system was necessarily superior: "In particular, nothing in our experience justifies the assumption that mechanistic systems should be superseded by organic in conditions of stability" (Burns and Stalker 1961). Thirty-five years later, it's difficult to identify a single industry that retains conditions of stability. As a result, organizations of all types are, as Burns and Stalker could have predicted, moving from their mechanical models to more organic ones.

In the years since my experience at Federal Express, popular business literature has examined all sorts of structures and behaviors that seem to grow from an organic model of organization. Peter Senge's ideas about learning organizations, Margaret Wheatley's thoughts about self-organization, M. Scott Peck's writing on work communities—all these draw on an organic model. In transforming this theory to a workplace reality, however, something went terribly wrong. Only a few organizations have made this transition successfully. In most organizations the theories have been subverted. Even in those that have worked hardest at change, AT&T for example, the specter of bureaucracy hangs over every attempt, disabling whatever actions they take to remake themselves for today's turbulent environment.

I'm convinced these companies are caught in the Einstein Dilemma. Asked why he was the person who realized that space and time were interconnected, Einstein replied, "Why was I the one? Normal adults never stop to think about such concerns as space and time. These are things children ask about. My secret is, I remained a child. I always asked the simplest questions" (Jones and Levenson, 1996).

Children ask these simple questions about their relationships to themselves, the universe, and other people as a matter of survival. Adults, on the other hand, have answered these questions and tested them over and over. The answers become the underlying assumptions on which we build most of our lives. They become so central to the way we see and think about life that we forget we ever asked them. When little boys in our society ask, "How should I look so people will like me?" the answer they get is, "You need to be tall and strong and have a full head of hair." Is it any wonder, then, that male leaders in both politics and business tend to be tall and athletically built and have a full head of hair?

Is that unfair? Obviously. Still we need these shared answers. Without them, working together would be impossible. Most of the time, those answers keep our world working smoothly. Our adult conviction that we know the answers only creates problems when the world changes so much that our old answers no longer work. That's what happened in physics at the beginning of the 20th century. As a result, an adult like Einstein had to re-ask basic questions so we could develop a new set of basic assumptions. This is the Einstein Dilemma. Caught between a changed world and the conviction that we already have the answers, we are trapped between old ways we know don't work and new ways we can't hope to understand. No matter how hard we try, most of us will remain trapped until we begin re-asking all the questions we were sure we'd answered.

Today much of the business world finds itself trapped in the Einstein Dilemma. The bureaucracies that thrived until about 25 years ago were built on a mechanical model. That is, when as children, we asked, "How do we put together lots of different people working together for a single purpose?" the answer was, "Put them together as if they were parts of a machine." And so from the first day we toddled into kindergarten, we learned to be one of many replaceable parts (students) whose job is to do what we are told by a leader (the teacher), someone who knows many things we don't. Our job was to follow the leader's instructions like good little walking, breathing machine parts. For most of us, this pattern would be repeated throughout elementary and high school, college, business school, and, finally, in our workplaces. We were passed and praised, then paid and promoted, for following instructions mechanically. If we were good enough at it, we would eventually become the leader and be able to tell others what to do.

Throughout the industrial age, this mechanical model of organization could be extremely effective. In a world of limited competition, relatively slow technological change, and scarce information, it made sense to have a few people at the top of an organization, who had access to a great deal of information and a superior vision of how to succeed in markets, giving the orders. The resulting bureaucracy helped AT&T make universal telephone service a reality. It enabled General Motors to become the world's leading automobile maker. It catapulted IBM to such dominance in the computer industry that competitors referred to the company, not as their competition, but as their "environment."

Over the last 25 years, however, the mechanical model of bureaucracy has broken down. With competition coming from all directions, technology improving daily, information flooding our world, no one person at the top of any organization (with the possible exception of Bill Gates at Microsoft) could direct an entire corporation the way Tom Watson, Jr. did at IBM during the 1960s. The alternative is a type of organization that capitalizes on the flood of available information by enabling people to self-organize and attack opportunities as they appear. Such organic corporations have an obvious advantage in keeping up with the ever-changing technology and customer preferences of today's markets.

However, as long as managers hold on to their old mechanical answers to the basic questions about how organizations should work, they can't expect to build such organizations. No matter how much they learn about organic behaviors, such as empowerment, and structures, such as teams or networks, they find themselves remechanizing those behaviors and structures. This is the underlying reason even Michael Hammer, the leading guru of reengineering, conceded that reengineering was a failure. Hammer had hoped that it would allow managers to rebuild their organizations so they could respond more effectively to today's rapidly changing markets. What reengineering actually did was to replace old, inefficient mechanical systems with new, highly efficient ones. But those systems were still mechanical, and as we'll see, mechanical systems make it difficult for people to innovate and adapt as we must if our organizations are to succeed in today's markets. Rather than reengineer, managers need to *deengineer* their organizations.[1] That is, they need to replace mechanical controls with more organic systems that unleash the enormous innovative energies most Americans bring to our jobs. When CEO Georg Bauer did that at Mercedes-Benz Credit Corporation, his people increased new business 84 percent, and productivity shot up 50 percent, all in only five years. Managers at any bureaucracy can generate similar results with deengineering.

Before they can build their new-style organizations successfully, however, managers must re-ask all those fundamental questions they'd figured out as children, so they can learn to think differently. The purpose of this book is to begin posing some of those questions and to examine how managers might begin answering them. If you want to learn about empowerment or teamwork, networks, or corporate redesign, this book isn't for you. There are plenty of books you can consult to learn about those topics. (Some of my favorites are listed in the chapter titled Further Reading.) My purpose in this book is to help you, as a manager, begin to develop a different, more organic way of thinking about your organization. To do that, I'll ask some of the fundamental questions about people working together I thought I'd answered long ago. Then I'll present the conclusions I've reached.

As you read, remember that my answers may not be right for your organization. My questions may not even be right. Every living thing is unique. As a result, every organically modeled organization is going to be equally unique. You'll know you've begun to understand an organic approach when you read a section of this book and think, "That can't work in my company. But if we did it a little differently...."

Some Basic Questions

The purpose of *Corporate DNA* is to help managers and others interested in an organic model learn to think about organizations as living things. To help you develop this habit of thinking, the book is structured as an extended thought experiment. That is, our explorations begin with simple questions that most of us thought we'd long ago answered, such as:

- How should organizations operate in today's markets?
- How should we integrate many people with different interests and skills into a single organization with a common purpose?
- How should we redesign our hierarchical bureaucracies so they'll be successful in today's information age markets?

Each of these megaquestions opens one of the book's three parts. The chapters in each of the parts explore a portion of the megaquestion, also stated as a question at the beginning of the chapter. Wherever possible, we'll contrast the mechanical answer that so many of us have developed to an organic alternative. We'll illustrate these alternative answers with the experiences of organizations that operate from both mechanical and organic models.

Prototype Organic Corporations

A handful of organizations serve as examples of how companies can use the design principles of living things to create competitive advantages. They represent only a few of the many companies that are using these principles today. I chose them because I came across them in my explorations and they provided powerful illustrations. None of them is perfectly organic. We are still at the bottom of the learning curve for what it means to operate organizations organically. So even the most advanced of them have enormous amounts to learn about this style of operation. Moreover, I don't hold up any of them as a model for other organizations to imitate. Because every living thing is unique, every organic corporation should be different. I've used these prototype organic corporations merely to illustrate how real organizations are using life's design principles to create competitive advantages in today's turbulent markets.

Part I examines how today's turbulent markets work. In Chapter 1, we ask what the basic dynamics governing those markets are. Our answer is that the combined forces of global competition and computer technology have made all the organizations in our markets so interdependent that they've come to behave like natural ecological systems. As a result, the basic dynamic is coevolution in a market ecology. Chapter 2 asks what this dynamic means for a key problem many managers face today—the apparent chaos of markets such as health care or telecommunications that are transforming themselves. Such markets, we find, develop very much the way natural ecological systems reform after a major disruption. By applying the principles of natural ecological formation, we can understand the processes that underlie the apparent chaos in the telecommunications or health care markets. Chapter 3 suggests how managers can apply these principles practically. In it, we work with a tool for representing market ecologies graphically, the ecograph. We also look at some of the questions managers should ask as they work to create competitive advantages for their organizations in today's markets.

Part II explores design principles managers can use to build companies that can thrive in the markets discussed in Part I. An organic model is extremely rich and suggestive. It can help us think through any issue from recruiting and rewarding people to eliminating waste from production processes. The chapters focus on five of life's key design principles to give an idea how you can use this way of thinking to examine your organization's unique challenges and opportunities.

Chapter 4 asks how managers can make sure everyone is working together for the benefit of the whole company. In it, we contrast the mechanical control bureaucracies exercise over people to the self-control organic corporations foster. Organic corporations foster such self-control by fusing the corporate vision and culture of mechanically modeled organizations into a corporate identity, which is infused into every structure in the company.

In Chapter 5, we explore the alternatives to using a company's structural and procedural information. We find that the alternative to bureaucratic placement of information only where it will be used is to make all a company's structural and procedural information available to anyone who wants it, as a corporate equivalent of DNA. When it is flexible, universally available, and aligned with corporate identity, corporate DNA becomes a tool for providing improved service, more intense corporate learning, and quicker coevolution in market ecologies.

Chapter 6 examines how companies can gather the information they need about events inside and outside the company. Together corporate DNA and a corporate nervous system enable organizations to be self-organizing. Because people in them can learn what they must react to and how to react to it, they can take advantage of challenges and opportunities as they occur.

The structure that enables living things to grow and adapt is the subject of Chapter 7. Our bodies are hierarchies of nested networks. Molecules network into organelles, organelles into cells, cells into organs, organs into organ systems, and organ systems into bodies. At each level, new capabilities emerge, and the units have the intelligence they need to do their jobs. Such an organic structure gives us a 3.5 million-year-old model for organizing people with only four or five levels. In this chapter, we look at how companies like 3M have used this structure to grow and adapt organically.

If people are doing what they think is right at any moment, how can management be sure all this activity is moving the organization in desirable directions? Our body's answer is the central nervous system, which gathers and interprets messages, coordinates activities, monitors overall health, and makes decisions for the entire body. In Chapter 8, we look at how senior management can function as a corporate central nervous system.

Part III looks at what bureaucracies working to reinvent themselves as more organic corporations can learn from the way living things grow and transform. In Chapter 9, we examine one key problem that complicates many corporate reinvention efforts—the confusion between mechanical change and organic transformation. Chapters 10 and 11 illustrate the differences between these two types of efforts by discussing the experiences of two organizations—Bell Atlantic in Chapter 10 and the Mercedes-Benz Credit Corporation in Chapter 11. Chapter 12 provides a handbook that applies what we learned in the previous chapters to the practice of corporate transformation.

As you read these words, the markets in which we work are transforming themselves. As managers we have a choice. We can fight the forces driving that transformation or we can embrace them. To managers intent on fighting transformation, I can only wish good luck. To those who would embrace the new world forming around us, *Corporate DNA* offers a different way of thinking, one that will make it much easier to navigate the turbulent markets swirling around us. The book you're now reading provides a picture of what your organizations will have to be like to prosper in the new world and a set of tools that will enable you to recreate your bureaucracies in this new image. After all, if you don't know where you're going, any road will take you there. This book offers a picture of the destination and a road map for getting there.

PART I

Market Ecologies

In the golden age of American business, in the 1950s, 1960s, and early 1970s, we Americans effortlessly dominated industries ranging from steel to health care, from petroleum to electronics, from automobiles to telecommunications. Each of these industries was controlled by either a monopoly—one phone company, one local utility—or a small group of competitors who played by the rules they themselves created—three major auto companies, seven sisters in petroleum. These markets remained stable because competition was limited (General Motors flirted for more than 20 years with a 50 percent market share of the auto industry); technological breakthroughs, like the computer or photocopying, were rare; and consumers were content with what they had.

Yet even as companies like GM were achieving their greatest successes in the mid-to-late 1960s, markets were shifting. For one thing, global competition was emerging. The Japanese challenged American dominance in steel in the late 1960s and in automobiles through the 1970s. The challenge in home electronics would follow. Soon every country in Europe and Southeast Asia seemed to be joining the chase. Even our dominance of the petroleum industry was challenged by the Organization of Petroleum Exporting Countries (OPEC) in the 1970s. At the same time, a technological revolution was accelerating the rate of change in these markets. MCI challenged the dominance of AT&T in long-distance phone service with microwave communications. Japanese electronics firms began using transistors for all kinds of products American inventors overlooked. Widespread use of computers accelerated this revolution to its current, breakneck speed.

Today the market stability in which most of us learned to manage has been replaced by turbulence. In fact, the most stable of the old markets—health care, finance-banking-insurance, and tele-communications, for example—have become the most turbulent, reinventing themselves in continually unexpected ways. The turbulence in these markets is so great that no one can guess what mix of competitors and services will emerge. What should managers do in markets where AT&T, now a declining leader in the long-distance phone service it pioneered, talks about merging with a major Baby Bell or other telephone company *in order to survive*? Where the purchase by a major insurance company of a leading health maintenance organization (Aetna and U.S. Healthcare) causes financial problems no one imagined? Or where Microsoft buys a $150 million interest in Apple Computer, the company with which it has been battling for a decade?

Even markets that seem relatively stable may not remain so when the technological revolution finally washes through them. Consider the automobile market. If you thought the invasion of foreign automobiles created turbulence, watch what happens in another ten years or so, when the fruits of the technological revolution start remaking it. What do you think will happen when light-weight braided composites—plastics stronger than steel—and high-strength ceramic motor parts become widely used in building automobiles? Using plastics and ceramics this way could result in cars considerably lighter and safer than those of today. Will markedly lighter cars finally make electric, hybrid electric-gasoline, or fuel-cell–powered motors economically viable? What if hydrogen-burning engines or solar energy becomes cost effective? And what if new parts were built to a standard that allowed you to order a car with a Ford engine, a Chrysler body, and a Toyota interior? Of course, no one knows whether any of this *will* happen, much less what it would do to automobile markets. It's much the same in nearly every market for every product and service in the world. Technology is changing so rapidly that it's increasingly difficult to plan for what will emerge. To succeed in such markets, we need a different understanding of how markets work and how our organizations can thrive in them. What, then, are the dynamics of today's turbulent, unpredictable markets?

That's the first question we need to ask as we examine what it means to think organically. An organic model suggests we should explore what happens when we think of markets as if they were natural ecologies. We do that in Chapter 1. There we find that to thrive, our organizations must coevolve in their markets. That is, as they adapt to shifts in their markets, their adaptations further alter those markets. So the need to adapt to what others in their markets are doing becomes continuous. In Chapter 2, we see what happens when we begin thinking of today's transformative markets, such as health care or telecommunications, in terms of the way natural ecological systems recreate themselves after a major disruption. In Chapter 3, we explore some of the tools organic thinking suggests managers can use to create competitive advantages in their market ecologies.

Learning a new way of thinking is difficult. Yet our markets have shifted dramatically. As managers, we have to ask whether the success of our organizations is worth the trouble of learning a new way of thinking. If it is, I invite you to join me in a journey exploring what I believe is the way our organizations must operate if they are to succeed in the turbulent markets of the 21st century.

CHAPTER 1

Coevolution Comes to Your Local Market Ecology

In fact, a world of nonstop change offers only short-term victories to those organizations that set out to beat the opposition. The long-term advantage lies with those organizations that focus on the environment as a whole, not just on the competition.

—William Bridges

Question: How can managers view today's markets in order to understand their turbulence and how organizations should operate in them?

On February 12, 1996, the *Wall Street Journal* printed an early valentine, for a love that would never be consummated, on its front page. It reported that AT&T and MCI were talking about working together to enter the market for local telephone service. Talk about future shock! The night before I'd watched these archcompetitors calling each other liars in their television commercials. Now they were talking partnership. At first I was shocked. But I quickly realized that this partnership of archrivals demonstrates how very turbulent many of our markets have become. Every day, it seems, new stories appear, recasting the basic structure of markets as different as health care, telecommunications, or banking-finance-insurance. Each is restructuring relationships between its members, introducing new technologies, and offering new ways to provide service.

In telecommunications alone, this restructuring resulted in a slew of mergers and interconnections. In just the early months of 1996, the following new connections touched every part of the market:

- The Bell Atlantic–NYNEX and Pacific Bell–SBC Baby Bell combinations to ease these companies' movement from local to long-distance telephone service

- The U.S. West and Continental Cablevision deal, the first combining a Baby Bell with a cable television provider
- The network of alliances developed for providing Internet access (AT&T with Netscape, Sun Microsystems with America Online; Microsoft with MCI and CompuServe; Sprint with America Online).

Since that time, developments have included an abortive attempt by AT&T to merge with the new Baby Bell, SBC/Pacific Bell; an attempt by British Telecom to purchase MCI, along with subsequent bids by GTE and WorldCom; America Online's purchase of CompuServe's customer base; and Microsoft's investments in both cable television giant Comcast and Apple Computer. I'm writing these words in fall 1997. By the time you read them, equally interesting developments will have further altered the industry.

And that was just established technologies. In addition, telecommunication companies have begun selling personal communications service—a less expensive, more technologically advanced service that works much like cellular technology. Before the end of the century, we can also expect satellite telephone networks, such as Motorola's Iridium, so you'll be able to communicate from any point on the globe to any other. We may even be able to make long-distance phone calls over the Internet. Still newer technologies seem likely to further transform this market. It's impossible to know, which is a manager's nightmare. How can even the most innovative managers make intelligent decisions for their companies when new technologies, competitors, and services make the market seem so chaotic?

It's a critical question. Because other markets are also transforming themselves. In health care, managed care companies like Columbia/HCA have built multibillion-dollar chains of for-profit hospitals. Not-for-profit hospitals have retaliated by merging or forming networks, such as the network led by Philadelphia's Jefferson Hospital; a pharmaceutical giant, Merck & Co., purchased drug distribution company Medco so it can manage pharmaceutical benefits to 50 million people; and another pharmaceutical giant, SmithKline Beecham, has been simultaneously negotiating to merge with either American Home Products or Glaxo Wellcome. At the same time, the distinctions between banking, insurance, and financial services have blurred. Megamergers, such as the one between Citicorp and Travelers Group, are consummated to take advantage of a market in which banking is less and less about transactions and more and more about providing financial services.

Can an organic approach to markets help us get a handle on what's happening in these kaleidoscopic markets? I think so. After all, the law of life—adapt or die—has become the law of the marketplace. By thinking of our markets as ecologies of organizations, we may be able to uncover patterns of cooperation, competition, and growth that are likely to be repeated in market after market. James Moore has already examined some implications of markets as ecologies. Moore emphasizes the full cycle of birth-maturity-decline through which ecologies and markets grow. He also focuses on business ecosystems, alliances that form to battle for share across markets (Moore 1996). Like Moore, we'll explore markets as multi-industry systems. An organic model, however, offers us an exceptionally rich metaphor on which to draw. So we'll take a different approach. We'll look more closely at why today's markets are operating more like ecologies and what that means for how we think of our organizations' operations. So let's begin with a look at why today's markets are acting so much like natural ecologies.

Markets and Natural Ecologies

In many ways, the idea of comparing markets with natural ecologies seems far-fetched. After all, markets and ecologies work very differently. Think about the element of time, for instance. It takes 20 to 40 million years to form new ecologies. Markets form in more like 20 to 40 years. *Tyrannosaurus rex* dominated its world in the Cretaceous period for something like 20 million years. General Motors dominated its market in the industrial age for about 40 years. So one market year is roughly equivalent to a million geologic years.

Organisms also require many lifetimes to evolve new forms as they respond to environmental change. Dinosaurs seem to have evolved into birds over millions of years. In one generation, some dinosaurs' genetic material may have mutated in a way that enabled their offspring to become more birdlike. But no dinosaur ever transformed *itself* into a bird. An organization, on the other hand, can evolve many times, as it adapts to its markets. AT&T, for instance, in its 1997 split into three companies, acted like a dinosaur trying to evolve into a small flock of birds. Another difference is that organizations have more control over their evolution than any species. We human beings cannot direct our own genetic mutations. If we could, my family would have long ago altered its DNA so that I'd still have a full head of hair. Organic DNA is encoded in our bodies, and we're only now learning, through genetic engineering, to what extent it's possible for us to manipulate our own genetic material. On the other hand, the organizational equivalent, corporate DNA (see Chapters 4 and 5), is *our* creation. It exists purely in our minds, and we have the power to change it whenever we want. So markets and natural ecologies have substantial differences.

Yet we have a lot to gain by examining markets *as if* they were ecologies. Both natural ecologies and markets are, after all, complex adaptive systems. That is, both are composed of many individuals, often grouped into larger units (flocks or companies, for example), which are continually making decisions. These individuals are themselves complex adaptive systems. Their decisions and their interactions link all members of the system to each other. When combined with the constant flow of information, a system of behaviors emerges from these interactions—population dynamics, for example—behaviors that could never have been predicted from the actions of any of the individuals or smaller groups in the ecology. In the African grasslands, for example, herds of zebra, antelope, and other plant-eating animals are in dynamic balance with their predators. Together, they form a system of interdependencies, in which the predators keep the plant eaters from overpopulating the grasslands, and the number of plant eaters limits the population of predators. Viewed as a system, the ecology has developed behaviors that could not exist at a less complex level.[1]

Similarly, people as individual consumers and as members of organizations come together to make up an economy. The buying choices of all these individuals limit the growth of any organization. Apple Computer, for instance, is in danger of disappearing at the end of the century, because more than 90 percent of buyers of personal computers have chosen the Microsoft-Intel standard. This market system is as interdependent as the ecology of the African grasslands. As Apple's share of the market shrinks, software writers who had been dependent on Apple computer owners must either switch to the standard or face extinction. Viewed as a system, the economy also develops behaviors that emerge only because of the interaction of various groupings. In this way, the competition between the Microsoft-Intel and Apple types of personal computers has resulted in much more useful machines than is likely to have existed if there had only been one standard without competition.

Such complex adaptive systems must continually learn and evolve through time. As evolutionary biologist Stephen Jay Gould pointed out, biological and human social systems each may be driven by a different set of principles. Yet "both are systems of historical change. More general principles of structure must underlie all systems that proceed through history . . ." (Gould 1991). What, then, can we learn by applying some of the basic principles of natural ecologies to today's markets?

Coevolution and Adaptive Ripples

Natural ecologies are interdependent systems that emerge from the interaction of the members of species of which they are composed. What's important in an ecology is not individuals *but relationships between them*. For instance, some acacia trees have hollow thorns and small food packets at the base of their leaves. A species of ants lives in these thorns and eats the food packets. In return, the ants protect the acacias from other insects and small plant-eating mammals. This relation seems to have evolved when some acacias mutated to produce the food packets. Natural selection favored trees that made the packets available, because the ants they attracted protected them from attack. It also favored the ants that protected the trees, because these ants had an easy source of food and, as the hollow thorns evolved, a protected place to live. Curiously, although researchers have found this relation throughout the Americas, Africa, and Europe, it hasn't developed in Australia where there are no small, plant-eating mammals to threaten the acacias (Grant 1984).

These species thrived by adapting genetically to meet each other's needs. That is, they didn't so much *evolve* as *coevolve*. In any ecology, many similar interdependent relations coevolve over time. As a result, we can't understand such an ecology by looking only at individual species within it. The real story of any ecology is in the coevolution of its interdependencies and the way the interdependencies hold the ecology together.

Because these interrelations form a web that interconnects all members of an ecology, any significant change by any member can send ripples of adaptation throughout the system. For instance, about 140 million years ago, the body design of plant-eating dinosaurs shifted. They evolved from high-browsers, such as the brontosaurus, which grazed on leaves high on trees, to low-browsers, such as duck-billed dinosaurs, which ate much closer to the ground. Until that time, plant life could grow slowly. Trees, for example, were generally safe until they grew high enough for high-browsers to graze on their leaves and could produce relatively few seeds, often as cones. Low-browsing dinosaurs, however, ate the cone-like seeds and grazed on young trees, making it difficult for the trees to mature and reproduce. Plant life had to adapt to this new reality or face extinction. Life's answer to this challenge appears to have been the first flowering plants, which developed at about this time. Flowering plants grow quickly and spread many seeds. They were the perfect adaptation to this change in the ecology (Bakker 1986).

In turn, the introduction of flowering plants had an enormous effect on their ecologies. For instance, insects began to thrive about the time that flowering plants spread on land. In addition, birds evolved from dinosaurs at roughly this time. It may be just coincidence that flowering plants and birds evolved at about the same time. Still, the appearance of flowering plants altered the world for birds and insects, both of which became highly dependent on flowers. Taken together, these changes transformed ecologies across the planet and led to the natural world we know today. This progression of evolutionary developments—low-browsing, plant-eating dinosaurs, flowering plants, new types of insects, birds—illustrates the way one change in a highly interdependent natural ecology sends out a ripple of adaptation that can travel through an entire system.

Adaptive Ripples in Markets

In *The Death of Competition,* Moore (1996) uses the automobile industry as a key example of how business ecologies are born, mature, and decline. One weakness in his analysis is that through most of the history of the industry, automobile makers made it difficult for other parties in their markets to coevolve with them. After an initial honeymoon with workers, automobile makers seemed to treat their employees as enemies, hiring goons to literally beat off attempts at organizing unions. They also seemed to compete with suppliers, playing them off against each other to drive down the price on most items. Until 20 to 30 years go, this way of connecting in markets worked. Today it mostly creates problems. For instance, GM continues to treat employees adversarially. As a result, it provokes repeated strikes and, unlike Chrysler or Ford, has pushed suppliers to cut costs in a most unpartnerlike way. It's no coincidence that GM continues to lose market share to these competitors. From our point of view, unless organizations recognize that they need other parties in their markets to work *with* them—that is, to coevolve for the benefit of *all* parties—they'll be in deep trouble.

This shift points to one of the key differences between yesterday's mechanical model of organization and today's organic model. The purpose of a machine is to generate the same products over and over as efficiently as possible. Living things, on the other hand, can exist only by nurturing coevolutionary relations in their ecologies. Organizations with mechanical models think of their purpose as creating products or services; those with organic models focus on managing relationships with other parties in their market ecologies. That explains why Intel and Microsoft could steal leadership of the personal computer industry from IBM and Apple. Whereas IBM and Apple believed that the most important thing in their market was the boxes they built for desktops, Intel and Microsoft were busy managing the network of computer makers, part makers, software writers, distributors, and customers.

One reason relationships have become so critical is that today's markets are much more integrated, and the organizations within them more interdependent than the ones we grew up with. To be successful in these markets, companies in every industry are developing mutually beneficial relationships with:

- *Suppliers.* In industrial-age markets, manufacturers intentionally cultivated many suppliers for any part so they'd never become dependent on any one supplier. Then they'd play one supplier off against another to nail down the best deal. No more. Today, just-in-time inventory control, whereby parts are delivered as needed, enables companies to drive down costs. But it also demands strong working relationships between manufacturers and their suppliers, relationships so close that the boundary between the two is all but dissolved. (For an example of how powerful this destruction of boundaries can be, look at the discussion of 3M's Integrated Solutions in Chapter 7.) Similarly, Wal-Mart became America's leading retailer by working directly with suppliers rather than buying through distributors. This required extremely close relationships with the suppliers. Suppliers and those they supply are becoming partners in each others' success.

- *Customers.* In the industrial age, manufacturers focused on products. Their experts "knew" what customers needed. That's the real meaning of Henry Ford's comment, "You can have any color car you want, as long as it's black." The job of marketing was to stimulate customers to want those products. Today, with increased competition, customer sophistication, and rapid new product introduction, the balance of power has shifted. Today companies as different as Ford, Hewlett-Packard, and Microsoft recognize the importance of giving customers what *they* want by including them in product development efforts. We are moving from a focus on *products* that will meet customer needs to a focus on meeting the needs defined by a *relationship* with the customer.
- *Competitors.* Even 20 years ago, the idea that archrivals, such as MCI and AT&T, might work together was ridiculous. But in 1991, the two companies that had battled to set the standard in personal computers—IBM and Apple—announced not one, but two joint ventures. In addition, all three major American car markers are now working together to create a commercially viable battery for the electric cars they want to develop. In today's markets, even companies that compete aggressively are more and more likely to join forces.

This growing interdependence is creating true market ecologies that demonstrate the same adaptive ripples as natural ecologies. One of the best examples of this phenomenon is the way the personal computer market—or at least the vast majority based on the Intel-Microsoft standard—restructures itself every time Intel introduces a new microchip. The microchip is the engine that drives a personal computer. Every time Intel introduces a more powerful chip, it becomes possible to build more powerful personal computers. The more powerful machines enable applications software, such as word processors and spreadsheets, to do more. Customers, at first delighted with new capabilities, soon begin to realize the limitations of their new software. Their increased expectations then set the stage for the next increase in chip power. And the cycle begins again (Figure 1–1).

Consider, for example, what happened after Intel introduced its 80386 chip.[2] Intel in late 1986 started shipping the 386 chip, substantially

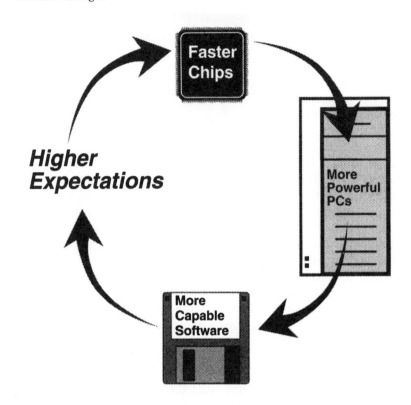

FIGURE 1-1   PC Improvement Cycle.

more powerful than its 80286, for IBM-compatible personal computers. The first computer maker to incorporate the new chip was Compaq. Using the earlier Intel 286 chip, Compaq had already become the leading IBM "clone" maker, manufacturing personal computers based on the IBM standard. In 1985, Compaq had been working to upgrade its personal computers. Learning that Intel was preparing a chip substantially more powerful than the 286, Compaq committed to building its new computers on the Intel 386. As a result, in September 1986 Compaq brought out the first personal computers with the new chip. Throughout 1987, other IBM clone makers switched to the more powerful 386.

As these new, more powerful personal computers became available, software writers could develop new, more capable software applications. In November 1987, for example, Microsoft released versions of its word processing program, Word, and its spreadsheet, Excel, for these more powerful machines.

IBM, on the other hand, was in no hurry to integrate the 386. Rather than thinking in terms of adapting to a rapidly changing technology, IBM managers thought in terms of controlling the market. After all, IBM had invented the personal computer standard when it contracted with Microsoft to supply an operating system and with Intel to supply a microchip. By 1984, IBM owned half the market for personal computers, 75 percent among businesses. However, IBM was losing share to clones, who turned out less-expensive machines on the IBM standard, because IBM had allowed Microsoft and Intel to sell the operating system and chip it was using to these other computer makers. In 1986, IBM was planning to regain control of this market by establishing a *new* personal computer standard with its PS/2 computer. So IBM held off on incorporating the 386.

Things didn't quite work out the way IBM managers had predicted. To their surprise, the clone makers' new 386 machines met market needs for more powerful personal computers and started eating further into Big Blue's market share. By the time IBM was ready to introduce its PS/2 in April 1987, it was forced to incorporate the 386 chip in its new offering. Unfortunately, even the 386 didn't help PS/2 sales. Because IBM was trying to set a new standard, the software that worked on old IBM 286 machines couldn't run on the PS/2. And because the PS/2 was so new, little applications software was available for it. IBM had tried to dominate the market rather than adapt to changes in it. So its PS/2 turned out to be a disaster.

But that wasn't the only effect of IBM's refusal to adapt to changes in its market ecology. At the time, IBM and Microsoft were competing to make IBM-compatible computers easier to use. Microsoft's operating system, MS-DOS, required users to type in commands, strings of letters and numbers that tell the computer what to do. Although some users enjoyed the challenge of having to memorize these commands, others preferred the alternative, introduced commercially with Apple's Macintosh computer in 1984. This user-friendly graphic user interface (GUI) operating system enabled users to perform computer operations by pointing to icons, pictures that suggested the operation, or by choosing items from a menu. For example, with a Mac, one could delete a file by dragging the icon of a file folder into the on-screen drawing of a trash can.

By 1986, IBM and Microsoft were competing to develop a GUI operating system for IBM-compatible computers. Microsoft introduced its first attempt, Windows 1.0, in 1985 to less-than-rave reviews. When the 386 came on the market, Microsoft switched Windows development to the 386. IBM, on the other hand, continued writing its operating system, OS/2, for the 286.

With a considerable lead in developing such an operating system, Microsoft was able to beat out IBM. In 1990 Microsoft introduced Windows 3.0, the first successful GUI operating system for IBM-compatible personal computers. Microsoft's superior knowledge of Windows 3.0 enabled the company to dominate the markets for word-processing and spreadsheet programs. Within a year of bringing Windows 3.0 on the market, the Microsoft share of these programs leapt from about 10 percent to about 60 percent.

Within six years of the introduction of the 386 chip, the personal computer market had been restructured. Starting with the new microchip, this adaptive ripple led to more powerful computers; more capable software; a new operating system, Windows 3.0, which cemented Microsoft's control of operating systems; and an enormous advantage for Microsoft in applications software. Microsoft and Compaq, with fast, effective adaptation, became stronger and healthier. Companies like IBM that refused to adapt, suffered. By the first quarter of 1996, Compaq's market share of personal computers in the United States stood at more than 12 percent. IBM's had fallen to less than 8 percent.

Markets Old and New

This new-style market (personal computers are only the first fully developed example) differs from industrial age markets in more ways than their greater interdependence. Consider the differences in the rise of Microsoft and that of Xerox. The photocopier technology that gave birth to Xerox was first commercialized in 1954. For more than 20 years, Xerox controlled that technology and virtually monopolized the market. It was only in the mid 1970s, as new technologies for photocopying became available, that Xerox had to compete.

Although both companies developed around new technologies, the markets of Xerox and Microsoft seem almost entirely different:

- Xerox faced no competition for 20 years. Microsoft faced competition from its inception. The current technological revolution is generating multiple new ways of doing almost everything. So it's almost impossible to imagine only one company in a market as potentially lucrative as photocopying. Even though Microsoft built a monopoly position in personal computer operating systems new developments, such as the popularity of the Internet, force it to readjust continually and bring out new products.
- Xerox could largely succeed as a stand-alone company. Microsoft, on the other hand, owes its success to relationships. Its first successes occurred as a result of its partnership with IBM and Intel. Later, Microsoft capitalized on the efforts of Apple and the IBM clone makers by writing applications software for both. Microsoft has been able to succeed only to the extent that it can help its partners succeed.
- As a stand-alone producer, Xerox could introduce improvements in its copiers on its own schedule. Without competitors, customers were entirely dependent on the company. Microsoft, however, suc-

ceeded by adapting to and taking advantage of every change in its market, *even when the changes ran counter to founder Bill Gates's vision*. For instance, in 1984 Gates asked the legendary question about why anyone would want more than 640 kilobytes of memory in a computer. By the mid 1990s Microsoft Word demanded nearly 40 times as much memory just for that one program!

Summary

We've begun exploring how our markets have become more like natural ecologies. The similarities between these two complex adaptive systems have been amplified in recent years, as market members—competitive producers, suppliers, and consumers—have become more and more interrelated. This interrelation has now become so intense that in many markets introduction of a product or new way of serving customers in any part can send adaptive ripples throughout the market. As a result, companies in such market ecologies face a different set of challenges than they did in yesterday's markets. Even a company that introduces a powerful new technology must now expect to face intense competition, must build or become part of a market alliance (James Moore's business ecosystems) and nurture relationships within it, and must continually improve on the technology.

Surviving in these market ecologies is most difficult in markets that are transforming themselves. The turbulence in these market ecologies is so intense that they often seem chaotic. Yet researchers now studying complex systems insist that chaos is actually a form of order that we don't yet understand (Kauffman 1995). Organic thinking can help us understand the dynamics that underlie the apparent chaos in transformative market ecologies. So we turn to the study of how natural ecologies recreate themselves after they are disrupted to see whether the dynamics of that process can illuminate what is happening today in transformative market ecologies.

CHAPTER 2

The Dynamics of Chaotic Markets: How Market Ecologies Form

The mass extinctions cleared out old communities, allowing a rediversification of creatures vastly different from those of before.
—Peter Ward

Question: What can we learn about the way today's transformative market ecologies are recreating themselves by studying natural ecologies?

Of all the markets transforming themselves today, health care may be the most turbulent. Like other transformative markets, health care is recreating itself with mergers and new forms of service. Yet something more is going on in health care. Consider, for example, the way Columbia/HCA, which seemed to be a dominant force in managed health care in mid 1997, was plagued early in 1998, by both federal fraud investigations and falling profits. Or SmithKline Beecham's on-again, off-again merger with American Home Products, then Glaxo Wellcome. What makes health care so turbulent is the war between managed-care insurers and health care providers for control of this $1 trillion-per-year market.

In one recent battle, in October 1997 about 200 physicians in southern New Jersey petitioned the National Labor Relations Board (NLRB) for union representation in bargaining with AmeriHealth health maintenance organization (HMO). The shocker here wasn't merely that physicians wanted to unionize. A few such unions already exist. What was surprising about this petition was the sense of desperation that seemed to drive it. After all, these New Jersey physicians were contractors with the HMO, rather than direct employees. The NLRB's initial ruling dismissed the petition (Moore-Duncan 1998) because, as independent contractors, the law clearly did not cover them. The physicians' lawyers must have recognized how little chance there would be that the NLRB would approve the petition. Yet the physicians were so frustrated by the HMO rules and regulations limiting their freedom in treating patients that they filed the petition anyway.

As with the confrontation between these physicians and Ameri-Health, the battle lines are clear-cut. For HMO executives, the issue is cutting the skyrocketing costs that drove health care costs to more than 13 percent of the gross domestic product by the late 1980s. As one HMO executive stated his position, "We see people as numbers, not patients. It's easier to make a decision. Just like Ford, we're a mass-production medical assembly line, and there is no room for the human equation in our bottom line. Profits are king" (*Wall Street Journal*, June 18, 1997). People running HMOs, concerned mostly with skyrocketing costs, are intent on reducing health care to a business, the human equivalent of, say, automobile repair. Patients are to be objects of a corporate assembly line; cost containment is the key measure of corporate performance. Decisions must be made objectively so patients don't receive unneeded, expensive treatment.

Health care providers, on the other hand, believe that cost control is only one element in this equation. For them, each patient and condition may be unique; so choosing the right treatment demands a relationship enabling the provider to understand the patient. Anyone who's had first-class medical care knows how comforting it is to be treated by doctors and nurses who know and care about us. Health care providers insist that their judgment be primary because their relationships with patients are the only way to know when standard treatments might not be appropriate.

The media love this confrontation because it gives them dramatic stories where evil insurance companies (as a general rule, no one likes insurance companies anyway) refuse needed treatment to innocent policy holders (it's better when they're mothers or children). Sometimes the insurers even know they need those treatments. Everyday, it seems, more stories appear about people who die or are deformed for life because of such callous treatment. As a result of the media attention, politicians further roil the waters with actions to prove they're on the right side of this battle. According to *The Economist* (March 7, 1998), more than 1,000 bills appeared in state legislatures last year to correct managed care's perceived abuses. President Clinton is getting into the act with the "Patients' Bill of Rights" now scheduled to appear around the end of March.

Through all this turmoil, however, a new health care system is emerging. The key questions we can pose to managers in that market are as follows: Can an organic model help us understand the dynamics of this market and the patterns beneath the turmoil? Can it help managers develop tools to make more intelligent decisions? We'll return to health care toward the end of this chapter. First, however, we need to look at how natural ecologies recreate themselves after major disruptions and what that means for transformative markets.

Ecologies recreate themselves in two ways. First, after mass extinction, entire ecologies are wiped out and life's interconnections must develop again from scratch. That's what happened 65 million years ago, when a comet apparently destroyed ecological systems across the planet, killing off the dinosaurs. Second, major disruptions can transform ecologies when a shift at one level has far-reaching effects, recreating existing patterns of life. For example, the evolution of low-browsing, plant-eating dinosaurs 140 million years ago set off exactly such a recreation. This distinction also applies to market ecologies. Markets for personal computers, for example, formed from scratch. There was no personal computer infrastructure, and the people who used mainframes or mini-computers were not, at first, interested in personal computers. On the other hand, the health care market was already mature when market disruptions forced it to transform itself.

The dynamics of these sister processes are similar, although transformation in mature systems is messier. So we'll ground ourselves in the process by looking at how ecologies form from scratch and apply what we learn to the growth of the personal computer market ecology. Then we'll examine ecological transformation and apply it to what is happening today in health care markets.

The Dinosaurs Are Dead! Long Live the Mammals!

You're probably familiar with much of the story of the death of the dinosaurs 65 million years ago. Most scientists agree that the dinosaurs were finished off by a comet that struck the earth, although it seems populations were softened by a series of small shocks—climate shifts, changes in sea level, and so forth—over about two million years. The impact of the comet seems to have produced what geologist Peter Ward called "a fiery hell of burning forests over much of the earth's surface, accompanied by giant tidal waves and great volumes of poisonous gas" (Ward 1994). As a result, about half of all species on the planet died out.

When the smoke cleared, a great deal about the environment had shifted for the survivors. For one thing, climatic conditions were very different from the ones in which the survivors had evolved. Moreover, many species had died off. As a result, the structure of relationships and interactions, sometimes referred to as a *foodweb*, was severely disrupted and may have collapsed. In this new world, the traits evolved by species over centuries to make them successful in their stable ecologies—that is, the ones that supported their interdependencies—no longer worked. The rules of survival became very different.

Plant life would be able to regenerate itself within a couple hundred years. Animal life, on the other hand, would take millions of years to replenish itself. This process of recreation works through the logic of succession, through a series of what I call *feeding levels*—first plant life, then plant eaters, then carnivores. Because it transforms energy in the environment into basic nutrition, plant life proliferated first. Plant species would interact with other plants, and with the remaining insects, reptiles, birds, and mammals. New species would invade from time to time. Some would become integrated into the newly developing ecologies. Others would fall out.

When the feeding level of plant life had become relatively stable, a similar process could begin on the feeding level of plant eaters. Freed from the interdependencies of old ecologies, life experimented with new animal forms to see what would work best in this new environment. As the level of plant eaters began to stabilize, carnivores would also become increasingly integrated into the ecological mix. Other levels, parasites, for instance, or hyperparasites that feed on ordinary parasites, developed. Eventually enough interdependencies redeveloped that ecologies "popped"—that is, a foodweb reestablished itself, interconnecting all members.

Before an ecology pops, new species can invade easily. Afterward, the ecological system becomes increasingly stable and more difficult to invade, as if an invisible wall had been thrown around it. Once they become fully mature, these ecologies can be invaded only by evolutionary developments such as the low-browsing, plant-eating dinosaurs or by invasion by species, such as rats or humans, whose behavior enables them to severely disrupt almost any existing ecology.

This process of evolving a new ecology took tens of millions of years. Moreover, it remained dynamic, producing remarkable life forms, such as the woolly mammoth and the saber-tooth tiger. With this process, life developed ecologies that have generally remained stable up to our own time. The following four principles[1] stand out in this process of formation and maintenance of ecological systems.

Punctuated Equilibrium

Evolution operates by means of punctuated equilibrium. It is the evolutionary reflection of the alternation between stable and chaotic states that researchers in complexity theory have identified in all complex adaptive systems. Long periods of relative ecological stability are punctuated with mass extinctions, such as the one 65 million years ago. It's as if diversity grows in stable periods and must be pruned during mass extinction to make way for new growth. After the pruning, life experiments to see what will work best in the new world.

Different Rules

After the events that cause a mass extinction, species find themselves subject to different rules for survival. Most species, unable to adapt to these rules, die off. Dinosaurs, for example, were unable to adapt to the different rules caused by shifts culminating in the impact of the comet. The dinosaurs' genetic packages were adapted very well for their old environments, but could not adapt to the environmental shift. Some mammals, on the other hand, were able to adapt, so they thrived. All in all, 99.9 percent of all species that once lived on Earth have become extinct. Over the course of evolution—3.5 billion years or so—life seems to have favored the species with the greatest ability to evolve and adapt to different rules, sometimes called *evolvability*.

Survival of the Luckiest

Why did some mammals win this extinction sweepstakes while others lost? It was not survival of the fittest. In fact, many of the animals fittest for the old environment may have had the greatest difficulty surviving in the new world. Those that did survive, mammals, for example, had developed characteristics that enabled them to adapt to the new rules as a side effect of their normal evolution. These survival characteristics may have had nothing to do with the characteristics these mammals developed to survive in the stable state of dinosaur-dominated ecologies. Luck, in addition to evolvability, played a key part in the extinction sweepstakes.

Gould describes two laws of life that we can consider elements of survival of the luckiest—contingency and incumbency (Gould 1991). With *contingency*, long strings of events that seem unimportant can result in major advantages. For instance, we are not sure why mammals survived and the dinosaurs died off. It may have been that mammals' smaller size made survival in the new world easier. Yet mammals became smaller because they had lost the battle to be dominant 140 million years before. If that's true, the survival of mammals was contingent on events that made their lives more difficult when they occurred. *Incumbency* makes it easier for living things to keep an advantage once they achieve it. Once mammals became dominant, it was likely that they would retain their dominance. Similarly, once dinosaurs became dominant in their ecologies, incumbency made it easy for them to maintain their dominance for more than 140 million years.

Succession

When ecologies start, they form by means of succession. The first things to stabilize in an ecology are often the ones on which other species are most dependent. Once this feeding level begins to stabilize, the feeding level most dependent on it can also begin to stabilize. Predators cannot thrive and form stable patterns until there is a stable population of plant eaters, and plant eaters cannot thrive until there is a sufficient population of plant life.

Rise of the Personal Computer

These principles offer an excellent way of thinking about the formation of new market ecologies. We'll illustrate with a look at the formation of the personal computer market—the most fully developed market ecology to date.[2]

Punctuated Equilibrium

Personal computers first appeared in the mid 1970s. Before that, all computing was done with mainframes, a market IBM dominated with a 70 percent share, and the smaller minicomputers introduced in the late 1960s by Digital Equipment Company. These computers centralized the power of large-scale computational tasks, such as payrolls for large corporations, in a single machine. This market was centralized in another way: Computer users were dependent on one company for both hardware and software, and one company's software could be used only on that company's hardware.

The event that opened the possibility of personal computers, the "comet" that punctuated the equilibrium of the market, was Intel's invention of the microchip in 1971. It became possible to put the brains of a computer on a piece of silicon the size of a thumbnail. As a result, the mid-to-late 1970s saw a proliferation of experiments in personal computers, as we would expect at the beginning of any ecological formation. The Altair appeared in 1975 and the Apple I in 1976. In 1977, Apple introduced its Apple II, Tandy its TRS-80, and Commodore its PET. In 1979, the first software "killer app," VisiCalc, a spreadsheet that users found extremely valuable, and the first important word-processing program, WordStar, appeared.

Different Rules

In 1981, IBM decided to enter the personal computer market. By the end of 1982, it was well on the way to setting the standard for the new industry, so much so that *Time* magazine declared the IBM personal computer "Machine of the Year" for 1982. Curiously, IBM succeeded initially by disregarding its own company procedures. IBM's corporate culture was ideal for the relatively stable mainframe computer market. The company would succeed in the different rules of the per-sonal computer market, however, by ignoring that culture.

IBM formed a group to develop the new personal computer. This group worked as a separate entity nearly 1,000 miles from corporate headquarters. The new group bought parts that were not developed by IBM—microchips from Intel and the MS-DOS operating system from Microsoft. The idea of using parts not built by IBM was unthinkable in its corporate culture. However, set off from the company, the personal computer team could react to the different rules of this market, rather than toeing IBM's mainframe corporate line.

The IBM personal computer group was able to adapt to these different rules, then, only because the company was in a hurry to bring out a new product. The company clearly did not understand the new rules and made critical errors from the beginning. Instead of insisting on some measure of control over MS-DOS and the Intel microchip, IBM allowed these companies to sell their products to other computer makers without restriction. As a result, IBM's 1982 success was balanced by the appearance that year of the first clones, personal computers that could run the same software as the IBM personal computer.

Companies like Compaq, Dell, AST, and Leading Edge, born amid the different rules of the personal computer industry and without IBM's bureaucratic overhead, were able to make personal computers less expensively than IBM, buying their microchips from Intel and their operating systems from Microsoft. When IBM was unable to keep up with orders for its personal computers, Compaq, in particular, moved in to take advantage and developed a reputation for high-quality, well-designed machines. In 1983, its first full year, Compaq had sales of $111 million.

IBM's inability to understand these different rules became even clearer in 1983, when Intel introduced a new chip, the radically faster 286. IBM's PC XT, based on the 286, had serious problems for its first nine months on the market. Compaq, on the other hand, introduced a line of high-quality 286-based machines and took over the part of the business market that wanted faster machines and couldn't wait for IBM to fix all its mistakes.

We've already seen how IBM resisted adaptation to Intel's introduction of the 386 chip two years later (see Chapter 1). Even though it controlled about half the market for personal computers in early 1984, IBM's inability to adapt to the different rules of the personal computer market marked the company for the decline it would experience.

Survival of the Luckiest

The story of the evolution of the personal computer market ecology is largely about the rise of Microsoft. Because Bill Gates cultivated his image as a visionary, it's easy to assume the success of Microsoft is a result of his vision. In many ways, however, the success depended more on Gates's ability to take advantage of events he hadn't expected. As in natural ecologies, the dominance of Microsoft is the result of survival of the luckiest.

For example, Microsoft's dominance in personal computer software was built on the operating system it supplied to IBM in 1981. Yet when IBM first asked Bill Gates about an operating system, he suggested Gary Kildall's CP/M, then the most technologically advanced. However, when IBM went to meet with him, Kildall was on a business trip, and his wife refused to sign IBM's confidentiality agreement. Later, Kildall didn't return IBM's phone calls. Only when it couldn't deal with Kildall did IBM ask Gates to supply the operating system. This is contingency with a vengeance.

Or consider the luck involved when in the mid 1980s Microsoft MS-DOS became the standard personal computer operating system. During the 1984 Super Bowl, Apple showed its commercial for the Macintosh, the first personal computer with a graphic user interface, which enabled users to do their computer work with visual symbols rather than strings of numbers and letters. The Mac operating system would remain more technologically advanced and user friendly than Microsoft operating systems for a decade. Yet because Apple decided not to license its operating system, no Apple clones appeared. The Mac operating system made Apple machines the technological elite and gave the company the highest profitability in the industry. But with clones excluded from that technology, MS-DOS became the standard. Once again, Microsoft's rise was contingent on events over which it had no control.

Succession

As with a natural ecology, personal computer markets stabilized through the logic of feeding levels—first hardware, then applications software, and now networking. The hardware level had to stabilize first. This level includes all the companies that contribute to the box on your desktop that enables you to run your applications software. In addition to the organizations that actually assemble your personal computer (Apple, IBM, or Compaq, for example), the hardware level includes microprocessor manufacturers (Intel or Motorola); operating system writers (Microsoft or Apple); as well as the makers of a variety of devices, from computer boards to printers to monitors, as well as the many components that each of them include. The hardware level must stabilize first, because applications software is written for a specific operating system, which enables the computer to run applications and do the basic jobs such as saving documents in files. As long as there was no standard operating system on the hardware level, it was impossible for the applications software market to stabilize. As the applications software market began to stabilize, the next logical level was networking, getting people to work together.

The first phase in the formation of the personal computer market was hardware stabilization, from 1975 to 1986. As with natural ecologies, there were a wide variety of experiments—from Tandy's TRS-80 and the Apple II to the Commodore Amiga. New entries to the market ecology came and went, depending on the ability of the companies to meet different rules. By 1984, the market was beginning to form around the IBM personal computer standard—Microsoft operating system and Intel microchip. Apple might have changed that with its Mac operating system. But by 1986, it had become clear that the Microsoft-Intel standard would dominate. Since that time, it has maintained a minimum 80 percent market share.

To take advantage of their incumbency, both Microsoft and Intel have continually upgraded their products—Intel with its series of X86 chips and the Pentium, Microsoft with Windows 3.0, Windows NT, and Windows 95. Both companies continue to raise the quality of the standard with which more than 80 percent of the market is compatible, much as species evolve to be more fit for their ecologies. As a result, the companies drive computer makers and software writers to continue developing in the directions they set, strengthening the interdependence between all the members in this standard segment of the market ecology.

The software applications level remained in flux a few years longer than the hardware level. In 1986, WordPerfect was the top word-processing program, selling three times as many copies as Microsoft Word. By early 1989, WordPerfect's lead had dropped to only a 50 percent advantage. Then, in 1990, Microsoft introduced Windows 3.0, which would sell 1 million copies in its first year. In an application of the power of incumbency, Microsoft software writers used their advanced knowledge of Windows 3.0 to develop new versions of Word and Excel, the company's already popular spreadsheet. Within a year, the company controlled 60 percent of the markets for both applications. By 1991, the applications software level of the personal computer market had stabilized.

A third level continues to develop, threatening to throw the other two feeding levels out of their hard-won stability. In the late 1980s, corporate personal computer users began to realize how much they could gain from having individual users networked so they could exchange documents or even work together. Novell made its name as a software company with programs that enabled companies to create such proprietary in-house computer networks. By late 1995, Lotus Notes had become the leader in networking software. That's why IBM bought Lotus for $2.7 billion, so it could make its advanced operating system, OS/2, more attractive by including Lotus Notes.

A funny thing happened to IBM on the way to the bank. By early 1996, the Internet, the *uber*network that links computer networks worldwide, which had been most popular with nerds, geeks, hackers, and other cult-like devotees, started to go mainstream. Intel's Pentium chip, increasingly powerful low-priced computers, and modems that enabled users to communicate data at ever-faster speeds, all came together. Suddenly it was easier and easier to get on the Internet. By early 1996, more than 11 million Americans were obtaining access through commercial services. Not surprisingly, the leading services—America Online, CompuServe and Prodigy—had been joined by a new offering from Microsoft. Then both AT&T and MCI offered their long-distance customers temporary free access to the Internet.

As a result of all this, one component of the Internet, the World Wide Web, has become so popular that even beer and automobile companies are including their Web addresses in television advertisements. The Web is a graphically oriented system that makes it relatively easy 34to acquire all sorts of information, in text, video, and music. School children are putting up their own Web pages. Today, you can obtain everything from vacation reservations to electronic magazines, called *zines*, on the Web. You can even be hired for a new job without leaving your home.

This growth in the Web calls into question whether IBM's purchase of Lotus is another sign of its inability to understand the different rules of the market. Lotus Notes gave IBM a powerful tool for helping companies create intranets, proprietary company networks, on the Internet. In Chapter 11, for example, we'll see how Mercedes-Benz Credit Corporation used Lotus Notes to help make its corporate transformation. So it seems likely that IBM has made hundreds of millions of dollars of sales leveraging Lotus Notes. At the same time, IBM's culture has driven away many of the most innovative minds at Lotus. If the market makes another shift, will the remaining people at what was Lotus be able to help IBM coevolve with it? IBM seems likely to need that help. It's had enormous problems in creating powerful software. In any case, buying Lotus no longer seems to be the sure thing it must have seemed when IBM purchased the company.

By the end of 1995, the interconnective feeding level of the personal computer industry was becoming increasingly competitive. Microsoft introduced a service to provide Internet access, The Microsoft Network, and has begun offering content for the Web, including its zine, *Slate*, and MSNBC, the cable news channel/Web site it developed with NBC. In the spring of 1996, it introduced its Web browser, Microsoft Explorer, and has since engaged in a pitched battle for dominance in that product with Netscape's Navigator. Microsoft pursued its battle with Netscape extremely aggressively, reportedly insisting, for example, that hardware makers bundle Explorer with the software on computers they sold or face retaliation. As a result, the U.S. Department of Justice is investigating Microsoft for antitrust violations, and, in March 1998, Senate investigators questioned Bill Gates as to whether his practices are anti-competitive. Gates, once again, seems to be winning the competitive battle. The question he seems not to have asked is whether the ill-will he's creating throughout his market ecology will come back to haunt him.

In addition to all this, we have the curious case of Sun Microsystems, a company best known for its workstations. These machines are desktop computers more expensive and powerful than personal computers and are used mostly for computer-aided design and scientific number crunching. The Sun Microsystems server has become the leading computer for connecting networks to the Internet. In 1994, Sun Microsystems introduced Java, a programming language that may someday allow your computer to borrow and use programs on the Internet. Today, the speed at which computer data is communicated is much too slow for borrowing programs from the Internet to be practical. If Java works the way some of its champions believe it will, this development on the third level of the personal computer market ecology could have much the same effect as the evolution of low-browsing, plant-eating dinosaurs 140 million years ago when it provoked formation of the mix of flowering plants, insects, and birds that we know today.

If Java does make it possible to store software programs on the Internet and borrow them only when needed, we'll no longer need computers with 32MB of RAM (random access memory) and a couple gigabytes of hard drive, the minimum acceptable as of August 1997. Moreover, because Java can run on any operating system, if we could borrow programs from the Internet, we'd no longer need a Microsoft operating system. In this way, Java is a direct challenge to Microsoft's dominant position. Already, several companies are selling stripped-down "network computers," sometimes called "thin-client devices," that could be used to borrow Java programs on the Internet. The leading maker of network computers, Network Computing Devices, sells machines mostly for use on corporate networks. However, with the current low price at about $700 per machine, and likely to fall, network computers might become attractive to home-computer buyers when rapid data communication makes it practical to borrow programs on the Internet. Other leading sellers of these machines include popular computer sellers IBM and Hewlett-Packard, both of which would welcome a wider market for network computers.

The market continues to shift too rapidly, however, for us to have any idea whether Java will be successful in challenging Microsoft. On one hand, since late 1997, $1,000 personal computers have become widely available. A recent report (*Philadelphia Inquirer*, March 12, 1998) even notes that new computers, with enough features for most buyers, are available for only a little more than $500. So the cost advantage of network computers is becoming less important. Still, Microsoft is taking the Java challenge seriously. In April 1996, it signed agreements with Sun Microsystems to let it develop programs in Java and has since designed a form of Java that runs best on its own operating systems, enabling it to re-establish the advantage Java had challenged. Sun Microsystems has taken Microsoft to court over this development, insisting their agreement prohibited this sort of development. So it's impossible to know what will eventually emerge.

Nonetheless, the parallels between the transformation sparked by low-browsing, plant-eating dinosaurs and what Java could do to the personal computer market ecology are striking. They suggest how much we may have to learn from further comparisons between natural and market ecologies. This market ecology formation from scratch, as with personal computers, doesn't happen very often. More frequently, we see existing markets, such as health care, transforming themselves. What, then, can we learn from exploring market ecology transformation and what that may mean for health care?

The Emerging Health Care Market Ecology

Natural ecology transformation begins in an environment with fully formed ecologies. When plant-eating dinosaurs evolved from high-browsers to low-browsers, they lived in a world already abundant with plant life and predators. Their evolution, however, seems to have created a crisis at the feeding level of plant life, provoking the evolution of flowering plants. Flowering plants, in turn, created a niche for insects, which, within several million years, developed in the abundance we know them today. Finally, the existence of flowering plants and insects made it easier for some dinosaurs to evolve into birds. Overall, the evolution of low-browsing plant eaters set in motion the series of evolutionary events that ultimately destroyed the ecologies in which dinosaurs had lived their first 70 million or so years and created those we take for granted today.

Even this brief overview suggests that the dynamic principles in ecology transformation are pretty much the same ones we saw in ecology formation:

- *Punctuated equilibrium* in the way the evolution of low-browsing dinosaurs disrupted ecologies that had been stable for tens of millions of years, even if it was not as dramatic as the comet that killed off the dinosaurs 70 million years later
- *Different rules* set by the low-browsing dinosaurs, threatening the survival of old-style plant life and making flowering plants dominant

- *Survival of the luckiest* in the way insects could suddenly thrive as a result of contingencies of the transformation
- *Succession* in the way the shifts in plant life made insect life more abundant and the way the abundance of flowering plants and insects contributed to the evolution of birds

Before we apply these principles to health care markets, however, it's worth remembering that market ecologies, like natural ecologies, are complex adaptive systems. When a complex adaptive system transforms itself from one stable state to another, it's impossible to predict exactly what the emerging stable state will be like. As Stuart Kauffman put it in *At Home in the Universe* (1995), in such emergent systems, "the players cannot foretell the unfolding consequences of their actions." If managers in health care cannot predict exact outcomes, they at least can get a feeling for the dynamics that drive the process. If they can understand the dynamics of the emerging health care market (or telecommunications or banking-finance-insurance), managers can make more intelligent choices in their attempts to coevolve within it. What, then, can this way of thinking about markets tell us about the health care market ecology emerging as I write these words?[3]

In the 1950s, when I was growing up, health care rested on an illness model. People sought their physicians' help when they were sick. The physicians were then responsible for healing the patients. Health care tended to be highly personal, and the main health care delivery feeding level was hospitals and physicians' offices. Patients had free choice of physicians, and the best physicians nurtured close relationships with patients. Through the late 1960s they even made house calls. Physicians were paid for the services they rendered, sometimes through health insurance, but more often from patients' pockets.

Starting in the mid 1960s, several forces came together to drive up health care costs. The key force was federal government spending, mostly through Medicare. Medicare covered most costs for the growing population of senior citizens, who use more health care services than any other demographic sector. As a result, the demand for medical services shot up. Mostly as a result of Medicare, federal government spending skyrocketed from $3 billion in 1960 to $72 billion in 1980, $196 billion in 1990, and $328 billion in 1995, according to the Office of National Health Statistics.

In the 1970s, a new generation of expensive, high-technology medical devices also became available. As hospitals competed for patients, each purchased a full array of the most up-to-date tools. Balancing their cost, use of these new tools often reduced the cost of care. Microsurgical techniques, for example, allowed surgeons to make small incisions that healed faster than conventional surgical incisions. A series of social problems, such as alcohol, tobacco, and drug abuse, violence, pollution, and teenage pregnancy, further drove up the cost of health care. In many cases, the people most affected were uninsured. Their costs were dumped on top of those who were insured. The end result was that as a percentage of gross domestic product, health care in the United States has nearly tripled, from about 5 percent in 1960 to more than 13 percent by 1990.

During the 1970s, the cost of health care rose high enough that most people acquired insurance to cover it. Many corporations were already offering health insurance as an employee benefit. In this way, insurance became a feeding level in the health care market ecology. It was at the insurance feeding level, where rising costs were being paid, that the transformation in the health care market ecology began. As the price of premiums rose at two or three times inflation through the late 1980s and early 1990s, large corporations demanded substantial change. Executives at General Motors even began talking about what had been unthinkable—nationalized health care.

To meet this challenge, the insurance feeding level of the market ecology evolved HMOs. Although the first HMOs started after World War II, the movement toward insuring people through them picked up steam in the 1970s. HMOs collect a fixed sum for each member. Members can then see a physician whenever they want, paying nothing or making a small copayment. With several physicians available, patients may not be able to see their physician of choice all the time, but they can work with physicians and nurses they know and have relationships with. In theory, HMOs were an attempt to shift toward prevention and a wellness model of health care. Providers would work with members to help them take responsibility for their own health, rather than seeking treatment only when they were sick.

The economic motivation, however, was to reduce costs. The old system, payment for service, rewarded physicians and hospitals for providing broad services but gave them no incentives to restrict spending. The new system, often called *managed care*, offered prepayment that made the profits of HMOs and the hospitals with which they worked absolutely dependent on their ability to restrain costs. So, for example, HMOs began using nurse practitioners to work with members in many cases in which physicians were not absolutely necessary.

By the early 1990s, with large corporations more and more upset at the rising cost of insuring their workers, managed care became increasingly popular for its ability to keep costs lower. As a result, HMO financial specialists began to control health care. As more patients joined HMOs, physicians found fewer independent patients and contracted with HMOs in larger numbers. To profit from this growing demand, for-profit hospitals began buying others to create hospital chains, such as Humana or Columbia/HCA, that were focused on reducing costs. By the mid-1990s, even not-for-profit hospitals were merging so they could reduce overlapping services and overhead. Chains of HMOs had become the dominant force controlling the delivery feeding level of the health care market ecology. Cost cutting, as we noted in the opening of this chapter, was their focus.

By early 1998, the reaction to the excesses of managed care's mechanical approach to health care was making a shift in that approach inevitable. The reaction arose from the patient-media-government feeding level. In the media, for example, stories about people who died or were disfigured because their HMOs refused treatment they needed were becoming more and more common. Because some HMOs stripped physicians of their ability to prescribe such treatment, some state legislatures, in Texas, for example, passed laws allowing patients to sue those HMOs for malpractice. In reaction to HMO policies that limited post-birth hospital stays to 24 hours, several laws passed allowing mothers to remain for at least 48 hours after giving birth. Columbia/HCA was under investigation for Medicare fraud. And by early 1998, President Clinton was preparing to announce a "Patients' Bill of Rights" for all Americans.

From our point of view, this reaction was inevitable, and the winner of the battle for control of health care delivery should have been a foregone conclusion, because low-cost managed care recognized only one of two different rules that now govern health care markets. Those rules were cost-consciousness and relationship-based markets. Like executives in the mechanically modeled organizations described in Part II, those in managed care focused almost entirely on controlling costs. Rather than encouraging the system to find innovative ways to deliver high-quality health care, their controls made delivering quality care more difficult. "Managed care is an intruder," in the words of Linda Rusch, vice-president for Patient Care at Hunterdon Medical Center in New Jersey. "It's helped us get the fat out of the system, but consumers also want quality."

As we saw with Microsoft and Intel, success in a market ecology depends on how well an organization can nurture relationships that will give it further opportunity. From this point of view, low-cost HMOs have performed miserably, completely ignoring the different rule of relationship management. In almost everything they've done, HMOs have excited anger and antagonism rather than nurturing relationships on which they can build. Many of these companies have pursued the bottom line so aggressively that they have alienated nearly everyone in their market ecologies. Patients are angry; legislators are livid; physicians are alienated at the loss of the autonomy they need to be effective healers; and nurses are more and more overworked, as their numbers are reduced to cut costs. Only employers who were mostly concerned with costs are happy with much of managed care.

If today's managed care model is dying, what will emerge as the health care system of the 21st century? Although it's impossible to predict exactly what it will be, our analysis of market ecologies can help anticipate the dynamics of that developing market. Let's finish this chapter by considering several factors that may drive this market ecology.

Relationships

Success in market ecologies depends on managers' ability to nurture relationships. But just what relationships should health care organizations be looking to nurture? With the old, mechanical view, people saw society's institutions as separate, temporary stops in their life journeys. We were born into families and generally supported by a church, temple, or mosque within our community. From there, we moved through education and on to either higher education or the work world. The work world could include education, business, church, health care, sports, entertainment, or government. At any stage in our lives, we might take advantage of any of these institutions. But all of them were largely separate. We went to the physician or a hospital when we were sick.

Today this view is inadequate. Social problems such as violence and substance addiction have so complicated the jobs of health care providers that it seems absurd to talk about the high costs of emergency departments, for example, without talking about the underlying social problems. Yet to make connections between social problems and their cost to the health care system, we need to view society as an organically interconnected system with all its institutions interlocked.

An organic perspective does exactly that. For example, bringing up healthy, happy children requires the active cooperation of family, religion, education, health care, and social service agencies. When we look at society this way, we see not separate institutions but interlocked, interdependent institutions that can succeed only if they work together. From this view, health care is not merely the job of physicians and nurses in offices, hospitals, and clinics. Nor are patients passive objects to be "cured" or "healed." Rather, an organic model suggests that people are autonomous and therefore must be responsible for their own health. The job of health care providers is to help people understand that responsibility and when necessary help them heal themselves.

For people to accept this responsibility, however, the whole community will have to become involved with health care. After all, many health care problems are largely a question of lifestyle choices. For example, recent research suggests that among the ten leading causes of death in the United States are tobacco use, suboptimal diet or activity level, alcohol abuse, firearm injury, and illnesses resulting from sexual behavior. These are problems that health care providers cannot address alone. They need to work with community leaders and educators to build community values that support healthy lifestyles, and they need to work with social service providers and local governments to reduce the social tensions that drive people to unhealthy choices. From the point of view we've been developing through this chapter, solving these problems will require developing integrated market ecologies that include all these members of the community.

As people take more responsibility for their health, they can help ease the cost crunch in health care. Enormous amounts of Medicare money go to caring for people in the months immediately before they die. Historically, providing care for the dying has been the family's responsibility. As an increasingly mechanical health care system began to offer to do more and more over the last 30 years, families became willing to allow dying to become a matter for hospitals. As it becomes clear that the system can no longer absorb the cost, however, an organic model of personal—and family—responsibility seems increasingly sensible.

The distinction between being healed mechanically and healing one's self is critical for another reason. An automobile mechanic can repair your car no matter how you feel about him or her. But allowing a physician to help you heal yourself demands trust. Lack of trust seems to be a leading reason why about half of all Americans, as the June 18, 1997 *Wall Street Journal* reported, do not follow through on their physicians' advice, often ending up sicker than they were initially. If people have repeated contact with health care providers, in many life situations, they are more likely to build strong bonds of trust with those providers. In fact, such a community-based health care system is developing in efforts throughout the country. The idea is to break down the institutional barriers between health care providers and the community so that we all share the responsibility for keeping ourselves and our communities healthy. Consider these examples:

- In Chittendon County, Vermont, the Champlain Initiative has brought together more than 250 persons representing every part of the community. Its mission is "Creating healthy communities." Its efforts will focus on issues ranging from improving child welfare and fighting poverty with economic growth to preventing isolation and encouraging increased regular physical activity.
- The Healthcare Forum is a national organization that provides education and research resources. Its vision is "to create healthier communities by engaging leaders in building new visions and models of care." It is urging its members, mostly participants in the health care market ecology, to take a leadership role by building community partnerships to address the wider spectrum of health-related problems.
- The Community Health Improvement Network of VHA, Inc., an organization that networks not-for-profit hospitals, is working to help hospitals across the country focus on education, prevention,

and early intervention in partnerships with local communities. In these partnerships, a brochures notes, "health care organizations increasingly are recommitting to work more extensively within the communities they serve to weave together a comprehensive set of health services to ensure coordinated, timely and appropriate access to care."

The results of efforts like these are so far mostly anecdotal. But they point to a real hunger among both health care providers and community members to form these relationships. The following are two such incidents from health care providers associated with VHA:

- Linda Rusch discussed this community model of health care with some of her nurses. They were so energized by what she'd told them that a group of nurses in a maternity unit started collaborating with the local prosecutor's office and a women's shelter. The nurses hosted a program on domestic violence and continue to be involved.
- Jim Dwyer, vice-president for medical affairs at the Memorial Hospital of Burlington County, N.J., worked with his local parish to create a health ministry. Finding that many of the needy were falling through the cracks of the managed care model, the parish developed a network of health care professionals who provided information and counseling to those who had fallen outside the system. Although the ministers did not provide services, they could help people find the resources they needed and offer personal reassurance. Dwyer said that the response from people in the community and requests from people outside it suggest that this kind of program addresses a growing need in many communities.

As health care providers begin winning the battle for dominance of health care markets, we can expect instances like these to proliferate.

One other VHA member hospital, Our Lady of Lourdes Medical Center in Camden, N.J., took a more comprehensive approach to community-based health care. Its experiences suggest how powerful a relationship-based approach toward providing services can be. According to Owen McNally, director of community health improvement, in 1994, the center was providing traditional community services—outreach to the elderly, for example—when it decided to take the lead in responding to a request for proposal for projects to explore how the tools of total quality management could be applied to improving community health. The center's proposal was one of ten chosen for technical assistance, creating the Camden Health Improvement Learning Collaborative.

Camden is a troubled city. Nearly 50 percent of the population is younger than 25, and more than 60 percent of the children live below the poverty line. Syphilis and gonorrhea rates are six times higher than New Jersey state averages, and other health statistics are equally dismal. The 85,000 people of Camden are served by three hospitals. Yet those people don't take full advantage of these hospitals.

Initially, the collaborative included people from five community organizations—Our Lady of Lourdes, the Camden City Board of Education, the Diocese of Camden, the University of Medicine and Dentistry of New Jersey School of Osteopathic Medicine, and the Area Health and Education Center. Representatives from these organizations began meeting monthly to discuss how to deliver health care to two communities in Camden. At first they talked about putting a primary health care center in each of the communities. But community representatives said their needs were different. What they really needed was help organizing the community so that people would be willing to take advantage of new sources of health care. So the collaborative hired a community health organizer for each community.

For more than three years, the collaborative has continued to meet and support this basic work in preparing the communities. It is now beginning to show results. Where community members used to be wary of each other and of health care providers, an increasing amount of trust has grown. Where health care providers in different facilities thought only in terms of competition, they now cooperate, applying for grants together. Soon after it was established, the collaborative received funding from the Kellogg Foundation, as one of 25 U.S. projects developing alternative ways of delivering health care services.

The collaborative has grown to 12 organizations, including the Camden Police Department and West Jersey Hospital, a long-time competitor with Our Lady Of Lourdes. It has also taken on a third community. The collaborative has defined its vision as "Building a healthier Camden by establishing a broad, collaborative community-centered process to effectivefy identify and address community needs." It is also ready to begin setting up a Neighborhood Living Room in each community. These facilities will be places where neighborhood people can obtain health care and learn about health issues and resources. McNally explained that one day a week, there might be a free clinic; on another day, a physician might be available. A neighborhood host or hostess will staff the facility, and people in the community will be invited to make themselves comfortable. A social worker will be available for counseling, referral, and case management. Each community will use the building as it sees fit, to hold adult education classes, for example, or after-school programs.

Rather than the current model, where community members must enter the "house" of health care providers, the Camden model enables those community members to come to their own "house," where a visiting friend can help them. With its emphasis on building relationships throughout the community, Camden's experiment should provide a more accurate picture of the future of health care delivery than the HMOs that currently dominate it.

Organic health care organizations will also explore specific partnerships within their communities. One technique they may want to use is the 3M Integrated Solutions program (see Chapter 7). This approach enables 3M to understand customers' needs to the point that the company can make significant contributions to those customers' success. In so doing, the company evolves from being a supplier to becoming a partner. Similarly, health care organizations can ask questions that move them toward partnering with other institutions. What are potential customers' central problems? A manufacturer of specialty chemicals, for example, might be interested in employee safety or potential problems with new manufacturing processes. A school system might want to find effective ways to communicate the dangers of drug addiction. Social service agencies might want to explore ways to reduce teen pregnancies.

As the barriers between institutions are breaking down on the delivery level, other feeding levels are coevolving to these shifts in health care market ecology. For example, the pressures of cost reduction have fallen just as heavily on members of the pharmaceuticals feeding level as in the delivery level. The members of this level of the market ecology include pharmaceutical manufacturers, distribution and benefits management companies, and pharmacies.

As at the delivery level, turbulence at the pharmaceuticals level is most evident in mergers. In late 1997 and early 1998, manufacturer SmithKline Beecham announced it would merge, first, with American Home Products, then with Glaxo Wellcome. To date, neither seems likely to be consummated. A couple of years earlier, manufacturing giant Merck & Co. had acquired benefits management company Medco to gain access to 50 million pharmaceutical customers. Driving these acquisitions are some major shifts at the pharmaceuticals level. For example, by 2002, patents will expire on drugs with $16 billion in sales in 1996. So manufacturers are scrambling to make up this quarter of U.S. revenues. All this has been complicated, as several insurance companies tried to cut their costs by cutting special deals with pharmacy chains that bought large amounts of their prescription drugs. Local pharmacies objected to being discriminated against and won their case in court. Similarly, in late summer 1997, some insurers started cutting their compensation to the point that many pharmacies insist they will be losing money on each sale (*Philadelphia Inquirer*, September 11, 1997).

These developments seem to be purely about money, final developments on a level where a mechanical model is about to turn organic. Because this level is so dependent on the delivery level, it seems likely that instability here will continue until some time after the delivery level begins to stabilize. Still, the different rules of organic market ecologies suggest we'll see more cooperation at this level. Insurance companies, rather than trying to squeeze the last penny out of pharmacies, might try to work with them to reduce costs at the pharmacies and *then* reduce costs as a percentage of the savings they help create.

More far-reaching developments seem likely. For instance, subjected to these different rules, the very conception of what pharmaceutical manufacturers do might shift. With the health care illness model, the best thing a manufacturer can do is develop a drug that customers would have to buy for the rest of their lives, all the better if the condition is widespread. As the model of health care moves to people maintaining their own health, pharmaceutical companies could begin to focus on strengthening the immune system or even genetic engineering to remove strands of DNA that encourage specific diseases. Once again, it's impossible to know precisely what will emerge as this feeding level finally stabilizes. However, an organic model gives managers a chance to explore possible directions their market ecologies will take. With those directions as a guidepost, they can begin encouraging small experiments to find what will work in their markets.

For some feeding levels, an organic model suggests enormous opportunities. Consider another level dependent on the delivery level, medical technology. The key driving factors at the delivery level appear to be enhancing community wellness and keeping costs reasonable. The medical technology level already has contributed to those goals. Advances in telecommunication now enable the world's most expert specialists to collaborate on surgical procedures anywhere in the world. Because physicians can broadcast magnified video of almost any part of the body, specialists halfway across the world can see what's happening better today than they could standing in the operating room ten years ago. This video consulting translates into improved community health and reduced costs.

As computers become more and more widespread, the market for devices for home diagnosis will explode. What would happen if researchers developed a device dental patients could place in their mouths to examine for cavities, gum problems, and other disease, and send the findings to the dentist's office for diagnosis? What if the device could use sound waves to clean teeth? What if a simple device could monitor critical signs for patients with high blood pressure or diabetes? Might use of such devices help cut costs, because patients no longer would need to visit the physician as much, and improve health, because the simplicity of such procedures would make periodic examinations easier and therefore more likely to occur? Today there are reliable, inexpensive home tests for conditions ranging from pregnancy to HIV infection. What might be possible once medical researchers begin applying the technological revolution within an organic model of health care?

This is not a comprehensive look at all the feeding levels of the health care market ecology. But it should be enough to help you see how an organic model, with its emphasis on coevolution in market ecologies, can help you understand even the most turbulent markets and decide what directions to try. This is a very different, more wide-open concept of strategic vision than the mechanical one with which we are familiar. Nonetheless, it provides a basic picture of the dynamics of transformative markets and how managers can develop flexible, adaptive strategies to take advantage of the very exciting opportunities these markets present.

Summary

Examining today's transformative markets in the light of how natural ecologies transform themselves after major disruptions gives us a very different understanding of what is happening in those markets:

- This model suggests that events over the last 30 years have punctuated the equilibrium of market after market we used to think of as stable. In health care, the forces of social change have combined with the technological revolution to drive health care costs so high that the market has been forced to begin recreating itself.
- Much of the turbulence in these markets seems to grow from the way organizations in them are operating by the mechanical rules of the era coming to an end, at a time when very different, more organic rules are taking root. In health care, the extreme cost consciousness of many HMOs is beginning to undermine them just as they seemed to dominate the market. Those unable to play by the different rule of relationships will see their market share drop and face extinction.
- The organizations that become leaders are likely, in fact, *not* to be today's most dominant. Survival of the luckiest suggests that the future leaders are those who have been building capabilities in relationship building, a talent that may have kept them from dominating their markets in the past. For example, not-for-profit hospitals most pressured by low-cost HMOs may be those forced most fully to develop relationships in the community. Throughout the period of transformation, we are likely to see organizations reach a point where they seem dominant, only to have that dominance slip away. The power of incumbency holds only once markets have stabilized.
- Finally, the feeding levels of market ecologies will stabilize by succession. In health care, developments at the insurance level created the need for change. However, the delivery level seems likely to be the first to stabilize. Once people in this market ecology

are clear about the pattern of health care delivery, organizations at the pharmaceutical and medical technology levels will have a much better idea of how they will need to serve their customers.

With this idea of the dynamics driving even our most turbulent markets in mind, let's now turn to some organic management tools. Creating competitive advantage in market ecologies, after all, will be the name of the game. What tools will managers have available to win the game?

CHAPTER 3

Creating Competitive Advantage in a Market Ecology

Understand the economic systems evolving around you and find ways to contribute.

—James Moore

Question: What decision-making tools can managers develop from the comparison of markets with natural ecologies?

One of the best things managers who want to understand what thinking of markets as ecologies can mean to them is to sit down at a computer, access the World Wide Web, and enter the address http:// www.amazon.com. They'll find themselves at Amazon.com, the first digital book store. Alberto Vitale, chairman of Random House, told The *Wall Street Journal* that this Web site represents "the beginning of a completely new way to buy books." But Vitale was only half right. The genius of Amazon.com is that it's a great deal more than an "easier [way] for people to find the books they want" (*Wall Street Journal*, May 16, 1996).

What makes Amazon.com a model of the future is not merely that it was one of the first successful businesses on the Web. Nor is it so special because its more than two million titles are ten times what you would find at the largest superstore. Amazon.com is a picture of the future because the books it sells may be the least valuable service it provides. At this Web site, you can read on-line reviews of books in which you are interested, get lists of related books, or ask for e-mail on new books about your favorite subjects. (When I asked to be updated on new books on organizational change in May 1996, within two weeks I received by e-mail information on 16 new titles expected out by the end of June.) Amazon.com is open 24 hours a day, seven days a week. It attracts customers from more than 60 countries, and 60 percent of its customers come back to buy again.

What Amazon.com is doing is building relationships based on the books it sells. When you go on-line with Amazon.com, you don't have to be a stranger. You can find out, from their on-line reviews, what other buyers are saying about the books you want to read. You can create an electronic relationship, obtaining new titles in your areas of interest, merely by asking. Perhaps most important, Amazon.com is amassing a database about customer preferences, which has almost infinite potential. With that database, the company can help readers form virtual book clubs to discuss their favorite subjects or form local face-to-face book clubs. It can connect readers interested in, say, New Orleans cuisine, with a travel agency to create a specialized tour of that town's best restaurants. The possibilities seem endless. Amazon.com has transformed the traditional book store into a way customers can more fully enjoy the subjects on which they buy books—by creating relationships with the company *and with other customers.*

To put it another way, Amazon.com is developing interdependent relationships within its market ecology. For managers, this need to shift focus from products to relationships is a key lesson we can draw from our discussion of market ecologies. In this chapter, we examine three such lessons, three of the different rules that apply in today's market ecologies. Then we look at how managers can use the idea of market ecologies to explore the unique opportunities today's markets present their organizations.

Mechanical Mistakes in Market Ecologies

It is possible, of course, to draw many more than three general lessons from our discussion of market ecologies. We'll limit ourselves, however, to three critical mistakes managers make in applying a mechanical model to today's turbulent markets.

Relationships Must Come First

Look back to the definitions of machines and living things (see Chapter 1). Machines exist to generate predetermined products. As a result, bureaucracies, modeled on machines, focus on product. Even when they provide services, as in education or insurance, the experts in a bureaucracy decide the qualities consumers need, create services around those qualities, and persuade customers to buy them. Even in public education, we see a struggle over whether teachers' unions will be allowed to act as the guild for experts who, with a mechanical model, are the only people qualified to design the educational corporate machine.

In the first stages of the market transformations we looked at in the last chapter, mechanical organizations are dominant. The mechanically focused cost-consciousness of managed health care isn't all that different from the attitude of leading banks that want to charge customers for every ATM use or teller contact. Similarly, major long-distance carriers and the Baby Bells often seem more interested in signing customers up and getting them to pay for sophisticated services, such as call waiting or caller ID, than in creating the relationships this theory of market recreation suggests are now becoming essential.

Living things, on the other hand, exist by nurturing mutually beneficial relationships with other parties in their ecologies. Similarly, organic corporations can thrive by using their products to nurture relationships. The biggest mistake bureaucracies make in today's market ecologies occurs because the bureaucrats don't understand this rule of survival and continue focusing on products. It's a major reason IBM lost its central position in the personal computer market. The company's managers believed that its technicians could build the best personal computers and that its marketing people could persuade customers to buy them. Intel and Microsoft, on the other hand, were more concerned with nurturing relationships with hardware producers, software writers, distributors, and customers. They wanted to develop top-quality products, too. But even when their products were sub-par—experts agree that MS-DOS, for example, was technically inferior not only to the Apple Macintosh operating system but also to Gary Kildall's CP/M—the ability of these two companies to create interdependent relationships with other parties in their market made them successful. Apple's greatest strength wasn't its technology. It was the intense loyalty the company cultivated among users. By building a more extensive network of interdependencies, however, Intel and Microsoft dominated this market.

The importance of nurturing relationships seems to be one of the key reasons so many companies are unable to do business on the Internet. Every beer and automobile maker seems to have an address on the Web. Most, however, remain unsuccessful in leveraging their presence on the Web into a competitive advantage. That's because they view the Web as another storefront, a place to sell products.

Unfortunately for them, the Web is not about products; it's about relationships. As Arthur Armstrong and John Hagel III observed in their *Harvard Business Review* article (1996), the most successful use of the Web, offering the greatest range of services, creates not one but four types of community—communities of transaction, interest, fantasy, and relationship. Only one type has to do with selling product. The others enable prospective customers to increase exponentially the value of products by creating relationships with other potential customers as well as the organization sponsoring the Web site. To be most successful, then, companies need to remember that their Web sites can be more than storefronts, where they persuade customers to buy their wares. Rather, they can be clubhouses, where customers add levels of value to those wares.

Not all buying on the Web will be relationship oriented. In fact, as buying on the Web becomes more familiar to shoppers, it's becoming easier for many companies, especially retailers, to use it as a showroom. By early 1998, retailers such as Lands' End and J. C. Penney were taking sales on the Web increasingly seriously (*Philadelphia Inquirer*, February 15, 1998). The shift to buying on the Web is even easier for customers who are used to buying from catalogs. The danger here is that these customers can use the Web to comparison shop for the best prices quickly and simply. To avoid competing almost entirely on price, retailers must use their Web sites to create relationships that enhance the value of what they sell.

If this ecological model is correct, building relationships should be equally important as markets form in health care, telecommunication, and banking-finance-insurance. We have already discussed the multiple connections being formed among telecommunications providers. The most successful are likely to be those that work with their customers to help the customers understand their telecommunication needs and to offer packages of services that meet those needs. Then the companies can coevolve with their customers. That is, they can collect feedback on service, help customers understand how their needs are evolving, and alter their service packages to continue meeting customers' unique evolving needs. These service packages become much more than products; they become results of the ongoing relationship between providers and customers.

We took a longer look at health care. Providers traditionally looked at their job as delivering a "product" in doctor's offices, clinics, and hospitals. Already they have begun to think instead in terms of creating lifelong relationships with customers, perhaps with entire communities. Such a relationship could begin with prenatal seminars available in community centers and schools, continue with nutritional and hygienic education starting in grade school, and even include community clinics in local schools and workplaces. This is only one possible way of thinking about delivering health care. The key is to examine how organizations can nurture relationships that increase their products' value to *all* of those who use it and make everyone better off because of them.

Market Ecologies Refuse to Be Controlled

Machines must be controlled because they're basically stupid. Each piece of a machine is designed with only the information it needs to do its job. The timer in your toaster "knows" how to release the spring that lets your finished toast pop up. That's all it "knows" and all it needs to. In bureaucracies, modeled on machines, managers practice command-and-control because they think of their organizations as peopled with dumb human parts that only know their standard operating procedures. Managers in bureaucracies also try to control their markets. That's why IBM held off on integrating the Intel 386 chip (see Chapter 1). IBM disregarded the network of relationships it had developed, preferring to control the market by setting a new standard. In ignoring its dependence on software writers, IBM doomed its new standard.

With an organic model we recognize the idea that we can control our markets is an illusion. Anyone with children, especially today, quickly learns how difficult it is to control living things. Similarly, we can't control our organizations, much less our markets. Some may object that Microsoft and Intel are doing just fine controlling their markets. It's true that Bill Gates seems to have borrowed some of his marketing tactics from John D. Rockefeller's efforts to control the oil industry. Yet the major successes for both companies depended on their ability not to control this market, but to adapt to changes over which they had no control.

In fact, both Intel and Microsoft seem driven by the realization that the market will accept their latest offerings only as long as those offerings meet the most recent needs of the market. As a result, these companies pour enormous resources into research and development so the next generation of products remains attractive to computer makers, software writers, and end users. When they make mistakes, as Microsoft did in ignoring the Internet as long as it did, these companies recognize those mistakes as quickly as they can and go on to something that will work. They don't dominate their markets by controlling them. Rather, they adapt better than anyone else, building a network of interdependencies around their key roles.

At the end of Chapter 2, we looked at what's happening to health maintenance organizations (HMOs) that focus on controlling cost without equal concern for quality. The results are predictable. Health care, after all, is literally a matter of life and death. And the news media love a good story about a large business whose greedy practices are killing their customers. So we're now seeing stories about people who died or became disfigured or disabled because their doctors, either too interested in their bonuses or reluctant to fight their employers, refused referrals. The resulting lawsuits and public revulsion will prove far more financially damaging than providing adequate care would have, and the system will adapt.

A relationship-based health care market ecology would respect the need for mutual benefit. The acacia and the ant (see Chapter 1) work together because doing so enhances the survival of both. Our health care system will minimize costs when everyone is convinced to help do so *as a matter of their best interests.*

Once Stabilization of a Feeding Level Begins,
It Is Difficult to Challenge Its Leaders

In 1991, IBM, Apple, and Motorola formed a partnership to develop a new type of microchip that could challenge the Intel-Microsoft dominance of personal computers. It would develop reduced instruction set computing (RISC) technology capable of running computers much more quickly than conventional chips. The partners believed that the Intel chips, which made use of conventional technology, had reached the limits for increased speed and power. The RISC chips, they believed, would allow them to begin shaping the market, as Intel had done since the mid-1980s. Moreover, because the RISC chip allowed computers to run both Mac and Windows operating systems, Apple hoped to neutralize the advantage of the Intel-Microsoft standard.

In 1993, the partnership introduced the PowerPC chip. Apple brought out a series of computers using these chips in 1994. Although these new computers were able to run Windows applications almost as quickly as Intel chips running Windows 3.1, Apple's market share would not climb above 12 percent. What Apple didn't appreciate was that well over 80 percent of application software was already interdependent with Microsoft operating systems. As a result, the main advantage of the PowerPC computers was to Apple computer users who wanted to use Windows applications. Especially with the introduction of more powerful Pentium chips and then Windows 95, there was little reason for anyone using a standard Intel-Microsoft computer to switch to an Apple. Today Apple personal computers account for less than 5 percent of the market. The IBM OS/2 operating system was similarly ineffective in challenging this standard.

From our ecological perspective, these challenges were likely to be futile from the beginning. The interdependencies on the first two feeding levels had become so strong that they were likely to resist almost any challenge. As long as Intel and Microsoft continued to upgrade their products, *any* challenge to the computer hardware standard from the hardware feeding level was likely to fail.

The best way to challenge that standard was from another feeding level. That's what Java has the power to do. By introducing a major evolutionary jump on another level, Java may restructure the entire market ecology, just as the evolution of low-browsing dinosaurs restructured ecologies at the beginning of the Cretaceous period.

Organizations in other newly forming market ecologies should take this lesson to heart. In health care, for example, a few networks of HMOs, insurance companies, and hospitals may dominate the market ecology by early in the 21st century. The challenge to their dominance won't come from this payment feeding level. It is already beginning to come from the delivery feeding level, where doctors are infuriated at being robbed of the ability to care for patients as they see best, and the patient-media-government feeding level, where outrage is being translated into legislation that will force insurers and HMOs to refocus on quality care and give doctors more freedom. Similarly, on the technology feeding level, major advances may allow people to connect medical monitoring devices to their television-computers. Already, devices exist that allow heart attack victims to receive remote defibrillation. Such devices might allow computerization of a great deal of routine health care, driving down costs and neutralizing the main advantage of HMO networks.

This kind of restructuring of market ecologies will be possible, no matter how stable they may seem, as long as new technologies continue to appear at the current rate. Our technological revolution could easily continue for another 20 years. As a result, until technology stabilizes, we're likely to remain in the chaotic state of market development, dominated by experimentation and continual change.

These three lessons hardly exhaust what we can learn from applying the principles of natural ecologies to markets. I've included them as examples of how managers' study of natural ecological formation can help them think through the problems of their markets. Let's turn now to a tool managers can use to help their companies adapt more effectively to the changes in their market ecologies.

A Visual Representation

We human beings are visually oriented animals. The vast majority of us think in pictures. To understand things, we need to visualize them—that is, see pictures that tell stories about them. Unfortunately, that creates an obstacle to thinking of markets more organically. Let's say we want to develop a picture of personal computer markets in the year 1995. Table 3–1 provides the information we want to use.[1]

The problem we face is that the main tools we have for presenting visual information about our markets are pie charts and bar charts. Look what happens when we present this data with pie charts (Figures 3–1 through 3–3).

We end up with three separate charts. Each tells us which company has how much market share in its own part of the personal computer market. The charts do not tell us a single thing about relationships between market members. This is part of a larger problem you'll find as you apply an organic way of thinking to your organization. We live in a world moving from a mechanical to an organic model. All around us are artifacts of the mechanical model—these pie charts, for example, which mechanically emphasize discrete segments. The presence of these artifacts makes it difficult to think organically.

TABLE 3–1   Personal Computer Markets in 1995.

PC Makers	Market Share (%)	CPU Makers	Market Share (%)	Operating Systems	Market Share (%)
Compaq	12	Intel	78	Microsoft	80
Packard Bell	12	Motorola etc.	12	Apple	12
Apple	12	AMD	6	IBM	5
IBM	8	Others	4	Others	3
Gateway 2000	5				
Dell	5				
Hewlett-Packard	4				
Others	42				

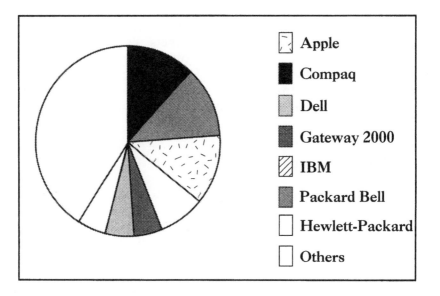

FIGURE 3–1   PC Manufacturers, 1995.

What we need is an organic way to visualize our markets, to *see* them as ecologies. The tool is the *ecograph*, a graphic depiction as a corporate foodweb of the key members of any market ecology. The ideal way to present this information would probably be as animated three-dimensional computer graphics that trace the history of a market ecology, for example, the personal computer market from 1975 to the present. That way we could watch its evolution from year to year. For our purposes, however, it's more important to examine how to build, and then to use, ecographs. So we'll build an ecograph for the year 1995 in the hardware level of the personal computer market ecology. Then we'll take

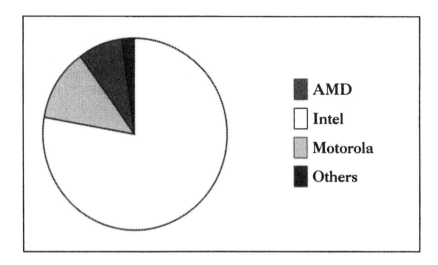

FIGURE 3-2   CPU Manufacturers, 1995.

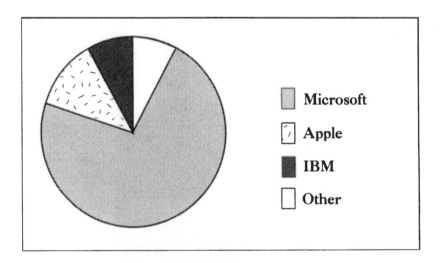

FIGURE 3-3   Operating System Writers, 1995.

a look at ecographs for the years 1982 and 1989 to see how this tool can help us understand the dynamics of this market ecology.

Developing an Ecograph

The purpose of an ecograph is to create a snapshot of a market ecology at any particular time. This snapshot must make the key relations within the market clear to its viewers. We'll look at this one use for ecographs. But it's not necessarily the only one. The ecograph is a new tool—I've been working with it only since the end of 1995—and you can probably come up with other uses and perhaps other ways to build them. In any case, you can develop ecographs of your market ecologies in the three following steps.

1. List Parties and Study Their Relationships

Most markets are extremely complex. A thorough mapping of all the parties in them would be confusingly complicated. So the first step in building an ecograph is to list all the parties and think about their relationships. In the next step, you can choose the most important ones, those you want to map.

The final ecograph for the personal computer hardware level in 1995 (Figure 3–4) includes only three groups—computer makers, chip makers, and operating systems writers. My initial list for this market also in-

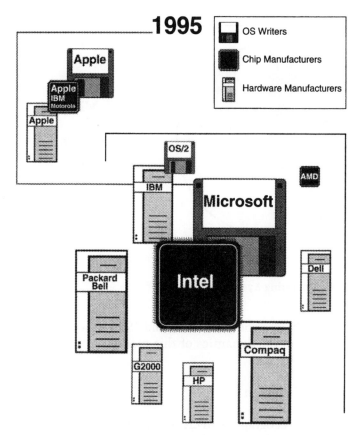

FIGURE 3–4   Ecograph for Personal Computer Hardware Feeding Level, 1995.

cluded customer segments, software application writers, and makers of all sorts of devices, such as hard drives, modems, memory chips, monitors, and sound and video boards. Once all these participants in the market were in front of me, and I began thinking about their relationships, I was ready to go on to the second step.

2. Identify Critical Parties

Which of the parties listed are critical to your exploration of the market? It depends, of course, on what you want to learn from the ecograph. A company with a new technology for building less expensive, higher-resolution monitors will focus on different players than a company developing a new software language for personal computers. A company with labor problems may need to include its unions, whereas one with good labor relations might not.

My purpose was to gain a deeper understanding of the forces shaping the personal computer market ecology. As a result, I initially identified four parties as critical—computer makers, operating system writers, chip makers, and application software writers. As you can see from the ecograph, I would eventually drop software writers. I did that for two reasons. First, including them would be too confusing. The amount of information depicted would confuse the issue rather than clarify it. Second, in working with this ecograph, I realized that software applications were a different feeding level and that the information would be more valuable if I focused only on the hardware level.

3. Map Critical Parties

Actually mapping the market is where the real work of creating an ecograph comes in. Give yourself as much time to play with mapping as you can. Expect to run into a lot of dead ends. At times, I'd give myself a day or two away from the ecograph after an especially difficult problem. In time, things come together. Here are some of the thought processes I ran through as I created the ecograph for personal computers in 1995.

Any ecograph tells a story. The story that would emerge from the personal computer hardware feeding level in 1995 was the marginalization of the Apple alliance. But it didn't start that way. I began by putting down representations of the personal computer makers. If I'd created a software program to do it, I could have made the shapes exactly reflect relative market share size. Instead, I drew the ecograph by hand, focusing on relationships. So size is only approximate. I played around with where to put the various computer makers, operating systems writers, and microchip makers until I became comfortable with the story the ecograph suggested.

It took a lot of time, many dead ends, and a lot of playing with these shapes before I came up with what would be the final ecograph. When I

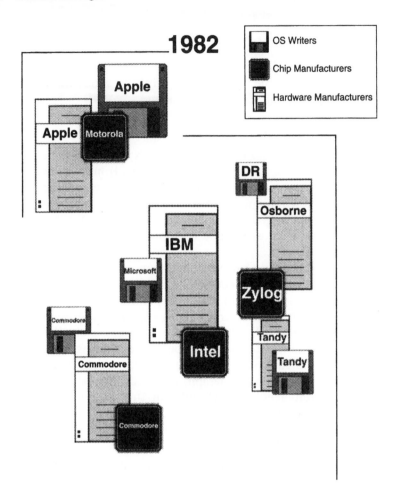

FIGURE 3–5   Ecograph for Personal Computer Hardware Feeding Level, 1982.

got to this point, I started drawing in major applications software makers. I realized, however, that including them would clutter the ecograph and make it difficult to understand, without significantly increasing its value.

The decision to leave out applications software produced a valuable insight. I realized that by mapping only computer makers, chip makers, and operating systems writers, I had created a simple ecograph of the hardware feeding level of this market. Having completed this ecograph for 1995, it was easier to map the markets for 1982 and 1989 (Figures 3–5 and 3–6), although both took serious effort.

Notice how much richer in information the ecograph is than the three pie charts. Because the information is so rich, it's possible to develop all sorts of insights into the process of building an ecograph. The

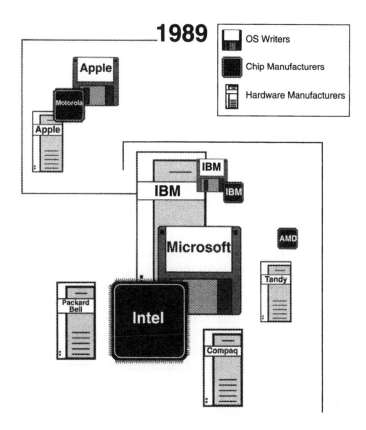

FIGURE 3-6 Ecograph for Personal Computer Hardware Feeding Level, 1989.

ecograph for personal computers in 1995 (Figure 3-4), for instance, suggests the power of standards setting that Gates recognized when he
started building Microsoft. When we look back over all three ecographs,
we can see this even more clearly. In 1975, Gates and his cofounder, Paul
Allen, argued about whether Microsoft should make hardware as well as
software. Gates insisted that the company stick to software (Cusumano
and Selby 1995). He seems to have been right. What made Apple machines so wonderful was the operating system software that, until Windows 95, was so much easier to use than the Intel-Microsoft standard.

The first thing I realized in studying these three ecographs of the
hardware feeding level was that in terms of market evolution, manufacturing computers themselves may be the least important part of
the process. The computer on my desk is a product, a convenience that
combines the two things I need, the computing power of the chip and the
manipulative capability of the operating system, integrated in a way that
enables me to perform the tasks I want to perform.

This insight further explains why IBM and Apple are having so much trouble. Both believed that the computer as product was what customers wanted. They were wrong. If you look at the ecographs for 1989 and 1995, you can see that Microsoft and Intel have succeeded not merely by producing operating systems and chips but by making themselves the center of *a network of relationships that makes the product valuable.*

These ecographs also clarify some of the principles of market ecology formation. Notice, for instance, all the experimentation going on in 1982, experimentation we expect at the beginning of ecology formation. The five computer makers we show use four chip makers and five operating systems. One computer maker, Commodore, is self-contained, producing its own operating system and chip. Two others, Apple and Tandy, make their own operating systems but go outside for chips. The last two, IBM and Osborne, go outside for both operating system and chips.

By the time we get to 1989, however, this feeding level has stabilized. Four of five major computer makers now cluster around the Intel-Microsoft standard. Only Apple remains outside. The ecograph for 1995 suggests the strength of this stability. Although we have three new leading computer makers, the basic map of the market remains unchanged.

There is no correct ecograph. One of the most important benefits of developing an ecograph is the freedom it gives you to explore and then express about your markets things of which you may not yet have become conscious. Other people will develop very different ecographs. This offers some valuable opportunities to teams working on strategic marketing plans. Break the teams into three or four groups and have each group develop its own ecograph. Compare the group ecographs and discuss the basic assumptions that make them different. Discussing these assumptions will deepen your understanding of your markets and provide additional information for shaping your strategies. Ecographs, combined with an understanding of how ecologies develop, also make it easier to understand the interrelations in our markets and how our actions ripple through them. Faced with the need to adapt to changes in the market, we can use an ecograph to choose between many possible adaptations.

Questions for a Market Ecology

To begin evaluating strategies for coevolving in their market ecologies, managers should start with a series of questions to clarify two strategic marketing issues:

- *Feeding Levels.* What are the feeding levels of the market? On which feeding levels does the organization wish to operate? Have these feeding levels begun to stabilize? If the organization has an advantage on a feeding level that is stabilizing, can it leverage the advantage on the next level, as Microsoft did in dominating first the hardware and then the software level?

• *Adaptive Strategy.* What overall strategy does your organization wish to pursue? Apple continued to attack the Microsoft-Intel standard well into the 1990s. In their partnership with IBM and Motorola to produce PowerPC chips, Apple executives continued to talk about defeating Microsoft. This at first may have seemed a logical approach. Yet an organic model suggests how much software writers and customers had come to depend on the Microsoft-Intel standard. With so much software already written for that standard, the ability of the PowerPC to run either would be attractive mostly to people already using Apple computers.

Ecology formation suggests that challenging a Microsoft demands a change that will restructure the entire market. The PowerPC chip was not radical enough to do that. On the other hand, it may be possible to launch a restructuring from another feeding level. Just as low-browsing dinosaurs restructured natural ecologies 140 million years ago, the introduction of Java, a programming language with the potential to make the Internet rather than individual machines the standard, may seriously challenge Microsoft's dominance.

Dominance of a feeding level is not the only strategy. By studying any feeding level, it's possible to identify many approaches. Organizations can look for ecological niches where they can enjoy more limited success, then work to leverage the success. In this way, Hewlett-Packard leveraged its reputation for high-quality printers to invade the hardware level. By producing low-priced, high-quality computers, Hewlett-Packard is winning an increasing market share.

Identity

Success in any market ecology demands one thing we have not yet discussed, an identity. We'll look at identity in Chapter 4, but it's worth considering briefly here. Living things must develop an identity, a characteristic way of succeeding in their environments. The great white shark, for instance, is the great killer of the deep, and all its parts—eyes, teeth, jaws, fins—are aligned to enable it to fulfill that identity. The most successful organizations also have clear identities. "Innovation" at 3M, "We are ladies and gentlemen serving ladies and gentlemen" at The Ritz-Carlton, "A computer on every desk and in every home, running Microsoft software" (Manes and Andrews 1994) at Microsoft, each expresses the unifying idea around which all of the company's corporate systems are aligned. Corporate identity is explored in more depth in Chapter 4. Here it's enough to point out that a clear identity may be the most important factor in creating competitive advantage in a market ecology.

The last strategic issue managers should consider as they build ecographs is this question of corporate identity. What is your current corporate identity? Will it help you pursue the strategic direction you've chosen or make it more difficult to do so? If you need to shift your corporate identity, what kind of identity will make your company more competitive?

Corporate identity is a lot more than image. Unlike image, identity does not focus merely on how we want the world to see our organizations. Identity defines the essence of an organization—how it relates to its markets, how it must treat its employees to make that identity an important part of each of them, and how it must shape every corporate system. 3M, for example, has been successful because every corporate system is aligned to produce innovation. As a result, the company regularly meets its goal of generating 30 percent of revenue from products no more than four years old. An ecograph of the market ecology gives managers a way of reconsidering corporate identity and what it has to be if their organizations are to develop competitive advantages.

Once managers understand the strategic marketing approach best suited to their companies, they can focus on potential adaptations. At General Motors in the mid 1990s, for instance, senior managers recognized a strategic need to reduce costs per vehicle if they were to remain competitive. The managers at GM could have chosen to work with the union, the United Auto Workers (UAW), to define a line of action that would have benefited both company and union. Instead management chose an aggressive challenge of the union. Because of the series of strikes that resulted from this position, GM may have seriously injured its chances for driving costs down.

Using an ecograph would have enabled GM managers to explore a series of such possibilities. First, they could have spread out the history of their markets in front of them as three-dimensional animation. Managers could then examine the potential effect of *any* adaptation on *all* the important members of their market ecology. In this way, they might have become aware of the potentially toxic side effects of challenging the UAW as well as the adaptive ripples this approach to the UAW might send through the market ecology.

Understanding market ecologies is only a beginning. If managers are serious in wanting their organizations to coevolve to take the greatest advantage of opportunities in their market ecologies, they must ensure those organizations can operate more like living things than mechanisms. Their organizations must become keenly aware of what is happening all around them and then be able to respond quickly. The best way for managers to make sure their organizations can do that is to begin thinking of them as if they were organisms.

Part II explores what happens when we think of these corporate issues in terms of an organic model. Although you may find some of the conclusions we reach helpful, the key value in Chapters 4 through 8 lies beyond those conclusions. As you begin to understand how to use an organic model as a different way of *thinking about your organization*, you can develop tools that will enable you to address any problem and take advantage of any opportunity you find.

PART II

The Organic Corporation

In Part I, we saw that organizations today can thrive only if they coevolve in their market ecologies. How, then, should managers run their organizations so that they can coevolve most effectively?

To coevolve effectively, organizations above all must be able to learn. Since 1990, when Peter Senge's *The Fifth Discipline* hit the bookshelves, building organizations that learn has been a key topic of management discussion. Many of you reading this book will remember the sensation Senge's book created, with its popular introduction of the idea of the "learning organization." What no one noticed then, including me, was the irony in the idea of redesigning our companies to be learning organizations.

The fact is that *all* organizations are born as self-organizing, learning systems—that is, they begin life acting as living things. To survive, new businesses must learn who their customers are; what products and services customers want; how to produce and deliver those products and services; and how their people should behave toward each other. As complex adaptive systems—entities whose many interacting parts enable them to learn and evolve— they try out everything they can to adapt to their environments and learn answers to these questions.

Once they've answered those questions, organizations need to change the basic way they operate. Their people must take the energy they've devoted to experimenting and put it in service of growing in the markets they've identified.[1] Here organizations must ask how they will integrate 100 or 1,000 or 100,000 people with different skills and interests in service of a single corporate purpose. They do so by building a formal structure that directs activity in the informal organization. This direction can take either of two forms: Management can get everyone working together by controlling them, or it can enable them to be self-controlled.

We build these formal structures with models, other systems that offer patterns for building our organizations. To control people, managers use a mechanical model of organization; to enable self-control, they use an organic model. Such models operate a great deal like the metaphors Gareth Morgan discussed in *Images of Organization* (1986). For Morgan, "our theories and explanations of organizational life are based on metaphors that lead us to see and understand organizations in distinctive yet partial ways. . . . [The] use of metaphor implies *a way of thinking* and *a way of seeing* that pervade how we understand our world generally." While this way of thinking helps us understand and manage organizations, it also limits us. Organizations are complex entities, and metaphors focus our attention on one element of that complexity at the expense of others. For example, in traditional bureaucratic management,

> [We] frequently talk about organizations *as if* they were machines
> designed to achieve predetermined goals and objectives, and
> which should operate smoothly and efficiently. And as a result of
> this kind of thinking we often attempt to organize and manage
> them in a mechanistic way, forcing their human qualities into a
> background role (Morgan 1986, italics in original).

Morgan's idea of metaphor is very much like what Senge discusses as mental models. I want to add one other thing. As the next few chapters show, our models also give us *the dynamic operating principles we build into our organizations.* Table II–1 lists some of the distinctions between machines and living things.

The *raison d'être* of a machine, the reason it exists, is to generate products for the benefit of its owners. Managers with mechanical models see their organizations as profit-making machines that should benefit shareholders. They believe those organizations should create products and get customers to buy them. Living things, on the other hand, exist by virtue of their ability to nurture mutually beneficial relationships in their environments. As a result, managers with organic models focus on using their

TABLE II–1 Distinctions Between Machines and Living Things.

	Machines	Organisms
Raison d'être	Generate products for benefit of the owner	Nurture mutually beneficial relationships
Information use	Put information where it will be used	Make information universally accessible
Integration	Analytical hierarchy of replaceable parts	Nested networks of units that contribute to health of the whole
Governance	External intelligence	Central nervous system
System-wide alteration	Redesign, reengineer	Evolve

products and services to build relationships with customers, suppliers, and even competitors. We examined this distinction and what it means for organizations in Part I.

In Part II, we look at three types of structures—information, integration, and governance—and how choosing a mechanical or organic model alters both the way the organization works and how its people behave. Over and over, we shall see the Law of Organizational Models in play (Figure II–1). The choice of a model suggests certain types of structures, and those structures result in specific kinds of behavior.

In Chapters 4 to 6, we look at the difference between the ways machines and living things distribute information. Machines put information only where it will be used; living things make the information of the whole available in all their parts. By severely limiting information, the mechanical model reduces workers to preprogrammed parts. By making information universally available, the organic model enables people to act autonomously.

Model ▶ Structure ▶ Behavior

FIGURE II–1 The Law of Organizational Models.

We explore this distinction in terms of the guiding purposes of organizations, referred to as *identity* (see Chapter 4); their structural and procedural information, or *corporate DNA* (see Chapter 5); and their ability to capture and communicate information about themselves and the world around them in a *corporate nervous system* (see Chapter 6).

In integrating all parts into a whole, machines produce analytical hierarchies, in which the whole is divided into separate, progressively smaller subunits. Living things, on the other hand, are highly interconnected hierarchies of nested networks, in which molecules nest in organelles; organelles in cells; cells in organs; and so forth. As a result, mechanically modeled organizations are made of mechanically separate units. An organic model, on the other hand, results in a hierarchy of nested networks in which individuals and units can easily connect. We explore the implications of this difference in Chapter 7.

In Chapter 8, we look at the differences in how these models of organization are reflected in the ways the organizations are governed. Machines must be designed, operated, and repaired by an external intelligence. As a result, managers in mechanically modeled organizations believe they must control and direct them—that is, practice command-and-control. Living things, on the contrary, are self-designing, self-operating, and self-repairing. They govern themselves through a central nervous system, which supports and maintains the whole rather than controlling it. In organically modeled organizations, then, managers support a system that enables people to do their jobs more autonomously.

Part III explores the difference between mechanical and organic models for making systemwide alterations.

Before we start applying organic design principles to organizations, we need to touch on one last issue. The purpose of a model is to give us the patterns we need to manage our organizations more effectively. Some readers may recognize inconsistencies in these discussions. Sometimes we discuss organizations as if they were single living things with DNA, sense organs, and a nervous system. Other times we discuss them as if they were tribes of individuals, as with 3M's 40-some product divisions (see Chapter 7). In Part III, we discuss them as evolving. Yet living things evolve over generations; a single organization can evolve itself. The fact is that there are differences between organizations and living things. What is important is not the consistency of our comparisons but how much those comparisons can help us manage.

With this in mind, let's turn to how we can apply the design principles of life to our organizations. We begin with one of the most critical issues in living systems. How can living systems, composed of units that behave autonomously, ensure they all work for the benefit of the whole? The answer is the shared identity with which their DNA is aligned. That identity is the subject of Chapter 4.

CHAPTER 4

Corporate Identity: The Image in the Mirrors

[With] no law other than the conservation of an identity and the capacity to reproduce, we have all emerged.
—Humberto Maturana and Francisco Varela

Question: How can management create a cohesive guiding purpose for the organization so that everyone is marching in the same direction?

According to a favorite story of former 3M CEO Lew Lehr, one 3M employee was developing a product that he *knew* would be a big winner for the company. The employee was so devoted to his idea that he ignored his boss's repeated warnings to stop wasting time on an idea that wasn't going anywhere. After watching this employee work on the idea for a year, with no payoff in sight, the boss finally fired him.

In most organizations, that would have been the end of the story. But not at 3M. The employee was so devoted to his idea that he continued working on it in an unused office, without pay. In time, he was rehired to complete the idea, and the product became a big winner for the company. The employee was eventually promoted to vice-president.

At first glance, most of us who grew up with a mechanical model will say this story is about the corporate culture at 3M. That's what Terrence Deal and Alan Kennedy concluded when they told this story in *Corporate Cultures* (1982): "A major element in the 3M culture, therefore, concerns doing what you believe in—and persisting at it." From an organic viewpoint, the employee's persistence is the least interesting thing about the story. Something else, something much more exciting, is going on.

The man who would not be fired is not just persistent. He's downright insubordinate. He disregards his boss's insistence that he stop working on the project, and he doesn't even pay attention when his boss fires him. He has entirely disregarded the authority of the hierarchy in favor of his personal judgment. It doesn't stop there. The market validates the employee in choosing his own wisdom over the company's authority when the product becomes a success. It's important to note that this product *was* successful. No one would tell the story if the product had failed. Still, the company rewards the employee for being insubordinate—and successful—by promoting him to vice-president.

If this were all, the story would still be pretty amazing. But the most exciting thing about this story may be the person who loved to tell it—the CEO. In relating this story, Lehr, the most senior person at 3M, is inviting people across his company to believe in their new product ideas to the point of challenging anyone in authority, even him.

How can a company of 74,000 employees succeed when its CEO invites people, not merely to challenge but also to work around the system and management's authority? The answer is that an organic corporation such as 3M uses a corporate identity—a description of how it succeeds in its markets—to let everyone know its purpose and then reinforces that purpose over and over. Every procedure and structure in an organization's corporate DNA, explored in Chapter 5, is aligned to give people incentives to act in ways that fulfill its identity.

The effect is a lot like a room of mirrors set up so that each one reflects the same image. Corporate identity is that image, reflected in all the structures and procedures of corporate DNA, all the corporate systems that move employees to act. Because all of 3M's 74,000 employees see the image of innovation wherever they look, Lehr could trust that although employees might disregard a manager's authority, they would always be true to 3M's corporate identity, innovation.

Before we go on to examine corporate identity and what it means for the way we think about our organizations, we need to look at how machines and living things create a sense of purpose. Then we explore how mechanically modeled organizations create their sense of purpose versus the different ways in which organic corporations create theirs.

Machines versus Living Things

Machines are pure tools of human purpose. We build them to perform specific tasks, no more, no less. Think, for example, about the difference between your car and a horse. Although you can teach a horse to go where you want it to, if you let it out of the corral, it will find its own way soon enough. Not your car. Your car will go only where you direct it to go, as long, of course, as you keep it in good repair. Open the garage door and your car will sit where it is until someone revs it up and takes it for a drive. A horse can find its own way. A car cannot. With no vision, ability to learn about the road, or understanding of itself, a car must be directed as it makes its way down the road.

Living things, on the other hand, understand, on a molecular level, what they are about. Each has evolved an identity, a characteristic way of succeeding that has been defined by its interaction with its ecological system. For example, there are about 350 species of sharks. Each species has its own identity, from the great white shark, the great killer of the deep, which naturalist E. O. Wilson (1992) calls "the most frightening animals on earth," to the mollusk-eating bottom dweller, the horn shark to the filtering shark, which sucks in shrimp and plankton-like sea creatures, much like some whales. Teeth, jaws, eyes, body, fins. In each species, all these evolved to enhance the identity of the species. Over tens of millions of years, the DNA of these sharks enabled them to try all sorts of variations on these systems. The systems that enabled the sharks to fulfill their identities survived. The ones that didn't work were weeded out through natural selection. In this way, DNA enables living things to evolve as a tightly integrated set of subsystems aligned to survive by fulfilling a single-minded identity (Wilson 1993).

Our human identity is manipulator of our environment. Opposable thumbs enabled us to make tools to recreate our physical world; our ability to exchange ideas enabled us to recreate our social world. No fangs or talons for tearing flesh, no thick coat of hair for warmth, no speed to escape predators, just the mental and physical agility to shape the world around us. For this reason, as Isaac Asimov (1994) noted, the parts of the brain "devoted to the lips, tongue and hand are (as one might expect) larger in proportion to the actual size of those organs than are the sections devoted to other parts of the body."

Corporate Vision, Corporate Culture

If we start with a mechanical model, how can we create an organizational sense of purpose? First we'd think of the organization as if it were a machine, a pure tool of its owners' purposes. As a result, such an organization would need an operator of the corporate machine with a vision to enable it to maneuver in its markets, just as your vision enables you to drive your car in heavy traffic. Moreover, because the parts of a corporate machine are human, its operator needs a way of communicating this vision, and the behavior it requires, to all those parts. The operator of the corporate machine we have described is a company's visionary leader. Part of that leader's job is to hold the vision that enables the company to take advantage of its markets and to model its corporate culture into the organization so that people can develop generally accepted behaviors that will help realize the vision.

This description of how a mechanical model translates into a sense of organizational purpose should be familiar. In *Organizational Culture and Leadership* (1991), Edgar Schein defines corporate culture as the way of thinking and acting that people in an organization learn and pass on, both individually and as a company. In the more familiar words of former McKinsey & Co. managing director Marvin Bower, it is "the way we do things around here" (Deal and Kennedy 1982). Schein goes so far as to insist that the *"only thing of real importance that leaders do is to create and manage culture..."* (Schein 1991, italics in original). At its best, such a corporate culture creates the human element with which visionary leaders make their organizations more than mere corporate machines.

At IBM, for example, the corporate culture was created by Tom Watson, Sr. and his son, Tom, Jr. "We want to give the best customer service of any company in the world," was how Watson, Jr. expressed what IBM stood for (Peters and Waterman 1982). That one sentence sums up the vision he and his father had for their company. Watson, Sr. built the company starting in the 1920s by selling mechanical, pre-electronic calculating machines. To realize his vision of customer service, Watson nurtured a hard-nosed culture in which people were expected to challenge each other, even him, when they thought they had good ideas. Balancing this was the Watsons' concern for employees. During World War II, for example, Watson, Sr. paid partial salary to employees who had gone off to fight the war. The resulting IBM culture combined intense loyalty with a challenge to do one's personal best. Not surprisingly, for most of its history, people loved working at IBM.[1]

The Watsons also emphasized taking care of the customer. In one story on the subject, Watson, Sr. was at a meeting to assess customer problems. He sat quietly as the participants made eight to ten piles of paper on the table, according to problem source—manufacturing, engineering, and so forth. Finally, Watson got up, walked to the front of the room, swept all the piles of paper off the table, and said, "There aren't any categories of problems here. There's just one problem. Some of us aren't paying enough attention to our customers" (Peters and Waterman 1982).

This corporate culture, valuing both employees and customers, ensured, first, that people loved to work for IBM and, second, that their shared behaviors and attitudes toward their customers made IBM's reputation for customer service legendary. Combined with Watson, Jr.'s vision of what the computer would soon mean—in the early 1950s, Watson, Jr. persuaded his father to move the company into electronic computers at a time when few experts could imagine a market for even 100 of them—this reputation for customer service enabled IBM to grab a 70 percent share of the mainframe computer market. IBM dominated the market so completely that competitors started calling IBM "the environment."

The weakness of corporate vision/culture as a way of ensuring a common purpose is that it belongs to the company's leader. Too often, a visionary leader who nurtured a culture is succeeded by an executive who has spent his or her work life navigating corporate politics. Without the vision of a leader who understands and nurtures the corporate culture, the company is reduced to a money-making machine, and attention is drawn from the customer and markets to internal politics. At this point, a mechanically modeled organization becomes a bureaucracy. That's what happened at IBM. Tom Watson, Jr. left in 1970 after a heart attack. His successors were sellers of mainframe computers, because the vast majority of company revenue came from mainframe computers. Their dedication to the mainframe business, without a vision of the shifting marketplace, killed IBM's chance to dominate a series of new markets.

Starting in the late 1960s, IBM researchers made technology break-throughs that would have allowed the company to dominate three computer markets. These breakthroughs included:

- The faster, more powerful reduced instruction set chips (RISCs) that Sun Microsystems would use to lead the market for computer work-stations, expensive desk-top machines used largely for scientific number crunching
- Parallel processing, the use of many microchips in a single computer so that difficult problems could be divided into more manageable parts, which made supercomputers possible
- An operating system for personal computers that in 1984 had most of the capabilities of Windows 3.0, introduced in 1989. (This is the one product that most enabled Microsoft to dominate personal computer software markets.)

With these breakthroughs, IBM could have dominated all three markets through the beginning of the 21st century. Yet the senior executives who followed the Watsons were more loyal to the mainframe business than to the vision/culture that made the company great. Because bringing any of these breakthroughs to market could have challenged the sale of mainframe computers, senior managers consistently blocked any commercialization effort. As a result, IBM saw its market share of personal computers drop from nearly 50 percent in 1984 to less than 10 percent in 1996. The company watched as Sun Microsystems became the leader in computer workstations in the middle and late 1980s. IBM never became a force in the supercomputer market.

With the loss of a visionary leader, the corporate culture of a company tends to focus on the past. When Tom Watson, Jr. left IBM, the culture focused increasingly on maintaining dominance in mainframe computers, which its senior managers knew best, and less on taking advantage of new market opportunities. John Sculley, former CEO of

Apple Computers, made this distinction in his book *Odyssey* (1987). Bureaucratic corporate culture, he wrote, "limits us by an emphasis on tradition, on yesterday's heroes, on myths and rituals whose sole value is that they derive from an earlier time." On the other hand, corporate DNA, which Sculley calls *genetic code*, "imprints notions of identity and values as culture does, but in so doing suggests a sense . . . that everything done today is an investment in the future, not an expression of the past" (Sculley and Byrne 1988).

Bureaucratic corporate culture venerates the past; corporate DNA, aligned with corporate identity, generates the future.

Corporate Identity

If we wanted an organization to behave as if it were a living thing, we would create a corporate identity to provide the sense of purpose similar to the corporate vision/culture of a mechanical organization. The corporate identity would describe how the organization succeeds in its markets, and all the procedures and structures of the organization would be aligned with that identity. With identity built into every corporate system, executive managers in an organic corporation wouldn't have to *manage* the corporate vision/culture, as they do in mechanical organizations. Rather, they'd need *to make sure all systems remain aligned with the identity.*

The term *corporate identity* does have another, more technical meaning. In that sense, corporate identity is the way an organization presents itself graphically, with its logo, on everything from delivery trucks to stationery to corporate publications. Many corporations have books full of rules on how corporate identity is to be presented. In this book, however, the term is used much as Wally Olins did in his 1989 book *Corporate Identity*. "Every organization," he wrote, "is unique, and the identity must spring from the organization's own roots, its personality, its strengths and weaknesses. . . ." Such an identity must be "so clear that it becomes the yardstick against which [the organization's] products, behaviour and actions are measured. . . ." Moreover, Olins warned that "identity cannot simply be a slogan, a collection of phrases: it must be visible, tangible and all-embracing" (Olins 1990). As we shall see, this is an excellent beginning for a definition of corporate identity. However, where Olins started by observing successful organizations, we begin with an organic model. As a result, we focus on how corporate identity becomes visible, tangible, and all-embracing when it is built into corporate DNA.

Similarly, in their book *A Simpler Way* (1996), Margaret Wheatley and Myron Kellner-Rogers discuss identity as one of the qualities essential to a more self-organizing type of organization. "Self-organization is the capacity of life to invent itself," they wrote. "This process of invention always takes shape around an identity. There is a self that seeks to organize, to make its presence known."

Thinking about corporate identity in terms of an organic model adds an element of concreteness absent in the works of Olins and Wheatley and Kellner-Rogers. Just as living things develop their identities as they evolve in their environments, an organization develops a corporate identity as it evolves in its market ecology. In this way, corporate identity is the characteristic way the organization has learned to thrive in its markets. As such, corporate identity is not merely about the organization's self. It reflects that self in its ongoing interaction with its markets.

Such an identity can be very different from the management fad for writing corporate mission or vision statements that became popular in the late 1980s. In some exceptions, such a statement did become a corporate identity. When Mercedes-Benz Credit Corporation began reinventing itself, its people defined the following mission statement: "To enhance the marketability of Daimler-Benz products through superior financial services and support." This statement describes the two elements of a strong corporate identity: (1) the contribution the company makes to its markets—enhancing the marketability of the parent company's products—and (2) what employees must do to help make that contribution—provide superior service and support. We'll explore how Mercedes-Benz Credit Corporation used this statement in Chapter 11.

Most corporate mission or vision statements avoid this kind of clear, specific description. The most notorious of such statements run, "We will be the best. . . ." You can fill in the rest. At Bell Atlantic, the Baby Bell providing local telephone service from Pennsylvania to Virginia, one version of the company's vision read: "Bell Atlantic's corporate vision is to be a leading international communications and information management company." In what would Bell Atlantic be a leader? Technology? Quality? Service? What does that mean for the way its people have to interact with their customers and each other? We simply cannot tell from the vision statement. This vision statement is a product of managers' mechanical model. The managers' vision reflects what they believe the corporate machine should be, mechanically cut off from its environment. Corporate identity, on the other hand, is always about the interaction between the organization and its markets. A bureaucratic vision or mission statement is the company looking at itself in the mirror; an organic corporation's identity is its handshake with its markets (Figure 4 1).

In this way, a strong corporate identity enables those both inside and outside the organization to understand what the corporation is about and what they can expect from it. This concept is similar to what James Collins and Jerry Porras call "core ideology" in *Built to Last* (1994). They

Corporate Vision

Corporate Identity

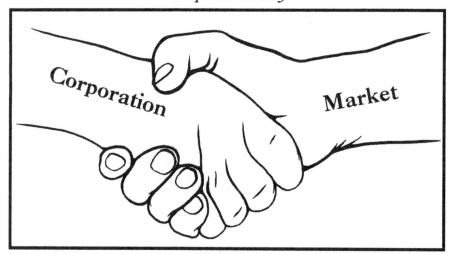

FIGURE 4–1   Corporate Vision and Corporate Identity.

are the "core values and sense of purpose beyond just making money." At 3M, that identity is Innovation. At the Ritz-Carlton hotels, it's "We are ladies and gentlemen serving ladies and gentlemen." In both cases, the identity describes the contribution the company must make in its markets. The identity suggests the types of systems and policies the company needs in every area from hiring to appraisal, product development to delivery. A strong corporate identity is reflected wherever a company's people look, as in a hall of mirrors, and thereby brings them together around a shared purpose. Because an identity allows managers to align all systems, the employees are not whipsawed by a series of contradictory incentives, as they often are in bureaucracies. As a result, both customers and employees know what to expect, and the corporate systems usually deliver it.

Managers at most organic companies, 3M for example, evolved their corporate DNA by trial and error over their histories, often without being conscious of what they were doing. Others, such as the founder of Federal Express, Fred Smith, developed their identities intentionally. In both cases, the corporate identity enabled the organization to try out different subsystems and processes, keeping those that enhanced the identity and dropping those that did not, much the way the great white shark evolved its systems around its identity. By developing a strong corporate identity, managers can enable people in their organizations intentionally to build and experiment with their corporate DNA to make those organizations even more successful.

For the rest of this chapter, let's look at two examples of aligning corporate systems around identities—a glimpse at some of the things people at 3M and Federal Express do.

Innovation at 3M

In the early 1990s, 3M raised its corporate goal for revenues from new products from 25 percent of sales from products no more than five years old to 30 percent from products no more than four years old. This goal drives the people at 3M to continually uncover new ways to meet the shifting needs of its customers and thereby to coevolve in its market ecologies.

3M can perform this way because its identity is *innovation*. Everyone at 3M knows the story of how innovation has been the driving, unifying force behind a corporation with tens of thousands of products. Innovation lies at the beginning of 3M's story—its founding in 1902 to manufacture a superior type of sandpaper and how that effort failed; the company's sometimes stumbling steps to develop new products to meet specific customer needs; and how the company finally began to succeed in the early 1920s with a more durable, waterproof sandpaper. Innovation goes on to describe the development of Scotch brand masking and cellophane tapes, of magnetic tape and medical gauze masks, and of the thousands of other products 3M sells.[2]

The story of Wetordry sandpaper, the first breakthrough product for 3M, set the tone for everything that followed. In January 1920, 3M president William McKnight received a letter from a Philadelphia printing ink maker, Francis Oakie, requesting samples of all the 3M mineral grits. Fascinated by the request, McKnight asked his eastern division sales manager to find out why Oakie wanted the samples. The sales manager learned that a neighbor of Oakie was leaving his glass-beveling business because the dust the work caused was damaging his health. So Oakie started wondering why he couldn't make a waterproof sandpaper that would allow his neighbor to eliminate the dust problem.

Convinced that Oakie had a winning idea, the sales manager wired McKnight to come to Philadelphia to check it out for himself. McKnight was impressed. By February 1921, 3M and Oakie had signed an agreement. Oakie moved to St. Paul the next year. He worked with others at 3M to overcome technical problems and perfect his idea. The new product proved a revelation in the automobile industry. Before the introduction of the waterproof sandpaper, it took two weeks to finish an automobile body. With Wetordry sandpaper, it took three or four days. The new product also produced a smoother, more polished finish to paint jobs.

This story demonstrates the 3M identity of innovation in a nutshell. It shows the openness of company management to unconventional ideas and its willingness to support people with personal vision. Moreover, it describes an attitude of cross-functional cooperation to learn new customer needs and then overcome the technical difficulties involved in meeting them. The story sums up the set of attitudes, values, and behaviors that enables the people at 3M to know each other as members of the same living organization.

To encourage innovation, 3M has institutionalized incentives in corporate systems throughout the company. The 15 Percent Rule, for example, gives most employees the opportunity to spend up to 15 percent of their time working on their own projects. This policy originated with 3M's visionary leader, William McKnight. McKnight initially gave this 15 percent of self-managed time to technical staff. Today some nontechnical managers also allow their people that free time. The 15 percent figure is not absolute. William E. Coyne, 3M senior vice-president of research and development, explained it this way: "The number is not so important as the message.... If you have a good idea, and the commitment to squirrel away time to work on it, and the raw nerve to skirt your lab manager's expressed desires, then go for it" (Coyne 1996).

People who identify a need can also take advantage of the 3M network for communicating about new technologies that might help them develop a product to meet the need. The company encourages curious employees to learn about new technologies developed in all parts of the company. In Coyne's words, "products belong to the divisions [that market them], but technologies belong to the company. Technologies should—no, must—be shared" (Coyne 1996). This belief in technology sharing is so strong that 3M will continue to share technologies with the new company, Imation, recently spun off to handle 3M imaging products.

The 15 Percent Rule and "bootlegging," by which employees beg and borrow resources to support new product ideas, have enabled thousands of 3M innovators to use the company's technical communication network to develop new products. Those products include Art Fry's Post-it notes in the 1970s, Patsy Sherman's Scotchgard fabric protectors in the 1950s, and Dick Drew's masking tape in the 1930s. Such innovators sometimes receive money to pursue these projects from a business unit with which their laboratories are linked. Innovators also can apply for a Genesis Grant, which is awarded by a panel of scientists rather than managers. Some frustrated researchers even walk into the office of the CEO to ask for money to continue a project, and receive it.

Even when employees are unable to win management support to commercialize a product, the company's emphasis on innovation encourages them to continue championing it, as in the story of the employee who wouldn't be fired. One reason that story may have been among former CEO Lew Lehr's favorites was his own experience. At one point, Lehr helped develop the first 3M surgical drapes. The product was slow to catch on, and Lehr's superiors told him to drop the project. Lehr, however, was sure it only needed time. He agreed to kill the project once inventories were used up, but didn't tell the factory to stop production until inventory built up. While inventory was dwindling, Lehr won more time by negotiating a major contract with a customer 3M wanted to keep happy. By the time all this happened, the surgical drape had begun to catch on in its market. Today this product earns several million dollars a year.

The moral of all this is that 3M's identity of innovation drives everyone to recognize that the most valuable products may initially seem the most unlikely. As a result, everyone is encouraged to take risks and fight for new products they believe will be successful, because the corporate identity, innovation, is more important even than being fired.

Management at 3M continues to focus on keeping its corporate systems aligned with innovation. For example, in 1996, the company developed a set of hiring guidelines, titled "Hiring Innovators." As successful as the company had been in realizing its identity, management *didn't* become complacent. It continues to study how the company can become even more tightly aligned with innovation.

"People, Service, Profits" at Federal Express

At first, I thought the corporate identity at Federal Express would be "absolutely, positively on time." That turns out to be an important element. But when you hang around Federal Express even for a few hours, you find it's only a part. Fred Smith started Federal Express in 1973 to provide overnight delivery to customers who needed to be sure their packages would arrive on time. To ensure that standard of service— "absolutely, positively on time"—he developed a philosophy to help employees focus on the highest level of quality. Smith's philosophy became the Federal Express identity, and the company states it in three words, "People, Service, Profits." If Federal Express treats its people like valued contributors to an important endeavor, those people will provide superior service. If the people provide superior service, the company will do well financially.[3]

This is the identity that every FedExer understands, the basis of the inspiring stories we hear about the company's 98 percent rate of on-time delivery. A delivery agent whose truck broke down, for instance, rented a snowmobile to get a package to a customer in a Nebraska snow storm. Another FedExer rented a private airplane to make sure one very special package was delivered on time. In some ways, they're all the same story— about a person, supported by the company, willing to take heroic measures to ensure the customer is served.

As with innovation at 3M, "People, Service, Profits" is at the heart of every corporate system at Federal Express. Each element of this identity is supported by specific systems. For example, to ensure that its people feel valued, the company developed a series of systems to encourage managers to behave appropriately:

- *Management Training.* Associates—what members of the rank and file are called—who want to become managers at Federal Express begin with a week-long course that details the company's expectations. They learn that 75 percent of managers' time must be spent supervising their people; that managers must appraise the performance of each person annually, talking candidly about real problems; and that less-formal feedback must be ongoing and can be unpleasant to deliver. They also learn that a manager who is twice late making annual appraisals is likely to be removed from management. The course drives home the difficulty of these demands through role playing. As a result, 80 percent of those enrolled in this class decide against joining management. By 1992, the annual dropout rate from management ranks had fallen from 10 percent to 2 percent.
- *Reverse Appraisal.* Every spring, the company's annual survey of associates begins with questions about ten critical supervisor behav-

iors, such as empowerment, coaching, favoritism, and open communication. When managers receive the results, they're expected to conduct a meeting with the people who report directly to them to discuss how they can improve their performance as managers.

- *Recognition.* FedEx also has a series of recognition systems that ensure managers give continual positive feedback when associates do a good job. Like many other companies, Federal Express has a corporate excellence award, the Falcon. But that's just the beginning. The company awards pins to any employee who receives a letter of customer commendation. It also awards three types of quality improvement pins—a bronze pin for people on a team whose idea is accepted by management; silver for a team that has succeeded; and gold for a higher level of accomplishment. Employees often wear their pins at work; some have so many they look like they need to mount their pins on scout sashes. Any employee can award any other employee a Bravo Zulu, the Navy semaphore flags for a job well done. The Bravo Zulu awards are points of pride, and associates put three, four, or five of them up on their cubicle walls. As a result, people walk around Federal Express facilities with the pride and self-assurance that come from knowing their work is appreciated.

Federal Express also supports the service element of its identity with a series of systems:

- The company provides extensive training for anyone taking on a new job, especially for its marketing and customer-service people, who receive six weeks of training before they go on the job. In 1992, 93 divisions within the company had their own training facilities.
- All employees have what the company calls recurrent training to keep them up to date. In the service centers, for example, service agents get four hours of paid study time before their annual job knowledge test. The day after the test, employees receive a printout telling them how they did, the areas in which they need more study, and what resources are available for study. Agents who fail the test are removed from customer contact to another job. They have eight hours of paid study time before the next test. Those who fail a second time have to find another job in the company. This annual testing, with the paid time associates are allowed for study, emphasizes how seriously the company takes the quality of service it provides.
- The Federal Express communications system includes the company's computer package-tracking system, which enables any sales representative to tell any customer where any package was at any given time. The computer system is complemented by the

corporate television network, which distributes a daily program with information on potential problems to employees throughout the company. For example, if jets have problems taking off from Anchorage one day, the associates unloading and sorting those packages in Memphis know about it and are able to rearrange their schedules rather than be surprised. We'll explore the concept of corporate nervous systems in the next chapter.

All three elements of the Federal Express identity are measured. *People* is measured through the composite of managers' scores in their reverse appraisals. *Service* is measured through statistical quality indicators (SQIs), a list of 12 customer-identified problems. Each problem is assigned a "yell" factor, indicating how much it bothers customers. A same-day late package is worth one point. A lost package is worth ten points. Every year, the company sets a goal for total SQI points. In 1992, it was 128,000 out of a potential 50 million. The company's SQI performance each week is posted in every workplace, along with the performance of that group so people are constantly aware of how they are doing. *Profits* are measured with an annual pretax income goal. If the company meets all three goals, all managers receive bonuses. Lower-level managers and professionals receive bonuses as long as the company meets people and service goals.

In all these ways, the identity of companies such as 3M and Federal Express are reflected in all their corporate systems. As a result, their corporate DNA expresses the company identity clearly and out in the open. In addition, it reinforces the behaviors the identities demand, aligning every corporate subsystem that might provide incentives.

Summary

Organizations built on mechanical and organic models develop cohesive, guiding purposes in different ways. Mechanically modeled organizations need a leader to provide a vision of the market and to model a corporate culture. In traditional organizations, this vision/culture belongs to the company's visionary leader, and managing it is among senior managers' most important tasks. Organically modeled organizations evolve an identity—a characteristic way of succeeding in their market ecologies— that they build into every company structure and procedure in their corporate DNA. This identity belongs to everyone in the organization, and senior managers must work to keep the structures and procedures of corporate DNA aligned with the identity.

In today's turbulent markets, organic corporations can use their identities to create a series of competitive advantages over mechanical competitors that use a vision/culture. Because a corporate identity is woven into the warp and woof of corporate subsystems, organic corporations can avoid the visionary leader trap. As with IBM, when the visionary leader of a mechanically modeled organization leaves, the company often loses both its vision and the protector of its corporate culture. On the other hand, organic corporations have identities woven into their daily work lives. As a result, 3M has had four CEOs over the last 20 years without the loss of direction that occurred at IBM. 3M continues to perform at a high level because its guiding purpose is built into every process and structure in the company.

For companies working to coevolve in their turbulent market ecologies, identities are a surer guide to corporate action than vision/culture. After all, in today's markets, even the best vision of a company's place in future markets can shift as new technologies enter the market. Identity, on the other hand, evolves from a history of interaction with the market. New technologies can come and go, but innovation at 3M or "We are ladies and gentlemen serving ladies and gentlemen" at The Ritz-Carlton remains a steady guide for absorbing and using those technologies.

An identity can focus managers' attention specifically on what they need to do to keep their organizations competitive. As with IBM, managing a corporate vision/culture is a leadership responsibility. Many senior managers never learn this capability. With an identity, senior managers have only to learn to keep corporate structures and procedures aligned with the identity. In doing so, they take a giant stride toward keeping their people focused on meeting the developing challenges of their markets in a way mechanically modeled organizations have often been unable to do.

In today's fast-moving markets, this ability to keep people focused on meeting developing challenges may be the most important advantage a corporate identity confers. By aligning everything about the company with their unique ways of succeeding in markets, companies such as 3M and Federal Express blaze the market trails their competitors must follow. In markets where the learning curve seems to become steeper and steeper, being a market trail blazer provides an advantage that is difficult to beat.

Let's turn next to the information that senior managers must align with their corporate identities—the flexible, universally available database of structures and procedures: corporate DNA.

CHAPTER 5

Corporate DNA as Database:
A Memory of Things
to Come

*In biological evolution, experience of the past is compressed in the
genetic message encoded in DNA. In the case of human societies,
the schemata are institutions, customs, traditions, and myths. They are,
in effect, kinds of cultural DNA.*

—Murray Gell-Mann

Question: How can managers ensure that people perform their jobs
according to the best available practices, rather than repeating the
mistakes of the past?

Don't Leave Home Without It

The quality advisor at the Philadelphia Ritz-Carlton hotel apologized for
what she was about to do. "This dress doesn't have any pockets," she
explained, reaching down to take her shoe off and remove a three-fold
pocket-sized pamphlet. "So today I have to keep my credo card in my
shoe."[1]

At The Ritz-Carlton hotels, *everyone* carries a copy of the credo
card, a constant reminder of what the company is all about and how its
philosophy shapes every action. It's a remarkable document. On the back,
in 18-point type—the rest of the card is in nine- or ten-point type—is the
corporate motto: "We Are Ladies and Gentlemen Serving Ladies and
Gentlemen." Read it once, and you *know* what this organization is all
about (Figure 5–1).

On the inside of the pamphlet are The Ritz-Carlton Basics, which
describe the key principles and procedures that form the company's
philosophy. Lateral service, for example, requires that when employees in

THE RITZ-CARLTON® BASICS

1 The Credo will be known, owned and energized by all employees.

2 Our motto is: "We are Ladies and Gentlemen serving Ladies and Gentlemen". Practice teamwork and "lateral service" to create a positive work environment.

3 The three steps of service shall be practiced by all employees.

4 All employees will successfully complete Training Certification to ensure they understand how to perform to The Ritz-Carlton standards in their position.

5 Each employee will understand their work area and Hotel goals as established in each strategic plan.

6 All employees will know the needs of their internal and external customers (guests and employees) so that we may deliver the products and services they expect. Use guest preference pads to record specific needs.

7 Each employee will continuously identify defects (Mr. BIV) throughout the Hotel.

8 Any employee who receives a customer complaint "owns" the complaint.

9 Instant guest pacification will be ensured by all. React quickly to correct the problem immediately. Follow-up with a telephone call within twenty minutes to verify the problem has been resolved to the customer's satisfaction. Do everything you possibly can to never lose a guest.

10 Guest incident action forms are used to record and communicate every incident of guest dissatisfaction. Every employee is empowered to resolve the problem and to prevent a repeat occurrence.

11 Uncompromising levels of cleanliness are the responsibility of every employee.

12 "Smile – We are on stage." Always maintain positive eye contact. Use the proper vocabulary with our guests. (Use words like – "Good Morning," "Certainly," "I'll be happy to" and "My pleasure").

13 Be an ambassador of your Hotel in and outside of the work place. Always talk positively. No negative comments.

14 Escort guests rather than pointing out directions to another area of the Hotel.

15 Be knowledgeable of Hotel information (hours of operation, etc.) to answer guest inquiries. Always recommend the Hotel's retail and food and beverage outlets prior to outside facilities.

16 Use proper telephone etiquette. Answer within three rings and with a "smile." When necessary, ask the caller, "May I place you on hold." Do not screen calls. Eliminate call transfers when possible.

17 Uniforms are to be immaculate; Wear proper and safe footwear (clean and polished), and your correct name tag. Take pride and care in your personal appearance (adhering to all grooming standards).

18 Ensure all employees know their roles during emergency situations and are aware of fire and life safety response processes.

19 Notify your supervisor immediately of hazards, injuries, equipment or assistance that you need. Practice energy conservation and proper maintenance and repair of Hotel property and equipment.

20 Protecting the assets of a Ritz-Carlton Hotel is the responsibility of every employee.

©1992, The Ritz-Carlton Hotel Company. All rights reserved.

THREE STEPS OF SERVICE

1
A warm and sincere greeting. Use the guest name, if and when possible.

2
Anticipation and compliance with guest needs.

3
Fond farewell. Give them a warm good-bye and use their names, if and when possible.

"We Are Ladies and Gentlemen Serving Ladies and Gentlemen"

THE RITZ-CARLTON®

CREDO

The Ritz-Carlton Hotel is a place where the genuine care and comfort of our guests is our highest mission.

We pledge to provide the finest personal service and facilities for our guests who will always enjoy a warm, relaxed yet refined ambience.

The Ritz-Carlton experience enlivens the senses, instills well-being, and fulfills even the unexpressed wishes and needs of our guests.

FIGURE 5–1   The Ritz-Carlton Credo Card.

---

any part of the hotel notice a service problem developing, they should stop performing regular job duties to pitch in and solve the problem. If someone from the restaurant sees customers beginning to back up at the front desk, that person should go behind the desk to make sure the customers are served promptly.

As a result, *everyone* at a Ritz-Carlton hotel needs to become familiar with *all* its procedures. The hotels offer many opportunities for people to learn them. Departments offer tutorials. Employees can take formal cross-training and become certified in processes in different work groups. Every department in each hotel also has a departmental Skills Mastery Manual—a binder with a full set of its procedures. The binders are available for anyone who needs to know how to confirm a reservation or clean a toilet bowl, set a table in the restaurant or order theater tickets for a guest. This is the place where, as Casey Stengel used to say, "You could look it up."

By putting Skills Mastery Manuals in every department, Ritz-Carlton hotels make the procedural information of the whole available to all its parts. This is what DNA does for our bodies. Put it all together—credo card, procedural tutorials, cross-training certification, and Skills Mastery Manuals—and you have a recipe for corporate DNA. Corporate DNA is a database of the procedural and structural information the people in an organic corporation need to work in a self-organizing way, aligned according to corporate identity. In the previous chapter, we looked at corporate identity. In this chapter, we look at corporate DNA as a database of procedural and structural information and compare it with the mechanical alternative.

Machines versus Living Things

Machines limit available information. Each part is designed with only the procedural information it needs to do its job. The spark plugs in your car "know" how to ignite the fuel in the cylinders. They contain no other information, and no other part "knows" how to ignite the fuel. Machine design links parts together to create cause-and-effect work processes that generate the product or service for which any machine was designed. By designing parts with limited information, we ensure the parts will do their jobs the same way every time, thereby increasing our ability to control machines and make sure they remain predictable.

Structural information is even more limited. That information remains in the blueprint of the machine, which belongs to the designers, who can make it as available as they choose. The type of machines we are discussing have no way to use this information. Recent research on "living" machines indicates that we can make self-repairing machines that contain their own structural designs (Kelly 1994). But the kinds of machines we learned about, and on which bureaucratic managers build their organizations, lack the intelligence they need to understand that design.

Living things, on the other hand, make the information of the whole—both procedural and structural—universally available in their DNA. DNA is life's ultimate tool for creative problem solving. On one hand, it's the language in which life writes itself. With only four symbols—the nucleotides adenine, thymine, guanine, and cytosine—DNA enables life to create every plant and animal, from bacteria and single-cell plankton to redwoods and elephants. But DNA is more than just that. Imagine designing a car that contains its own blueprint, the instructions it needs to build itself, and the knowledge it needs to operate, repair, and even change to take advantage of changes in passenger preferences and road conditions. That's what DNA lets us do.

Organic DNA has two qualities that are critical to corporate DNA, because they enable people to help their organization coevolve to market shifts. First, DNA is *universally available*. It contains information on every process and how to build and operate every other structure in our bodies, distributed to every part. You have the same DNA in your wrist as in your liver. As a result, on the molecular level, each part of our body has access to information about how every other part works. No one knows why life uses information so redundantly. Still, this overabundance of information seems critical to the way living things operate.

The other quality is that DNA is *flexible*. Small changes in the order of nucleotides—mutations—occasionally occur. The body has a genetic editor that eliminates most of them. Many of the mutations that remain add no survival value. So the organisms in which they occur do not survive. Only a very few of the changes that become part of the DNA code have survival value. Those few, however, let us adapt to changes in our environments. As Jonathan Weiner notes in *The Beak of the Finch* (1994), adaptation can occur very rapidly, shifting the nature of entire populations of animals from generation to generation. Over millions of years, these changes allow living things to evolve new structures and new species, as the dinosaur evolved into the bird. This flexibility is essential. Living things coevolve in reaction to changes in the climate and other living things in their ecologies. As each species adapts, it subtly changes the ecological balance. Then other members of the ecology must adapt to the changes. Flexible DNA makes coevolution possible.

Information in Mechanically Modeled Organizations

Build an organization on a mechanical model, and we would expect employee parts to have only the information they need to do their jobs. In turn, management would connect these living parts in a cause-and-effect chain to create defined products. We would further expect that the way employees do those jobs could only be changed when the information they needed to do their jobs was changed by the external intelligence—operator of the corporate machine—that controlled them. Finally, although they might have access to the corporate blueprint, we would expect them to have little use for it and, most certainly, no ability to change corporate structure.

Anyone who's worked in a bureaucracy will recognize that description. In a bureaucracy, employees are not expected to know much beyond the information needed to do their jobs, usually stated as inflexible, tradition-bound standard operating procedures (SOPs). An employee's job is to practice SOPs, even when a better, less costly way to serve the customer is obvious. Bell Atlantic CEO Ray Smith used to talk about his initiation to the SOPs of the old AT&T finance department. In his early days in the department, Smith found a way to save the company thousands of dollars annually. He told his boss, who replied, "Ray, that's great. But that's not the way we do things around here."[2]

SOPs are a key way bureaucratic managers can maintain control and predictability. When an employee is limited to one way to perform each procedure, managers can reduce that employee's behavior to a mechanical response. The extent to which people's behavior is controlled sometimes becomes comical. At IBM, for example, SOPs limited the frequency with which a writer could reuse a joke in executive speeches. The higher the level of the speaker, the longer the writer had to wait to reuse the joke (Carroll 1994).

We all know what happens when organizations use information mechanically. Have you ever asked someone in a bureaucracy for an exception to the rules and felt the not-too-subtle message that you were getting in the way of the bureaucrat's doing his or her job? The reason you felt that way is precisely because you were keeping that bureaucrat from doing his or her job. A bureaucrat's job is not to serve customers. Rather, it's to practice SOPs and follow the boss's orders. That's what people in a bureaucracy are paid to do. In many cases, only the person in the job knows the SOPs for that job. As a result, SOPs end up belonging to the people who practice them, as does any information that comes to them as they perform their SOPs. This is one reason so many bureaucracies have been so disappointed with their total quality management (TQM) programs. Only limited improvement is possible within any one job or within a given business unit. Yet because people feel they own their procedures, they're often suspicious of cross-departmental improvement or suggestions for improvement from people in other departments.

Bureaucracies are infamous for what happens because of this fragmentary way of storing information. For instance, several years ago, I had a telephone line installed in my home office. It worked fine for a couple of days, although I did get a few calls for a Foot Locker store. Then over the weekend the line died. I spent half the following Monday calling the telephone company, over and over, explaining the problem to one service representative after another, unable to get back to the previous person with whom I'd spoken. Finally, I realized the telephone company had given me the same phone number as a local Foot Locker store.

By the end of the day, I was furious. Not because the Foot Locker and I were given the same number. Technical mistakes happen. I was enraged that I had spent half a day calling over and over to service representatives whose real job was to follow a series of SOPs, not to help me solve my problem. It would have been a simple matter to record my trouble report in a computer database so any service representative could have access to it. But the company's managers were so fixed in their mechanical model that no one thought to implement such a customer-friendly precaution. The job of anyone in a bureaucracy, after all, is to perform a set of SOPs, not to address the customers' problems.

This story demonstrates the Law of Organizational Models at work. The mechanical model of bureaucracy results in mechanical structures, such as one for storing information. And those structures produce certain types of behaviors. Model determines structure, which implies behavior.

Information at Organic Corporations

If we were to design an organization to use procedural and structural information the way living things do, we would expect to build a corporate equivalent of DNA. That is, we would expect the organization to make all its procedural and structural information available to all employees. We would also expect to have mechanisms for keeping that information flexible so it could continually coevolve with its market ecologies. In fact, when we look at the way companies such as The Ritz-Carlton or Federal Express store and access information, we find exactly this kind of corporate DNA—a flexible, universally available database of company procedures and structures.

The Structure of Organic and Corporate DNA

Organic and corporate DNA share a problem: Both contain enormous amounts of information. Yet that information must be stored in a compact, easy-to-access form. Your body stores all the instructions it needs to perform all the activities, from conception to death, that make up your life in your DNA. A single, stretched-out string of that DNA would be about a yard long. However, it is structured so it can fit in your cell nuclei, each of which is only one one-thousandth of a centimeter in diameter. Similarly, a corporation such as 3M or Motorola may have hundreds of thousands of procedures in locations across the globe. To be fully effective, these procedures must be quickly accessible and easy to update.

DNA's structure enables our bodies to fit all those instructions into this extremely compact space. We don't need to examine how DNA works. We do need to understand how organic DNA stores so much information so compactly so we can draw some conclusions about how to store corporate DNA in a similar way.[3]

Deoxyribonucleic acid (DNA) is composed of four building blocks, the nucleotides adenine (A), thymine (T), cytosine (C), and guanine (G). These bases combine in sets of three, called *codons*. Each codon has a specific meaning. Many of them, when translated into RNA, produce one of 20 amino acids—for example, the codon AAG produces the amino acid lysine. A series of these codons come together to form a gene. Several other codons give directions to start or stop reproducing a gene—for example, UGA means "stop" (U stands for uracil, which replaces thymine as a base of RNA). Genes come together, with stretches of genetic material that appear to be meaningless, to form chromosomes. The human body has 23 pairs of chromosomes.

DNA appears in the body as a double helix, a twisted staircase composed of two mirror-image strings of bases—exact reflections of each other. Adenine and thymine are mirror images, as are cytosine and guanine. The double string of nucleotides that constitutes DNA enables cells both to replicate themselves by copying their DNA and to produce ribonucleic acid (RNA), which enables DNA to send chemical messages. The double helix is wrapped tightly in supercoiled loops so it can fit within cell nuclei. This structure suggests the following guidelines for designing corporate DNA:

1. Start simply. DNA is made up of only four symbols. So it seems important to write corporate processes in simple instructions that anyone in the organization can understand. Who, for instance, could misunderstand The Ritz-Carlton credo "We are ladies and gentlemen serving ladies and gentlemen"?

2. Combine simple instructions in relatively small sets that represent individual sections of more complex procedures, just as the bases of DNA combine in codons. The Ritz-Carlton Skills Mastery Manuals are composed of many pages, each with several simple statements that describe a single process.

3. Group the corporate codons into larger sets of instructions, much like our genes, that define groups of related procedures. In this way, The Ritz-Carlton uses Skills Mastery Manuals to collect procedures for entire departments.

4. When necessary, "supercoil" the procedures so they are compact and easily available. It would be possible, for example, to store all the procedures of even the largest corporations in a computer database available to each department.

What's important is not that corporate DNA exactly reflect the structure of organic DNA. The key is to move from small, simple components to larger, more complex ones. In that way, the components can be available in terms of easy understanding as well as physical accessibility.

Universal Availability

Corporate DNA contains the full set of internal information that people in any organization need to work in a self-organizing way, distributed universally. Just as DNA in living things contains instructions for all the other structures and all the processes in that organism, corporate DNA should include instructions on every structure and every process in the organization. Just as your DNA is distributed to every nucleated cell in your body, everyone in an organic corporation needs access to its corporate DNA.

At first, this may seem unreasonable. For example, why would desk clerks at a hotel need to know how people in housekeeping clean rooms, except to answer guests' questions? The answer is that in today's turbulent work world, something very near magic begins to happen when people who care about the places they work can get the procedural information they want when they want it.

Consider the desk clerk and the housekeeper. One Ritz-Carlton hotel was having trouble streamlining its housekeeping procedures. Someone in housekeeping discussed the problem with a friend at the front desk. After that conversation, the desk clerk started thinking about what would happen if housekeeping used a computer system similar to the one the front desk used to track guests. The desk clerk submitted this suggestion, which became the key to a more efficient way housekeeping developed to clean rooms.

The universal availability of corporate DNA is a lot like the current movement toward open-book management. Pioneered by Springfield Remanufacturing Corp. CEO Jack Stack and promoted in an open-book newsletter edited by John Case, open-book management has three essential parts. Everyone in the organization must:

- Have access to and understand the financial information—sales, goals, budgets, income statements, and forecasts—that used to be sole possession of senior managers
- Be held accountable for their units' financial performance in addition to quality goals
- Receive compensation and rewards for the success of the business as a whole

In Case's words, "The system is thus wholly transparent: people see and understand the numbers that determine success, learn the part they play in making those numbers, and know in advance how they will be rewarded if the unit achieves its goals" (Case 1997).

The power of this system is obvious. Open-book management enables everyone in an organization to develop a sense of ownership while cultivating trust between management and rank-and-file workers. For any organization building its corporate DNA, making this financial data and the methods for compiling it available is essential. But why stop with financial information? If we want everyone in an organization to develop a sense of ownership, why not make all nonproprietary information available to anyone who wants a look?

When managers do make information universally available, remarkable things happen. At Mercedes-Benz Credit Corporation, the subsidiary that finances Daimler-Benz products in North America, a corporate transformation replaced the hierarchical mechanical model of the company with a more organic one. The new model includes the use of Lotus Notes to keep anyone in the company who is interested aware of new company structures and procedures as they develop. Among other things, making this information universally available began to unravel some long-held misunderstandings.

Like the situation at many companies, the group in the field and the group at corporate headquarters at Mercedes-Benz Credit Corporation didn't fully understand or appreciate what the other group did. Lotus Notes, however, gave the two groups access to what was happening with the other, and its discussion database gave them the opportunity to learn more about each other. As people in the field saw how people at corporate headquarters were working to reinvent their services and make them more valuable and supportive, this lack of understanding began to evaporate. Over time the two groups developed an understanding of and appreciation for each other. They also worked harder to meet the needs of the other. At one point, people in the field explained that they didn't like their counterparts being called *corporate,* because corporate's job was to support efforts in the field. As a result, corporate became the North American Support Center, and the two groups began to build a sense of trust and cooperation that had never before existed.[4]

Financial, procedural, and structural information—all this and more must be easily available in the public record of an organization's corporate DNA. Any company that doesn't make this information easily available is going to start losing customers. Today we have too much competition for every product and service, and people are simply too busy to make a dozen telephone calls to get one piece of information. Because of my problem with the telephone company, I am waiting for the day I will have an alternative for local service. Compare my telephone company to Federal Express. One telephone call to FedEx can tell you exactly where your package is. You can even log on to the FedEx site on World Wide Web and find out directly.

Flexibility

In the early 1990s, I taught quality improvement to several work groups at a Baby Bell. All my students shared one reaction to the material. Whenever I mentioned the importance of written procedures, they reacted with only slightly less panic than a victim in a vampire movie reaching for a cross. For people in a company that had once been part of the old AT&T, the Mother of All Bureaucracies, the word *procedure* was synonymous with SOP, the invariable instructions by which people were supposed to do their jobs.

For my students, procedures were restrictions that made it difficult to serve customers. Yet procedures are essential. We have to know the best way to do any job, even if it's the best way anyone has yet found to do it. Still, at a time when technology is rapidly changing the way we do everything, when we face new competition from every direction, and when customer needs are constantly changing, we also need to reassess how we perform every aspect of every job. Otherwise we'll lose the ability to meet customer needs in a competitive way. The TQM movement recognized this need for flexibility in assessing and meeting customer needs. In this way, we can see TQM as one way for our organizations to coevolve, adapting corporate DNA to shifts in the markets in which they operate.

At the heart of TQM is the idea of continuous quality improvement, based on statistical analysis. For W. Edwards Deming, the grandfather of TQM, especially, continuous quality improvement was the key to dominating markets by means of increasing productivity, lowering costs, and giving customers the products they wanted. For Deming, this was a simple, yet elegant process: Define quality in terms of what your customer wants; improve the processes by which you make and deliver the products and services your customer wants when those processes are statistically out-of-control; and when you have made any of those processes near defect-free (statistically in-control), reinvent the process to make and deliver your products and services so they more fully meet your customers' definitions of quality. As you give your customers more and more of what they want, their needs change, which, of course, begins the process again. Around this process, Deming wove his management philosophy, summarized in his Fourteen Points and Seven Deadly Diseases. For Deming, TQM integrates the quality improvement process with management philosophy (Deming 1982).

Deming's philosophy reflects an organic model in several ways. For example, the constancy of purpose Deming proposes in his first point reflects the focus that a corporate identity creates for companies like 3M or The Ritz-Carlton. Deming's insistence on choosing suppliers on the basis of long-term relationships rather than on price alone (point four) and on eliminating numerical quotas (point eleven) suggest his move away from the mechanical view of organizations as money-making machines. Other points, such as "drive out fear" (point eight) and "break down barriers between staff areas" (point nine), also suggest the organic community structure explored in Chapter 7.

Deming's process of continuous quality improvement provides a vehicle for organizations that are consciously coevolving in their market ecologies. Too often, other business thinkers have focused only on the first two steps of this process (defining quality and improving existing processes). As Michael Hammer and James Champy insist in *Reengineering the Corporation* (1993), "The aim is to do what we already do, only to do it better. Quality improvement seeks steady incremental improvement to process performance." To this aim, they contrast the radical redesign of reengineering. But that ignores the third step in Deming's process—reinventing processes that are statistically in-control.

In the early 1980s, Ford became one of the first U.S. corporations to implement Deming-style quality improvement companywide. What resulted was both incremental improvement and radical redesign. On the incremental side, Ford enabled any production-line worker to stop the line when there was a problem that had to be solved. Although the effects of this change were certainly radical, giving real power over the process to production-line workers for the first time in nearly 70 years, the change itself was an incremental improvement, a minor change.

Other changes included radical redesign. For example, Ford's installation of Windsor Export Supply radically changed the way the company processed invoices, reducing the work cycle from 15 days to six. The team approach Ford used to introduce the Taurus also utterly changed a time-honored procedure (Walton 1986). The widespread introduction of Deming-style quality improvement was a key reason Ford became the productivity and profitability leader in the U.S. automobile industry in the late 1980s and early 1990s. It also begins to suggest the kind of flexibility we would expect in a company that saw its procedural information as corporate DNA.

One final note on Deming-style TQM: From our organic viewpoint, the word *improvement* in continuous quality improvement may be misleading. In rapidly evolving market ecologies, the best "improvements" are the adaptations organizations make to coevolve with other members of the market ecology. To improve the quality produced by a process, you do not necessarily need to increase productivity or lower cost. What is most important is that the process is now better able to meet the shifting needs of the customer. In this way, TQM becomes the vehicle organizations can use to coevolve with their market ecologies in a more self-conscious and purposeful way.

Using the Model

DNA gives us an extremely rich model for how our organizations can use structural and procedural information. In this chapter, we have only begun to scratch the proverbial surface. Consider two other areas. Mutations enter the mainstream of the evolution of a species in two circumstances—*radical change* and *geographic separation*. First, the environment changes radically, and species must find new ways to survive. We looked at what happens in this case in Chapters 1 and 2. Second, a small portion of a species is geographically isolated. Without radical environmental changes, mutations normally are filtered out by means of natural selection before they have developed the hardiness they need to compete with the genes of the entire species. When a small group is geographically isolated, however, such mutations have time to take hold and develop, unchallenged by the entire species. When these isolated groups again come into contact with the rest of the species, the changes they have developed may be strong enough to spread across the species.

Geographic separation gives us an interesting reading on the success of 3M as an innovator. As discussed in Chapter 7, the key structures at 3M are its 40-some product-oriented divisions. Each of these divisions is considered its own business, and many have their unique cultures and corporate DNA. As a result, the company has the equivalent of 40 geographically separated areas that can test changes in the corporate DNA, enable them to develop the hardiness to survive, and then expose them to the other divisions. In effect, this is the process by which the technology of microreplication (see Chapter 7) spread across 3M to become a billion-dollar-a-year source of sales.

DNA performs another job for our bodies. It acts as a marker that lets our bodies recognize when they have been invaded by something foreign. Our bodies trigger their immune systems when they recognize a virus or bacterium with a different DNA. In this way we maintain our integrity as living things. The tendency for organizations to reject different corporate DNA is another interesting application of this model.

Organizations often develop an immune reaction when foreign DNA is introduced. Consider the IBM personal computer division. IBM management located this division in Boca Raton, Florida, far away from corporate headquarters in Armonk, New York, and allowed it to operate as a separate unit, developing, in effect, its own corporate DNA and disregarding the most important rules of the company. The personal computer this division created was so popular that by 1984 it became the industry standard. However, once the division was successful, IBM began to integrate it, subjecting it more and more to the corporate policies in the company DNA. As a result, new features in the IBM personal computer took longer and longer to develop, and quality fell. Soon the IBM personal computer, which had close to a 50 percent market share in 1984, was losing that market share to its clones. By the mid 1990s, the IBM market share was less than 10 percent, and the division was losing $1 billion a year.

As long as the IBM personal computer division could exist as a separate unit with its own corporate identity and DNA, it was able to coevolve successfully in the new personal computer market ecology. However, once the division was pulled back into the corporate organism, its different corporate DNA marked it as an invader, and IBM's corporate immune system made it impossible for the personal computer division to continue operating differently. In organic terms, because the division's success came from the difference in operation—a different corporate DNA—IBM's corporate immune system began killing the unit it had created.

Corporate immune reactions have become common in many companies with the flurry of "change" programs introduced over the last 20 years. Managers with mechanical models tend to think of these techniques as components to be added to their corporate machines. Chapter 10 explores how mixing a new corporate DNA with the old threw Bell Atlantic into a struggle between change agents, with their new corporate DNA, and defenders of the old.

Managers who think in terms of corporate DNA recognize that more than adding a new component is involved. Otherwise, the company's old corporate DNA will have an immune reaction to the new DNA needed for, say, interdisciplinary teamwork. The same thing will happen over and over. If introducing interdisciplinary teams, or empowering employees, or practicing quality improvement is really essential, the organization needs to reconsider its whole database of procedures and structures and perhaps even its corporate identity.

Summary

We have examined how the differences in the way machines and living things use their structural and procedural information is reflected in organizations modeled on them. Machines are designed so each part has only the information it needs; living things make the information of the whole available in all its parts. As a result, mechanically modeled organizations need visionary leadership to succeed. Organizations modeled on living things, on the other hand, have all the information their parts need as corporate DNA. Organic corporations can therefore coevolve in their market ecologies in a self-organizing manner, because their parts operate autonomously.

For organizations operating in turbulent markets, the advantages of storing and accessing information as corporate DNA are clear. At The Ritz-Carlton hotels, for instance, no one owns, and therefore controls, job procedures, as workers do in bureaucracies. The procedures are common property. Any employee, working anywhere in a hotel, can borrow any department's Skills Mastery Manual for the evening. By treating this information as common property, organic corporations create a series of competitive advantages:

• Service is quicker and customer needs easier to satisfy when no one ever says, "But that's not part of my job description."

- The organization is constantly learning new ways to do things that enable it to coevolve with the changing needs of its markets. Because no one owns job procedures, anyone in any work group can make suggestions about improving procedures anywhere in the organization. No suggestions are automatically discounted, as they often are in bureaucracies, and people are continually improving the way their organizations work.
- Common ownership of procedures creates a sense of ownership of the whole enterprise. Everyone works for the good of the whole rather than for their departments and against people in other departments, as so naturally happens in bureaucracies.
- The comparison with organic DNA gives managers a way of thinking through problems as different as how to encourage greater innovation and how to incorporate new ways of doing things without exciting a corporate immune reaction.

With corporate DNA aligned with corporate identity, any organization can create the sense of purpose and a base in procedural and structural information its people need to act autonomously. It is through the autonomous action of each person and their interactions that an organic corporation coevolves in its market ecology. To coevolve successfully, however, one last type of information is needed, an ongoing flow of information on current events, both inside and outside. We need to turn now to how an organic way of thinking suggests we supply such information to our organizations—that is, through a corporate nervous system.

CHAPTER 6

Corporate Nervous System: In Conversation with the World

It is the quality and complexity of this nervous system that more than anything else dictates the quality and complexity of the organism.
—Isaac Asimov

Question: How do the people in an organization know about events in their organizations and market ecologies to which they will have to respond?

The day after I sent a manuscript by means of FedEx to St. Louis, I sat down at my computer and went on the World Wide Web. After all, it was 10:30 A.M., and by now the package should have reached its destination. I entered http://www.fedex.com, and sure enough up came the Federal Express home page. From there I navigated to the page where I could track my package and entered the tracking number. Within a few seconds, the page was telling me that my package was on the truck to its destination.

Something was wrong. I had paid a premium to have the package delivered by 10:00 A.M., "absolutely, positively on time." Was the company's electronic representative telling me that the delivery was already half an hour late? Before I could work up any real anger, however, I remembered, with that special type of disappointment Emily Latella made famous on *Saturday Night Live*, that my package's destination was in the next time zone. When I checked again an hour later, I was not only informed that the package had arrived but also learned the name of the person who had signed for it.

I was delighted. Not just at the niftiness of the technology, although that was part of it. I was delighted at the sense of being let in on a secret, on the internal working of this company with which I had done business.

It was as if I'd been allowed to plug in to the nervous system of the company to see the world from its special perspective. Which was what happened. I'd been drawn into an electronic conversation with Federal Express that allowed me to learn the exact state of our transaction. As a customer, that conversation made me very comfortable—I knew what was happening in a world that too often keeps me wondering what is going on.

Mechanical versus Organic Communication

In one way, the nervous system does exactly that for our bodies: It allows us to conduct a conversation about what's going on all around and within us as it's happening. The nervous system interprets information so that it makes sense. It delivers messages to the parts of our bodies that have to react. Moreover, it allows us to monitor whether our reactions are what we want them to be. By allowing us to sense and test our world in an ongoing manner, the nervous system enables us to operate comfortably, and to be successful, in our surroundings.

This is very different from what happens in a machine. After all, there is little reason for a machine to have access to information about events going on around it. Machine operators usually make that connection with the world. Some machines do have a simple connection with the world around them, as with a thermostat. And machines are being built today with more sophisticated sensors, for "self-healing" telecommunications networks, for example. But when most of those managing today grew up, this kind of sophisticated sensor system was virtually unknown. In addition, the kind of machine parts we have discussed had extremely limited intelligence. As a result, they would be able to understand only the simplest information about the world within or without.

The Body's Communication System

Our bodies actually communicate through the interaction of two systems—the endocrine system and the nervous system. The endocrine system consists of hormones that regulate the body's internal operations—pituitary growth hormones, for example, or epinephrine, which prepares us to react to danger. The nervous system has two parts. The *peripheral nervous system* carries electric signals from the sense organs and other body parts to the spine and brain and back again. The *central nervous system*, brain and spine, integrates messages from the peripheral nervous and endocrine systems and coordinates the activities of the body as a whole.

It might be interesting to look at a corporation in terms of both systems—corporate nervous system to collect, integrate, and communicate information on current events, and a corporate endocrine system to help control and communicate about internal work processes. For our purposes, however, we can overlook the corporate endocrine system. Some of it is encoded in corporate DNA. Much of the rest can be considered a part of the corporate nervous system.[1]

Unlike machines, our bodies can't survive without a constant flow of information about current events. When you reach to pick up a glass of orange juice, a storm of messages descends—from your eyes, hand, and arm to your brain; from your brain, through your spine, to the muscles of your hand and arm; and from the skin and muscles of your fingers back to the brain. This storm of messages enables you to measure the speed with which your hand approaches the glass, how close it's getting, and whether you hold the glass tightly enough. Through this ongoing conversation between your nervous system and your surroundings, you can be comfortable that you'll get your drink without much problem. Pay insufficient attention to the information from this conversation, as all of us sometimes do, and you may end up with a lap full of orange juice.

The conversation between your nervous system and the world is the process you use to learn, and it shows why people who believe DNA *determines* our behavior misunderstand how our bodies work. We could say that our DNA determines our behavior only if every sense impression invariably triggered a specific procedure in our DNA. But that's not the way our bodies work. The first time we experience a sense impression, touching a hot stove, for example, a specific procedure is triggered. If that procedure lets us maintain our integrity, as when we automatically pull back from the hot stove, we continue to behave that way, and our behavior has been determined by our DNA. Few sense impressions, however, are that simple. When a baby senses a wet diaper, that sensation will most likely trigger crying. But if the parents respond to the crying with angry outbursts, the baby will try different responses until he or she learns a response that works better with those parents. The baby's DNA has not determined its behavior. The behavior is learned though the conversation the baby's nervous system facilitates between the environment and the baby's DNA procedures.[2]

With this conversation, the baby tries to learn what he or she must do to become confident that he or she will be changed, just as each of us has become comfortable that we'll get a drink without spilling the orange juice or dropping the glass. Without this conversation, we can't really be sure what will happen. That's why the loss of feeling in a hand or foot can be such a terrifying disability. The nervous system creates an ongoing feedback loop, monitoring and reacting to what you are doing. It's a remarkably complex symphony of impulses. The retinas of the eyes, alone, have more than 150 million nerve receptors. Hundreds of millions of messages are continually being received, integrated, and acted upon— even to perform the simplest task.

The nervous system does perform a series of other jobs for our bodies. It integrates a picture of our world for us, tells us which pieces of information we should pay attention to, helps us interpret that information, monitors our health and internal systems, coordinates body-wide activity, and makes decisions for the whole. These are the jobs the central nervous system, the brain and spinal chord, performs. In this chapter, we focus only on the peripheral nervous system, the network of nerve cells that lets us gather information, brings it to the central nervous system, and conveys information from the central nervous system back to the parts of the body. In Chapter 8, we return to the central nervous system as a metaphor for how senior management can play its role.

As with DNA, what's important is not the exact way the body conveys this information. We want to focus instead on two design principles that we can apply to help our organizations work better:

- *Continuous Feedback.*   Your nervous system enables you to create an ongoing, real-time feedback loop. In this way, you can be continuously aware not only of what is happening in your environment but also of the degree to which your reactions do what you want them to. For organizations, this suggests the need to have constant feedback on the effects of our actions and the ability to change them at any time.
- *Measurement.*   Creating a degree of comfort in our environment demands that we continually measure our reactions to it. Our bodies learn the correct amount of pressure with which to hold a glass by experiencing what is too little and what is too much. This need to measure everything we do in our organizations continually is one of the revelations that made the idea of total quality management (TQM) so powerful.

Bureaucracy and Information as Power

If you think of an organization as a machine and its employees as parts, the idea that the parts need redundant information about what's going on around them will seem absurd. For one thing, employees as machine parts would not have the intelligence to interpret the information. "Managers think; workers do." No matter how many times I hear this statement, it shocks me. But the fact that it is repeated so often indicates how widely accepted it is. Besides, it's the job of senior managers, as operators of the corporate machine, to understand markets and order any activities needed to meet changes in them. The information senior management gathers is its property, and management communicates only what it believes people in the company "need" to know. One company I worked with in the early 1980s had an "open communication" policy. People joked that this policy actually meant, "We will communicate openly what we want to communicate when we want to communicate it."

In bureaucracies information should flow up the organization from those in the field to senior management. Part of every employee's job is to report to his or her supervisor about what's happening. In the real work world, however, information rarely flows freely up the hierarchy. For one thing, in a bureaucracy, raises, bonuses, and promotions are decided by your boss. So a smart employee learns not to communicate anything that would irritate the boss. As a result, bad news drops out of the system quickly. Perhaps even more damaging, managers' mechanical model sometimes makes it impossible for them to accept information. At one company where I taught quality improvement, the workers on the warehouse floor knew every problem in their operation and had worked out cost-effective, sometimes elegant solutions to them. Yet when they went to their manager and explained, they were thanked and told, almost ritually, "Managers think; workers do. Go back to your jobs."

For bureaucrats, information is power. As a result, senior managers dispense what they know in a miserly way. Others throughout the organization follow their lead. At one Baby Bell during the early 1990s, service representatives didn't learn about a new telephone service the company offered until customers, responding to advertisements, called to ask them about it. Managers in product development, advertising, and sales were so used to treating information as personal property that no one even thought to examine who might need to know more about this new product introduction.

Because natural communication with customers is distorted as it goes up the hierarchy, bureaucracies need other ways of communicating. So they gather information about customers in artificial ways, such as market research and focus groups. They treat their customers as little machines that can be studied objectively, whose needs and desires can be learned for the asking. Yet there's no way to know when the people companies question are telling the truth or when people in a focus group are more anxious to please the group leader than give accurate information. Still these companies assume they can take what they learn, advertise in the right way, and expect customers to buy their products. This mechanical communication with customers doesn't work. If it did, advertising would be a science, not an art form. Advertisements only occasionally persuade customers to buy products. Yet companies that think mechanically continue their market research and advertising as if they were 100 percent effective.

Corporate Nervous Systems

If we think of communication organically, on the other hand, organizations should continuously process a wide variety of information ranging from the success of internal systems to how their people are responding to the challenges and opportunities markets present. People in these organizations can operate autonomously because they can learn what they must react to in their market ecologies, from their corporate nervous systems, and how to react, from their corporate DNA. Then they can further learn from their corporate nervous systems how effective their efforts have been. Finally, they can communicate what they learn to others throughout their organizations.

Organic corporations can profitably make at least three types of information available to their people: what's happening within the organization, what's happening in the company's markets, and what's happening in the wider world in which it operates. Most of the examples of corporate nervous system fulfill both functions of our own peripheral nervous systems. They both collect information from sense organs for processing by the central nervous system and make the processed information available wherever it can be useful.

Making Internal Events Available

To remain healthy, a living thing must be aware of how well its internal systems are working. If your body were unaware that your blood pressure had fallen, it would have no reason to manufacture chemicals, such as angiotensin II, that help raise blood pressure. Monitoring blood pressure and producing the chemical is the job of the central nervous system, specifically, the part of the brain called the hypothalamus. Obtaining the information the hypothalamus needs to monitor blood pressure is the job of the peripheral nervous system. An organic model suggests that a corporate nervous system must begin with networks that enable people to communicate what goes on in the organization. Organic corporations use an almost-infinite variety of networks to make internal news available to people who might need it. Most often the type of corporate nervous system an organization implements depends on its corporate identity.

Federal Express, for example, has a complex corporate nervous system designed to support its identity, "People, Service, Profits." Its system of bar-code package tracking ensures a high level of service. Any associate or customer can learn what's happened to any package through either the company computer network or the World Wide Web. This system supports the company's profits by providing detailed feedback on the effectiveness of the company's operations. Management can use this information to locate patterns of problems, correct the problems, and drive down costs.

That's just the beginning. Any FedExer who wants to know about how well any unit, or the company as a whole, is performing can consult statistical quality indicators (SQIs). In Chapter 4, we looked at how SQIs measure a dozen key mistakes the company can make. The company's SQI performance is published every week, and each department posts its performance, along with its goal, so anyone can see it. The annual SQI total also is compared with a goal set at the beginning of the year and used to help determine management bonuses. As a result, no one ever has to ask how effectively company systems are meeting customer needs.

3M has different needs. Because of its emphasis on innovation, people in the company need to be able to learn about new technologies as researchers develop them. As a result, 3M has a network of technical communication that enables people to learn about the latest developments. This formal network was built on a shared need to know. That need also led to a powerful informal network in the company's scientific community. Through this informal network, Art Fry first learned about Dr. Spencer Silver's work in adhesives—work that Fry used to create Post-it Notes.

Feedback can be "informal" in a different way. At Rosenbluth Travel, for example, CEO Hal Rosenbluth wanted to learn how people felt about the agency's work. He asked 100 associates to make a crayon drawing of what the company meant to them. Although 95 of the drawings were positive, five indicated problems, and Rosenbluth was able to intervene and address those problems. He was able to do that because he had introduced a creative feedback loop to complement the company's more formal information network (Rosenbluth and Peters 1992).

Market Feedback

The next level of feedback is keeping up with what's happening in your markets. Creating feedback loops with customers, suppliers, competitors, and other stakeholders is a critical part of an effective corporate nervous system. The forms such networks can take are limited largely by the imagination of managers.

Desktop computers make it possible for companies to gather enormous amounts of information about what customers are buying. Probably the best known example of their power is Wal-Mart's transformation of retailing through the use of bar-code information. Wal-Mart was the first retail company to use bar-code scanning for inventory control. Because the company could learn what was being bought at any store as soon as items were scanned at the cash register, Wal-Mart was able to replenish stock on the shelves almost instantly. The company leveraged this information with regional distribution centers. It bought directly from its suppliers, stored its stock in the distribution centers, and then sent the merchandise out to its retail stores as bar-code information indicated items were needed.

Wal-Mart rode the competitive advantage it created through this corporate nervous system to become the leading retail company in the United States. This advantage has several facets. First, by avoiding distributors, Wal-Mart drives down its costs and is able to develop special relationships with suppliers, such as Procter & Gamble, which has employees dedicated to serving Wal-Mart who work at Wal-Mart's headquarters in Bentonville, Arkansas. Second, Wal-Mart cuts costs by turning over its merchandise more quickly than its competitors. In the late 1980s, Wal-Mart stores received deliveries to replace stock an average of twice a week. Some stores received deliveries every day. Competitors such as Sears and K Mart replenished stock every two weeks. According to George Stalk and Thomas Hout (1990), Wal-Mart's use of bar-code information as part of its corporate nervous system enabled it to grow three times faster than its competitors and earn a return on capital twice as large. Third, because the company knows on a day-to-day basis what customers are buying, it can give those customers more of what they want and are buying rather than offering what company buyers believe customers want.

Notice how different this is from the way mechanically modeled organizations gather customer information. A company such as Wal-Mart doesn't have to question and study customers and then trust the customers are telling the truth. By gathering information at the point of purchase, companies that use a corporate nervous system can get the word where it most counts, where customers make purchasing decisions.

The retail clothing industry especially thrives on gathering information at the cash register. Buyers for conventional retail stores have to commit to new fashions up to six months before they can sell them. A specialty retailer called Mothers Work, Inc., however, developed an alternative approach using a variation on the Wal-Mart computerized inventory-management system. Through 1996, Mothers Work ran more than 450 maternity clothes stores, making most of the clothes they sold. Its computerized system enables managers to track every single garment. As a result, whereas many people in the fashion industry rely on gut feelings, Mothers Work had the numbers to test any assumptions about what customers want: "Every merchant we hire wants to expand into colored blouses," reported founder and president, Rebecca Matthias. "But I know [from our bar-code data] the most important thing our customer wants to buy is a white shirt" (*Wall Street Journal*, June 17, 1997).

Compiling this information about what customers actually want gave Mothers Work an enormous competitive advantage in its markets. For example, the hot color in maternity clothes for summer 1996 was lime green. Most stores had to commit to their purchases months before they realized this. Mothers Work, on the other hand, was able to recognize and act on this information almost immediately. Because it makes most of the clothing it sells, the company was able to stock its stores with relatively small lots in a variety of colors. By early May it had realized that lime green was outselling orange five to one. Most of its competitors didn't realize this until mid June. Moreover, once the company did realize lime green would be the most popular color, its factories could crank out racks of clothes in that color, knowing it would very likely sell. Most other stores were stuck with the colors they'd ordered six months earlier.

Mothers Work illustrates the enormous power of extending a corporate nervous system to customers. With it, a business can get real-time information on what customers want *now*.

Although computer systems can present valuable opportunities to collect customer information, sometimes it also pays to do it the old-fashioned way, with personal contact. Consider the case of Tommy Boy Records. By the early 1990s, Tommy Boy had become the generally acknowledged cutting-edge leader in rap music. It also became one of the industry's profitability leaders with margins running as high as 27 percent. Tommy Boy's leadership resulted largely from the company's integration of an advanced computer tracking system with immersion in the markets it serves (Tucker 1993).

Tommy Boy didn't just meet the market's needs. To some extent, it helped shape those needs, actively participating in the coevolution of its market. Company founder and chairman Tom Silverman was the first in the industry to use the bar-code information of a company called Sound Scan, which compiles sales information from compact disc sales around the country. Silverman also used the numbers from Sound Scan most creatively. "What I'm trying to do," he told *Fast Company* magazine (Tucker 1993), "is really learn the dynamics of how people buy records and how records are sold." Ultimately, Silverman hoped to learn "the psychology of how people buy. What makes them *have* to own the record?"

That seems pretty ambitious. But, for Tommy Boy, squeezing the meaning out of these numbers wasn't enough. Complementing Silverman was his president, Monica Lynch, who immersed herself in the culture of rap music. By attending rap concerts and hanging out with her customers, Lynch added a picture of the continually changing market Tommy Boy served. Together, Silverman and Lynch worked "to understand the American public and understand what they are looking for, what would appeal to them, why they would buy a record, and not try to impose our vision on them," as Silverman explained it (Tucker 1993).

With this kind of information, broken out by city, and even by communities within a city, Tommy Boy was able to market its records as these communities were ready for them. Silverman also learned to aim the company's marketing first at the most visible people in their markets and then to build word-of-mouth campaigns for new artists in clubs and record stores. Only then did Tommy Boy take its recordings to radio and MTV. As a result, with a nervous system evolved specifically for its market, the company conducted a complex conversation with its customers. By making full use of that conversation, Tommy Boy could influence its market ecology, to coevolve with it, appealing to its needs, playing on them, and, finally, meeting the needs it had helped create.

How can we leave the issue of conversing with customers without mentioning the Internet? Potential customers are flooding onto the Internet. (One estimate I found—on the Internet, of course—was that by the end of June 1997, 51 million people in the United States were on-line and that 20 million of them considered it indispensable.) As a result, every business from tire sales to beer makers has a presence on the World Wide Web. Although most of these companies want to use their Web sites as electronic storefronts, almost as many use them to gather customer information. However, the questionnaires Web surfers are enticed to fill out usually are another form of traditional market research.

As we saw earlier, the power of the Web is in forming relationships. Companies, such as Amazon.com, that form these relationships can collect enormous volumes of information on customer likes and dislikes at the point where it most matters, the point of purchase. Especially in the computer software industry, companies, Microsoft for one, use their Web sites to obtain feedback on their products. They can even distribute upgrades to customers unhappy with their initial purchases. This is the kind of intimate communication with which companies can learn most intensely from their customers.

Searching the World

It's no longer enough to have an accurate picture of local markets. In a time of global competition, managers need to understand what's happening in all the markets they might be serving, even those that are only now forming. They also need a good idea of the policies governments in those areas are developing. Perhaps the best example is mainland China. If you have products and services the Chinese need, you have some difficult questions to answer. Does China represent, for you, more than a billion potential customers? Or is it a morass of political intrigue and unpredictably shifting economic policy? The Chinese have a well-deserved reputation as tough negotiators. For example, when AT&T tried to set the rules for a billion-dollar underwater cable project, Chinese negotiators ended up relegating AT&T to a smaller role than it wanted by bringing in a rival, Baby Bell SBC Communications (*Wall Street Journal*, July 23, 1977). Is this the kind of market in which you *really* want to make a serious investment?

To make decisions such as this, some companies have special units devoted to scanning conditions around the world. Others leave it up to individual managers. Companies can plug a wide range of sources into such an extended corporate nervous system. Publications such as *BusinessWeek*, with its coverage of business news worldwide, offer one source for this information. Magazines such as *The New Republic* explore the economic implications of political decisions from Beijing to Ontario. The *Wall Street Journal* or the *Manchester Guardian* offers daily coverage of many of these same issues. A wide range of consulting firms in every industry offers more focused pictures of the events you might need. Smart organizations complement this second-hand information by sending employees to Singapore or New Delhi or Budapest.

With the World Wide Web, however, an explosion of available information has created a new challenge. There's plenty of information chronicling every turn of the market and analyzing every policy decision. The *Wall Street Journal* has a service on the Web that can provide you with information in areas that you specify. Whole magazines and books now have Web sites where you can read them. The twin problems business people face are how to get the desired information when they want it and how to ensure the information is accurate. A nervous system is only as valuable as the accuracy of the information it provides. The value of accuracy is one key reason consulting companies such as DataQuest in the personal computer industry are so successful.

As the amount of information available to us continues to grow, the ability to obtain the best information quickly will become an increasingly powerful competitive advantage. It also presents an opportunity to entrepreneurs who might be able to develop "one-stop shopping" to provide the widest variety of information full time. Such a company's services might begin with a daily, on-line digest of news and analysis from a wide variety of publications. The service might increase its value by including a system that rates the sociopolitical leanings of the writer and the relative accuracy of each piece. In addition, it could offer a service that would retrieve past news and analysis as well as archived data, such as market share statistics. It also might offer original analysis the client desired.

Almost all this information is available. Not all is easy to find. By offering a single on-line address or telephone number, the information service could make life simpler and easier for its clients. In addition, by offering a rating system to help define reliability, the service would further increase its value. In this way, it would extend its clients' corporate nervous systems.

Such a service would be an experiment in coevolution. After all, simply by making this kind of information available, the company that provides it would help its customers change the way they do business, enabling them to gather more information about the world faster and more accurately. This change would create new information needs. The company providing information could monitor electronically kinds of information clients need and compare it with the needs of other customers looking for trends in the market. The employees of the information-providing company could work closely with customers to define new information needs as they developed and, of course, fill those needs. In this way, the information-providing company could climb the learning curve of its new business, coevolving with each client and the market as a whole, evolving its products, or even means of delivery, as clients' needs evolved.

Summary

Mechanical and organic models suggest very different ways to process internal and environmental information. Machine parts don't need access to information about what's going on around them; they are built to be controlled by an operator. Managers with a mechanical model see little need to share what's happening inside or outside the organization. Living things, on the other hand, need an ongoing flow of information. As a result, organizations built on an organic model need a way of gathering and distributing information—a corporate nervous system.

Thinking in terms of a corporate nervous system offers important competitive advantages to organizations, especially in today's rapidly shifting markets. By gathering information as part of their day-to-day routines and making it available whenever employees may want it, such organizations can expect to:

- Develop a keen sensitivity to how the organization is working. By opening a variety of channels to communication with employees, organizations can more quickly learn when systems are beginning to break down. Management's openness to this sort of information is critical. If it addresses the sorts of problems that Hal Rosenbluth identified with his call for crayon drawings, it can prove, first, that it cares about employees and what they see as important and, second, that it will do something about employee concerns. The health of any organic corporation depends largely on how much employees believe that management cares and will address their concerns.
- Remain intensely aware of what their markets' needs are, how those needs are evolving, and how well they are meeting them. Companies can gather this information from the widest variety of sources. It would be possible to integrate the computer information of a Wal-Mart with the everyday experience of the employees of 3M and the measurement system of Federal Express to develop an in-

creasingly rich and therefore valuable body of information on both the evolution of the market and a company's ability to coevolve with it.

- Build a more accurate picture of world markets. At a time when developing markets are becoming increasingly lucrative, organizations need a way to evaluate both market and political developments quickly as well as accurately. In a way, this may be the next frontier for the "news" industry. Services that can help organizations capture the information that enables them to make appropriate decisions and then to get ongoing feedback on subsequent events will provide enormous value.

All three of these advantages share one characteristic. They push the organization to a level of truthfulness that is rare in bureaucracies. Bureaucracies compartmentalize information, making it easy for those who control the information to deny events they don't want to face. An effective corporate nervous system makes this kind of denial difficult. When everyone has access to measurements of the company's effectiveness in meeting customer demands, it's much harder to insist that everything is fine if it's not. In today's markets, a clear picture of what's going on is absolutely essential. As a result, the conversation with the world that a powerful corporate nervous system enables is no luxury. It is a means of survival.

Effective communication isn't the only fact of corporate life that makes this kind of truthfulness possible. Equally important is a structure that encourages people to work with and learn from each other. That brings us to the question of structure: How will we put people together in units and interconnect those units when we think of our organizations as if they are living things?

CHAPTER 7

Structured to Grow: Organic Community Structure

[The] web of life consists of networks within networks. At each scale, under closer scrutiny, the nodes of the network reveal themselves as smaller networks. We tend to arrange these systems, all nesting within larger systems, in a hierarchical scheme by placing the larger systems above the smaller ones in a pyramidic fashion. But this is a human projection. In nature there is no "above" or "below," and there are no hierarchies. There are only networks nesting within other networks.

—Fritjof Capra

Question: How should management structure people in an organization in order to integrate all their talents and knowledge most effectively?

So far we've focused our journey into organic thinking on information: how a company articulates its identity so everyone knows how it succeeds in its markets; how it can align its procedural and structural information around that identity and then make it universally available as corporate DNA; and how it can develop a corporate nervous system to ensure a steady flow of current information.

Our next stop is structure: how an organization knits its individual members into a working whole. This knitting together is twofold. It includes both the formal structure pictured in the organization chart on your office wall and the way that structure encourages people to act toward each other. Together, structure and the behavior to which it leads form the community structure of a company—the formal structure mentioned briefly in the introduction to Part II. Community structure is the principle we explore in this chapter.

What IBM Wouldn't RISC

In the 1960s, an IBM senior scientist named John Cocke became fascinated with how to make computers considerably faster. He started simplifying the software instructions that drive the operations of a computer processor. The product of his work is called the reduced instruction set computing (RISC) microchip. If IBM had been able to commercialize Cocke's breakthrough the way 3M commercializes its innovations, IBM could have revolutionized both the market for personal computers and the market for computer workstations, the more expensive desktop machines used for scientific number crunching. The failure of IBM to take advantage of Cocke's contribution illustrates the power of bureaucratic community structure to undermine even the most brilliant technical breakthroughs.[1]

In 1968, Cocke led a team that built the ACS, the first of three prototype RISC-based computers. The ACS was extremely fast and potentially low-cost. Yet IBM management canceled the project because, Cocke was told, the ACS could not run the software used by the IBM 360 family of mainframes—the company's key product. By 1975, another team led by Cocke built a prototype low-maintenance computer they called the ServiceFree, a small, potentially inexpensive, and exceptionally fast machine. Even though—or is it because?—Cocke insisted the computer could initially run nearly 50 times faster than IBM's fastest mainframes, management also killed ServiceFree in the prototype stage. Finally, in 1978, a third team produced a minicomputer prototype, called the 801. The power of its chip sent ripples of enthusiasm through to top technical people at IBM. Still the project ran into a wall of resistance. Facing active hostility from the mainframe division, the 801 hovered in IBM's never-never land between prototype and commercial development.

In the early 1980s, IBM management finally approved use of the 801 microchip for two projects—the Olympiad workstation and the Fort Knox minicomputer family. Both became political volleyballs, and Fort Knox never went commercial. In 1986, Olympiad finally did produce a "commercial" product, the RT PC workstation. However, the project had been so compromised that the machine ran too slowly and cost too much. Six months later, Sun Microsystems introduced its SPARCstation, which became the standard for computer workstations. Finally, in 1988, 20 years after Cocke's first RISC-type computer, IBM brought competitive RISC-based computers to the market—the RS6000 line of workstations. (Big Blue, the computer that defeated world chess champion Gary Kasparov in 1997, was an RS6000 machine.) These were excellent machines. Yet the company had squandered enormous amounts of time, money, and human energy in a political dance that never created a new product or satisfied a customer.

You can find a fuller discussion of IBM's refusal to commercialize not only RISC chips but also several breakthrough technologies, in *Computer Wars* by Charles Ferguson and Charles Morris (1993). They summarize IBM's political dance in biological terms: "A kind of reverse Darwinism was stunting development. Any new idea could be vetoed by the divisions; but if a project actually got under way, it had to run a gauntlet of corporate mandates, which, often as not, crippled the original idea."

In our terms, IBM seemed intent on *not* coevolving in the new personal computer market. Looking back, the resistance of the IBM management at first seems irrational, even suicidal, the product of a dysfunctional corporate culture. From the point of view of the players in the drama, however, every act of resistance made perfect sense. In fact, the community structure of IBM—the combination of the formal structure pictured in its organizational chart and the incentives that kept its people working together—gave those managers valid reasons to resist the company's technological breakthroughs. *The IBM community structure drove these managers to protect their careers by acting against the long-term best interest of the company.*

In Chapter 4, we saw how IBM started moving toward bureaucracy in 1970, when it lost its visionary leader, Tom Watson, Jr. Without the humanizing affect of the culture Watson managed, IBM's fragmented, machine-like community structure overwhelmed its ability to introduce products based on the breakthrough technologies its laboratories produced. In this chapter, we look at how thinking about an organization as if it were a machine creates a community structure that can drive people in a company like IBM to act self-destructively. Then we examine how thinking organically gives us an alternative. Once again, this is the Law of Organizational Models at work. The choice of a model results in specific types of structure, which drive certain behaviors.

Mechanical versus Organic Structure

Machines are excellent tools, partly because they reduce the complex, interconnected structure of our bodies to simple cause-and-effect relations. For an idea of how different these structures can be, think about two ways of climbing a hill—driving your car and running.

Driving

Like most machines, your car was designed as an analytical hierarchy. That is, it's made up of subsystems (the engine, chassis, fuel-delivery, and exhaust systems, for example), each with a specialized function. The subsystems, in turn, are composed of parts. In this way, the engine includes cylinders, pistons, spark plugs, and inlet and outlet valves. These parts may be made up of smaller components, down to individual screws, rods, and ball bearings.

For your car to work, each part must perform the limited task that it was designed for and pass the product of its efforts on to the next part in a simple, cause-and-effect process. When you start going up a hill, you press the accelerator pedal, which increases the flow of gasoline to the carburetor, which mixes gasoline and air in the proper proportions. The carburetor delivers the mixture through the inlet valve, and as a piston descends the mixture is sucked into a cylinder. The piston moves up and compresses the mixture. A spark plug ignites the fuel. The explosion forces the piston back down, pushing the drive shaft to move the wheels. To maintain your speed as the hill becomes steeper, you need to press harder on the accelerator pedal to pump more gasoline mixture into the cylinders. The process speeds up, and you get more power.

Three facts about this process, the basic process for most machine operations, stand out:

- *Limited Intelligence.* Your car, like most machines, is a tool whose parts have no intelligence. As a result, like any machine on which we would model an organization, your car needs an external intelligence to guide it. Your vision ties your car to the road, and you as driver must initiate any changes by which your car adapts to shifts, such as a steeper hill or a bend in the road. If the technology changes, your car cannot incorporate, for example, fuel injection or cruise control, by itself. You must install them, or your car will remain as it was.
- *Cause-and-Effect Processes.* Each part is designed to do only its small task. The piston can't ignite the air-fuel mixture, and the outlet valve can't deliver the fuel. As a result, each part is entirely dependent on the ones that provide input for it. If the carburetor mixes air and fuel in the wrong proportions, the spark plugs can't do their job properly. As long as all the parts are properly maintained and connected, your car should drive as smoothly as the day you bought it. The whole is the sum of the parts.
- *Analytical Connection.* Parts that are not connected in a process function separately. If the radiator cap is too large and falls off, the spark plugs aren't affected. The situation is the same with larger subsystems. The chassis can be rusting away, but the engine runs perfectly. Of course, if the radiator cap falls off and the fluid drains from the radiator, the engine eventually overheats, and the spark plugs can't do their job. That's not so much a mechanical problem as it is a problem with the owner's maintenance of the car.

Running

What happens when you run up a hill is very different. Unlike the analytical hierarchy of machines, your body is structured as a hierarchy of nested networks (Figure 7–1). That is, *at each level of structure, small units network to form more complex units, which network to form even more complex entities.* At each level smaller networks nest in larger ones. Simple molecules such as water network with other molecules to form complex molecules, including proteins such as DNA. Simple and complex molecules form a series of structures, called *organelles*, such as the nucleus and mitochondria, which form cells. There are about 200 different types of cells in the body; they form substructures that make up organs. Organs are interlaced with blood vessels and nerve cells. Here we reach the body's most complex levels. Organs network in organ systems—the esophagus, stomach, small and large intestines, and liver in the digestive system, for example—and the organ systems form the body as a whole.

When you start running uphill, the increased effort you exert with your leg muscles demands more energy. Your heart beats faster, and you breathe harder. Red blood cells rush into the alveoli of your lungs, where hemoglobin, a protein molecule, exchanges fresh oxygen for waste carbon dioxide. The red blood cells are pumped back to the heart and then out to all parts of your body, including the muscle cells of the legs, through the network of blood vessels that compose the circulatory system. When the red blood cells reach your leg muscle cells, the mitochondria in your cells exchange waste carbon dioxide and water for fresh oxygen and glucose (blood sugar). In the mitochondria, you burn the oxygen and glucose to form adenosine triphosphate (ATP)—the body's form of energy—producing more waste water and carbon dioxide. The ATP enables muscle cells to contract in cooperation with other cells in the muscles and other muscles throughout the body.

While all this is going on, you're taking in an enormous amount of information—looking for twists and turns in the road or for furry animals or listening for the horn of a car behind you. Your central nervous system continuously integrates all this information into a total impression that you use to guide yourself. The key factors are very different from those involved in driving your car up the same hill.

- *Distributed Intelligence.* Whereas your car is a tool with parts that have no intelligence, in your body every molecule, cell, and organ is intelligent. At each level, units make decisions about the jobs they do. As you run uphill, the muscle cells in your calves "know" how to burn sugar for energy and how to contract and expand to drive you up the hill. Your red blood cells "know" how to pick up oxygen in

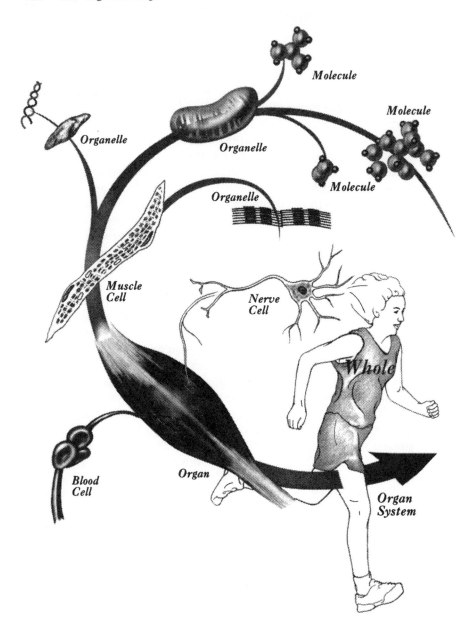

FIGURE 7–1   Runner as Hierarchy of Nested Networks.

your lungs and bring it to the calves so they can burn the sugar. Your respiratory system "knows" how to release burned fuel as carbon dioxide and bring in the oxygen that lets you burn more fuel to make more energy. Your nervous system "knows" how to send the messages that coordinate your activity. However, while your central nervous system continuously coordinates those activities, it does not control your body's adaptation to changes in the world around you. Rather, it signals cells to run harder, and they must decide whether to fulfill that request.

• *Systemic Processes.* In your body, each part has a specific task, but processes are not analytically separated, as they are in machines. Different body systems are constantly interacting. They can do this because, unlike machines, in which the boundaries between units are solid and impermeable, the boundaries between the parts of living things are semipermeable. Some substances can pass, for example, through cell walls. Because of this semipermeability, muscle cells not only are in contact with blood vessels and nerve cells but also can import oxygen and electrical impulses from them. In this way, muscles, circulatory system, respiratory system, and nervous system continuously interact. From the time you roll out of bed in the morning until you pull the covers up at night, every activity, even one as specialized as thought, depends on this ongoing interaction of body systems.

This ongoing interaction makes it difficult to control living things, because a stimulus to any one system can be communicated to any other. Think, for example, how differently people react to stress. Some have stomach problems; some suffer from depression; some develop skin conditions. Because all our systems are interconnected and every individual is unique, the only way to know for sure how a living thing will react to any stimulus is to observe it.

• *Interrelated Structure.* In machines, only parts with cause-and-effect relations are connected; what happens in one part may have no consequence in another. In living things, on the other hand, anything that happens anywhere can have consequences almost anywhere else. To put it another way, at each level, the behavior of parts affects the whole, and the behavior of the whole affects the parts. For example, if a person experiences a great deal of stress, that stress can make the immune system less effective. This reduced effectiveness may expose the entire body to disease, tuberculosis, for example, and the disease can affect one particular system, as tuberculosis attacks the respiratory system.

This reaction to stimuli at one level after another is how our bodies adapt to changes in our world. When a living thing experiences a new stimulus, this inside-out adaptation introduces an element of uncertainty. Each unique living thing experiences that stimulus in its own way. As a result, this structure makes it even more difficult to control living things. With this basic understanding of the contrasting structures of machines and living things, we turn to what happens when we translate them into organizations.

Mechanical Community Structure of Bureaucracy

As we saw in the introduction to Part II, managers who decide to give their informal organizations direction through control adopt a mechanical model. They impose a machine-like analytical hierarchy that knits their employees together almost exactly as if the employees were machine parts. Corporations depict this formal structure in the organizational charts most readers will recognize. These charts often become so complicated that they look like electrical diagrams. In *My Years with General Motors*, for example, Alfred Sloan includes several of the organization charts he developed for his company, each of which is so detailed it becomes confusing. The chart in Figure 7–2 simplifies a company to three main units or sectors (Industrial and Consumer, Life Sciences, and International).

For clarity, the chart shows only the Life Sciences Sector broken down into subunits, its three market groups. Of those market groups, only the Traffic and Personal Safety Group is broken into five divisions. If we wanted to show this organization accurately, the divisions would further be broken into departments, and, in some cases, the departments into smaller units. Eventually, we reach the individuals, rarely pictured in these charts, actually doing product research or selling products.

I've included this organizational chart for two reasons. First, these charts depict organizations as mechanical units, composed of separate boxes. The chart thus implies that each unit is separate, and its boundaries impermeable. If each unit does its job and managers connect it with the appropriate other units, the organization should run as smoothly as a finely tuned roadster. Second, in a way this chart is a trick example. The organization partially pictured here is 3M, which we use later as an example of organic community structure. Still we can present that structure as mechanically as the organization charts Alfred Sloan developed for General Motors in the 1920s and 1930s. I've used 3M to make this point: What's important in the real world of work is not the breakdown of units into smaller units, but the way all these units are interconnected. What really differentiates 3M from Sloan's General Motors is the way their different community structures work.

In a mechanical community structure, the job of managers is to connect employee parts in large processes and to maintain control. Senior managers, as corporate machine operators, have to look for changes in the market. When they see them, they send orders down the chain of command, much the way you step on the accelerator so your car will pick up speed as you start going uphill. Managers determine, for example, how much revenue the company can expect to earn in a fiscal year, and they begin cascading this expectation down the chain of command. At each level, these expectations are translated into the need for action, whether in manufacturing, sales, or service. The action management demands

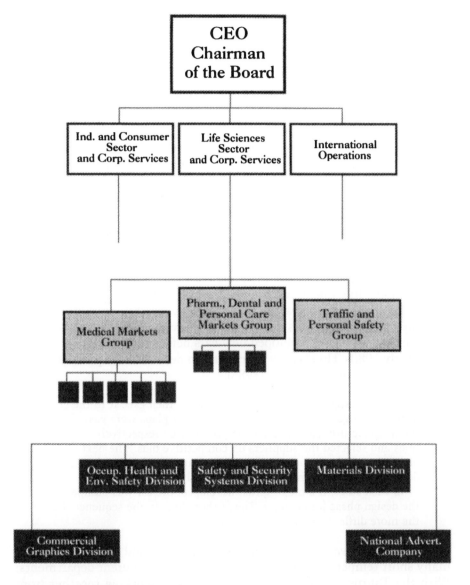

FIGURE 7-2 Organization Chart.

continues to be broken down at each level until specific orders reach individual workers.

As with machine parts, employees have specified tasks to perform. They are expected to perform those tasks and hand their products off to the next person in the process. People in sales, for example, obtain their price lists and quotas. Then they go into the field and sell their wares. The job of the salesperson is to sell the quota's worth and bring back the orders. In a mechanical community structure, that salesperson is not likely to have responsibility for suggesting new products customers might want, for actually making any products, for shipping the products or billing the customer, or for assuring the customer receives good service if there are problems. Each worker performs standard operating procedures and makes a mechanically limited contribution to a larger process.

Mechanically formal structure can imprison employees in their positions. The boundaries of units are considered as impermeable as the metal parts of a machine. These boundaries are barriers to cooperation in the natural flow of people in the organization as a complex adaptive system, a company's informal organization. In fact, people are sometimes disciplined for communicating without going through official channels. In this way, the formal structure controls the flow of information that would naturally occur in its informal organization. As long as each subunit does what it's been ordered to do, managers believe, the company should perform up to expectations. As a result, managers are responsible only for the performance of their own units. They believe that their organizations, like machines, are the sum of the parts.

Even when bureaucracies were most successful, this mechanical structure made operations much more difficult than they had to be. Consider the way Ford developed new cars before it designed the Taurus in the early 1980s. Here's how Mary Walton described the process in *The Deming Management Method* (1986):

> As it was, designers designed a car on paper, then gave it to the engineers, who figured out how to make it. Their plans were passed along to the manufacturing and purchasing people, who respectively set up the lines and selected the suppliers on competitive bids. The next step in the process was the production plant. Then came marketing, the legal and dealer service departments, and then finally the customers.
>
> In each stage, if a major glitch developed, the car was bumped back to the design phase for changes. The farther along in the sequence, however, the more difficult it was to make changes.

The result was an enormous waste of time and effort, as well as many short tempers and bad feelings between the different departments. With the Taurus, however, Ford had all groups working together from the beginning. The result was a triumph of fast development and high quality.

The real problem is that the mechanical structure of bureaucracy does not reflect the way people actually work. Anyone who has worked in a bureaucracy knows that the informal organization does most of the work. People see the work that has to be done and do it in spite of the bureaucracy. A mechanical structure erects obstacles that make it difficult and time-consuming, sometimes even impossible, for people to do what they see has to be done. This is the cost managers pay for maintaining control.

Yet, the control bureaucratic managers believe they exert is an illusion. Anyone who's lived with a teenager or a pet cat knows that it's impossible to control a living thing. To create the illusion of control, bureaucracies develop community structures that coerce employees to act as if they are being controlled. Those community structures are based on a few key assumptions about how to treat people as replaceable parts. The resulting human resources policies seem to be aimed at squeezing the most out of employees. This seems to be what Michael Hammer meant when he described the problem with reengineering this way, "It's not so much getting rid of people. It's getting more out of people" (*Wall Street Journal*, November 26, 1996). That's exactly the point: *These policies were created so people can be controlled by management—that is, coerced into following orders that would squeeze as much work as possible out of them.*

The human resources policies that give bureaucratic managers control rest on a series of assumptions built into corporate life:

- Your boss holds your career in his or her hands. With a mechanical model, the organization needs people to follow the orders of their superiors. To coerce you to do so, bureaucracies make your boss responsible for your raises, promotions, even your ability to transfer to another unit. A boss can offer you desirable or undesirable daily tasks, allow you to take training courses or go to conferences, and generally treat you in a way that makes you love or dread coming to work. As a result, sensible employees give their bosses whatever makes the boss happy. A boss who yells at people for bringing bad news soon finds that nothing ever goes wrong. A boss who cheats suppliers is likely to find employees supporting him or her in that behavior. In *The Addictive Organization*, Anne Wilson Schaef and Diane Fassel (1988) compare this behavior with that of alcoholics and the codependents who learn to cater to their warped realities.
- You should be rewarded and recognized for your contributions to the unit to which you belong and should constantly compete for those rewards. If the company operates like a machine, people doing their daily jobs don't have to worry about contributing to the welfare of the whole. Each person's job is to contribute to the performance of the unit the boss leads and, perhaps, the next larger unit. As a result, the purchasing departments of bureaucratic corporations are notorious for infuriating everyone else in the company. In one company, employees got in trouble for buying personal computers *at lower prices* because the seller was not on a list of approved vendors. When people are rewarded for doing their jobs *as defined by*

their departments, they don't have to consider whether what they do benefits the company as a whole.

In a bureaucracy, rewards take many forms—a one-time award, an annual bonus, a raise in salary, or a promotion. In almost all cases, work performance is seen as a competition for limited dollars and cents. Annual raises, bonuses, and promotions are often based on how your manager rates your performance, another good reason for following orders and flattering your boss. By limiting the number of people in any unit who can achieve the top rating in performance appraisals, many bureaucracies encourage employees to compete further for their bosses' favor.

- Competition for limited corporate rewards makes life a battle of everyone against everyone else, although that's often covered up with a culture of niceness. I once heard the CEO of a Fortune 500 company criticize his senior management team for being too nice. They never took clear, sharp positions, he complained, or argued the issues. This culture of niceness covered up an ongoing competition for money and position. Some organizations, such as ITT under Harold Geneen, encourage open internal competition. The situation is complicated when it's covered up by a culture of niceness because dishonesty becomes a way of life. People are careful not to tell their bosses anything that will irritate them, and because the bosses depend on *their* bosses, it's dangerous to tell irritating truths to anyone above you on the chain of command. Ultimately no one can ever be sure when anyone is telling the truth.

In addition, people don't share important information because rewards *are* given competitively. In one bureaucracy, because few people in a department could achieve the top rating for bonus purposes, the manager of media relations regularly withheld information about product introductions from the manager of internal communication, who had the office next to her. The lack of information decreased the effectiveness of the manager of internal communication, and made the manager of media relations look better in comparison. The damage was twofold. Customer service employees were not always told about new products, and no one was ever certain what information was true. People could only trust that any activity was politically motivated.

As we've seen, organizations built on a mechanical model that still have visionary leaders often don't behave this way. At IBM Tom Watson, Jr. could humanize the corporate community with a culture that got people working together for a purpose they all agreed was worthwhile. It's only when they lose their visionary leaders that mechanically modeled companies deteriorate into bureaucracies—fragmented, mechanical communities in which the welfare of each unit becomes more important than that of the whole.

Given the corrosive effects on behavior that these policies have, is it any wonder managers at IBM killed John Cocke's RISC prototypes? Since the 1960s, mainframe computer sales had generated the majority of revenues for IBM. As a result, senior managers in the company were almost always mainframe salespeople. Having spent their careers developing loyalty to the mainframe division, how likely were they to encourage a product that might undermine the market for mainframes? Beyond that, managers in the personal computer or minicomputer divisions saw Cocke and his supporters as outsiders trying to tell them what to do. How likely were they to support outsiders who wanted them to try a technology that had never been commercially successful? Why risk something new, especially when its success might undercut the mainframe managers' positions in the competition for corporate rewards?

Organic Community Structure

An organic community structure can provide its informal organization as much direction as a mechanical community structure provides a bureaucracy, but does so by creating a sense of self-control. It frees the informal organization to express itself fully, encouraging its innovative pursuit of corporate identity. It does so by building a formal structure as a hierarchy of nested networks, like that of a living thing.

At first glance, mechanical and organic structures may seem nearly identical. That's why we pictured 3M's structure as a standard pyramidal organization chart. But look what happens when we compare the nested networks of 3M with those of the human body:

Human Body	3M
Molecule	Individual worker
Organelle	Functional department
Cell	Product division
Organ	Market group
Organ system	Market sector
Whole body	Corporation

For more than 70 years, 3M has structured itself as a hierarchy of nested networks, with most employees nesting progressively into at least five levels—department, division, group, sector, and company.[2] The company has three operational sectors—Life Sciences, which manufactures and markets products ranging from surgical tape and personal safety masks to respirators and reflective sheeting for highway signs; Industrial and Consumer, with products like Scotch brand tapes, sandpaper, and Post-it Notes; and International Operations. It also has a Corporate Services unit

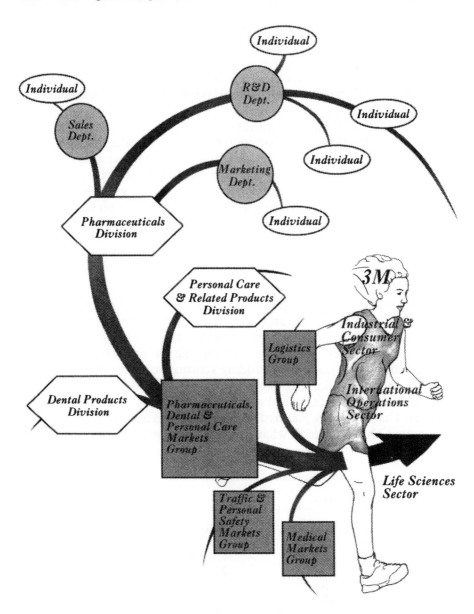

FIGURE 7–3   3M as a Hierarchy of Nested Networks.

that offers company-wide services in areas ranging from quality and finance to human resources, legal affairs, and marketing. The Life Sciences and Industrial and Consumer sectors are composed of several groups, and each group of a number of divisions (Figure 7–3).

For example, the Pharmaceuticals, Dental, and Personal Care Markets Group of the Life Sciences Sector includes divisions for the three types of products mentioned in the group name. 3M has in the neighbor-hood of 40 such divisions, which act like independent businesses. Each division develops, manufactures, and sells its own products, and each has a structure and a culture appropriate to its market. Most divisions in-clude functional departments—laboratories, manufacturing, marketing, sales, logistics, and so forth—as well as cross-functional teams. As shown in Figure 7–1, we can draw the 3M organizational chart so that it looks normal to anyone who has worked in a bureaucracy. But the reality is a lot more chaotic.

Everything in a bureaucracy is supposed to be done in small, easy-to-control chunks of action, which managers then integrate into larger and larger processes. The organizational chart tells them who does what and who is responsible for putting which pieces of which processes together. That's how people become prisoners of their boxes on the organizational chart. On the other hand, people at 3M consider their structure a convenience. According to one spokesperson, "The only rea-son the sectors exist is the convenience of analysts. The scientists don't care; even the marketing people don't care" (Stewart 1996). Whereas a mechanical community structure is designed to contain and control the informal organization of a company, an organic community struc-ture seems designed to enhance the natural activity of its informal organization.

The formal structure of 3M is more a platform that supports than a prison that contains. People in the sales area of the Health Care Services Division are not trained in sales alone. They receive intensive training in the technology of their division so they can describe their products to customers. Being located in a functional department within a division enables employees to network throughout that division. Although no one in a division knows everything about the division, most people at least know someone who can fill them in on what they don't know.

Similarly, technical and manufacturing people regularly visit cus-tomers' manufacturing facilities to learn about their operations. These visits often result in suggesting uses of 3M products those customers hadn't imagined. For example, Geoff Nicholson, staff vice-president for Corporate Technical Planning and International Technical Operations, pointed to the automobile industry. About 15 years ago, technical staff were visiting a customer's factory and learned that the rivets the cus-tomers were using to hold side molding to doors were rusting. The technical staff went back to the laboratory and developed an acrylic foam tape that replaced the rivets and solved the problem.

The units at 3M are as semipermeable as the cells in your body. People in all departments are expected to know about the other depart-ments of their divisions and, when they have the opportunity, to roll up their sleeves and get their hands dirty in other departments. People in marketing, sales, laboratories, and manufacturing constantly talk and work with each other to ensure customers receive the products they need.

One of the most exciting things about 3M's structure is the way it continues to evolve. The newest evolution at 3M is Integrated Solutions, which began in 1995. Initially a response to changing customer needs and changes in markets, the program has leveraged the advantages of the company's organic structure. As a result, anyone representing 3M to a customer can call on the company's entire portfolio of products and technologies.

Dominic Tallarico, a member of the management team that heads Integrated Solutions, explained that the program was created to solve several challenges the company faced:

> On one hand, each division had its own sales force and line of products. But our customers preferred a one-face approach. On the other, most customers have no way to know all our 50,000-some products. At the same time, they want solutions presented to their problems, in the customer's language, not a long discussion of our products.

To meet these challenges, 3M developed teams of salespeople from several of the divisions that any company would buy from, building on the existing semipermeability of units. The number differs depending on the customer. Each team determines how many divisions should be represented. By teaming sales staff in this way, 3M was able to increase both the knowledge base and in-company network that any one of them brought to the customer. According to Tallarico:

> Our sales people receive excellent training in their divisions. So they begin with an understanding of the technology behind their products. With field experience, they begin to see patterns of solutions. On top of that, they've built themselves into the human equivalent of neural networks that enable them to answer all kinds of questions. When we put three or four of these people together, we enable them to see things our customers never dreamed of.

The program works this way: 3M builds a sales team, usually led by one division salesperson who has an excellent relationship with the customer. After they receive further training in team selling and each other's divisions, team members ask the customer for permission to map the customer's work flow and promise a report with recommendations about how the customer can reduce costs and increase productivity. The team then maps the customer's work flow with help from marketing. In preparing the map, team members talk with the customers to identify key problems and help the customer determine how critical the problems are to their operation. Tallarico added that customers find the resulting reports an eye-opening experience that gives them the opportunity to do things they had not imagined. In his words:

We had one customer that manufactured buses. By the time we made our report, we were able to offer them material and process science solutions that gave them the opportunity to do things they didn't think would be possible. The company now wants 3M in on the design and specification stage of its development process.

In another case, a team was making its recommendations to the vice-president of operations for an airline. "We showed them a facsimile of one of their aircraft and told them how we could help to increase productivity up to 300 percent in processes they thought had no problems," Tallarico said. "When he saw the improvements we were suggesting, the vice-president got so excited, he offered us one of the company's planes for a year so we'd have a model to work from."

As a result of Integrated Solutions, 3M is developing the ability to coevolve with customers more intensely and directly. The program enables them, in effect, to become partners contributing to their customers' success. As their customers' needs evolve, as they implement 3M's suggestions, 3M will have a relationship that enables it to learn of evolving needs, help meet the needs, and suggest or even invent new products the customer can use.

In this way, 3M's evolution toward ever-more-organic forms is creating opportunities for growth that had not existed and that the company could never had known about if it hadn't developed Integrated Solutions. From our organic point of view, 3M is taking advantage of its nested network to operate by the principles we've seen with living things:

- *Distributed Intelligence.* Unlike employees in a bureaucracy, the people at 3M are expected to think for themselves. That was the purpose of the 15 Percent Rule introduced by William McKnight, the first company chairman. McKnight saw the people who worked for him not as replaceable machine parts but as fully intelligent human beings capable of learning things management might miss. In his words:

  Those men and women to whom we delegate authority and responsibility . . . are going to want to do their jobs in their own way. . . . Mistakes will be made, but if a person is essentially right, the mistakes he or she makes are not as serious in the long run as the mistakes management will make if it is dictatorial and undertakes to tell those under its authority exactly how they must do their job (Coyne 1996).

It's only with this basic faith in the intelligence of each individual that the institutional insubordination we saw in the story of the man who wouldn't be fired makes sense. No bureaucracy would put up with that behavior, because bureaucrats can only maintain control of their corporate machines as long as their people accept authority.

- *Interconnectivity.*   Whereas the parts of a bureaucracy generally work separately and distinctly, different parts at 3M never stop working together. At the division level, for example, people in the marketing, laboratory, and manufacturing areas are continuously working with each other and sharing information so they can develop and fabricate products that will keep their customers' loyalty. Nicholson noted that 3M wants not merely to meet the needs customers understand but also to surprise them with products that meet their needs in ways they hadn't expected, such as Post-it Notes. That desire to delight is at the heart of the story about replacing door molding rivets with 3M adhesive tape. And it didn't end with that one application. When the tape was successful with U.S. automobile makers, marketing people in Europe and Japan checked with local automobile makers and learned how their specifications differed. They brought the information back to the laboratories, where differentiated tapes were developed for this purpose. At 3M, every part is connected with every other.

As a result of the technical communication system 3M uses to make new developments available across the company, a new development in one part of the company can generate hundreds of millions of dollars of sales as people in other parts find new uses for it. One major success at 3M is its microreplication technology, which approached one billion dollars annually by 1996. The technology, covering surfaces with millions of tiny structures that enable the surfaces to behave in specific ways, was developed in 1964 to improve the performance of overhead projector lenses.

The technology slowly made its way through 3M. By 1970, it was being used to improve the way traffic signals reflect light, and in the late 1970s, for solar concentrators. By 1983, the potential of the technology was clear, so the company created an optical technology center to speed the process. By 1995, the technology was being used to make products ranging from brightness-enhancing film for computer screens and computer mouse pads to a variety of fasteners and a product the company calls "the reinvention of sandpaper." At 3M, just about everyone tells you that the products belong to the divisions but the technologies belong to the company. It's this sense of being interconnected by means of its technologies, as well as by its people, that enables 3M to continuously innovate in a way that was impossible at the IBM of the 1970s and 1980s.

Because every part of 3M is connected with every other, management cannot hope to control what happens at the company. Roger Appledorn, the 3M scientist who invented the first product using microreplication, put it this way: "We didn't sit down and say, 'Microreplication is the next thing to do; let's go do it.' It doesn't work this way. It evolved. It reached a critical mass. And it suddenly proliferated" (Stewart 1996). In other words, managers don't see 3M as a machine to be controlled with behavior that can be predicted. They see the company as a living thing that grows and evolves in unpredictable ways. Because its structure is so tightly connected with its market ecologies and because 3M's identity is so powerfully embodied in every corporate system, managers at 3M can trust that people will do the right things.

- *Inside-out Adaptation.* Because of its interconnectivity, 3M has the same inside-out adaptation as a living thing. Microreplication began as an adaptation to the market's need for higher-quality overhead projector images. It took nearly 30 years for this innovation to make its way through the company. But today, microreplication has improved the offerings in nearly one of every four divisions at 3M. Meanwhile, the company recently spun off its data storage and imaging business. That action will change the flow of energies and resources within the company in ways that are entirely unpredictable. Those changes will alter what happens in units throughout the company, once again in thoroughly unpredictable ways.

To sum up, the structure of 3M is radically different from that of bureaucracies. Bureaucracies design their formal structures as *the* way they get things done. The structure at 3M is much looser. It exists not to do specified work but to encourage people to detect and meet customer needs in the most innovative way—that is, to be continuously coevolving with its markets. The constant interaction between people within single departments, between people in different departments within the same division, and, in Integrated Solutions, between people in different divisions, gives 3M more the feel of your body running up a hill than your car driving up it.

This organic structure would collapse into the mechanical structure we find in bureaucracies, however, without a series of assumptions about human behavior that maintain an organic community structure:

- People must behave autonomously. A mechanical model gives bosses near-complete power over their people; an organic model gives individuals autonomy. After all, like units in a living thing, each individual has the distributed intelligence necessary to do his or her job. 3M's trust in its employees is emphasized every time someone tells the story of the man who wouldn't be fired, Lew Lehr's manipulations, or any of a hundred stories that make this point: What's important at 3M is not your boss's authority, but your intuitions about how you can contribute to the company's success. Autonomy is possible because, first, each individual brings his or her personal experience to the job; second, each has access to corporate DNA and information from the corporate nervous system; and, third, each lives by the corporate identity. By making their own decisions, people constantly learn what the company's customers and markets need. As they share that with others, ideas for new products and new ways of serving customers can flow wherever the organization needs them.

• People are rewarded or recognized noncompetitively for contributing to the operation as a whole, not just to their units. The organic system of rewards at 3M differs from that of many bureaucracies in a couple of important ways. The objective is rarely to win a competition with others, as in a bureaucracy. Rather, 3Mers try to come up with some-thing authentically valuable to customers. Employees who need money to develop an idea for a new product are not competing with other employees. Researchers have authority to spend what they need to meet the goals of their units. If a project falls outside the goals of their units, researchers can apply for Genesis Grants for start-up funding. If they're refused Genesis Grants and still believe their projects are important, some researchers go to the executive suites to ask for money. And they can expect the executives to listen, because in most cases, the executives have been in a similar position.

Organic corporations such as 3M also don't rely on cash incentives. "We steer clear of monetary rewards," explained Nicholson. "People who do technically good jobs will get promotional opportunities. But peer recognition is the most important to us." That recognition ranges from informal gestures, such as a supervisor's taking staff members to dinner or a ball game, to formal programs such as the Carlton Society, the 3M hall of scientific fame. Even promotions have a nonmonetary side. At 3M, the company treats the career path as a way for employees to achieve personal fulfillment, not to meet the company's goals. 3M doesn't insist that everyone be promoted into management. Those who find their scientific work more fulfilling can take advanced technical positions. For people who develop successful new products, the reward can be managing their product units as they grow.

Although it's essential that people do their functional jobs, the emphasis at 3M is to contribute to the company's corporate identity of innovation, not merely to do one's job. Art Fry, the engineer who invented Post-it Notes, for example, was working in what was then the Commercial Tape Division when he got the idea for this product. If Fry had worked in a bureaucratic company, his manager would have resented his investing time and energy in a product that wasn't part of the division business plan. What's important is not the numerical goal of any unit, but the company's pursuit of earning 30 percent of revenues every year from products no more than four years old.

- Because everyone shares in the pursuit of new products that will prosper in the market, the focus is on growth as the company coevolves rather than on internal competition. A nested network is the perfect structure for growth. Each division has to justify its size with the demand for its products, not a bureaucratic competition for limited resources. As its market grows, a division can grow into a group, which is how the Tape Division, which initially made masking tape, grew to become the Tape Group, which makes more and more types of tape. As the market for electrical wiring tape grew, that part of the Tape Group was spun off to become the Electrical Wiring Group. For Nicholson, "3M's history is a history of growth, of dividing and multiplying."

To achieve this constant adaptation, employees at 3M cooperate in a highly honest environment. To adapt, living things must continuously take in feedback on everything happening around them. If that feedback isn't accurate, the living things will make bad decisions and stupid mistakes. Bureaucracies process enormous amounts of inaccurate feedback because of the dishonesty woven into their community structures. Such dishonesty would be enormously destructive at 3M. At least half the company's new-product projects fail. With large amounts of honest feedback, the company can close down unsuccessful projects before they get out of hand.

The results of a truthful environment go far beyond the ability to adapt to market change. A place where people are encouraged to be honest is more enjoyable and less stressful. In addition, politics demands a lot less attention when people trust each other. In many ways, this trust is the most important product of an organic community structure. It not only produces a happier work force but also frees large amounts of energy for pursuing business goals that, in a bureaucracy, would be invested in political gamesmanship.

3M is only one company with an organic community structure. One of the most exciting things about looking at our organizations with an organic model is the infinite number of variations it suggests. Do you want your organization to be like a panther or a redwood tree, a coral reef, an elephant or a snapping turtle? That's up to you. There is no "best" size or structure for a living thing, only a size and a structure that are effective in a given environment.

Summary

In this chapter, we contrast how mechanical and organically modeled organizations integrate their people with a community structure. Managers with a mechanical model use analytical hierarchies to control the activity of their informal organizations and make sure they move in the required direction. Managers with an organic model use a hierarchy of nested networks to enable their informal organizations to pursue the corporate identity through self-control. While both models have advantages, an organic community structure presents organizations with a series of interconnected benefits for operating in today's turbulent market ecologies:

- An organic structure gives people the support they need to behave autonomously, thus encouraging any interest they have in finding new products and new ways of doing things. Instead of being treated as replaceable parts, people are encouraged to contribute as creatively as they desire to goals they share with everyone in the organization. Because they feel valued by the organization, they feel good about contributing to its success.
- The semipermeability of organic units encourages connections between people and projects to emerge as they're needed. Whereas a mechanical structure limits communication, organic structures provide opportunities, such as 3M's technical communication, whereby people from different parts of the company can come together around common interests. This free flow of information makes it easier for people to translate their ideas for innovation into real products and process improvements.
- The openness and sense of common purpose fostered by an organic structure make it easier for people to trust and be honest with each other. This honesty is essential for both the organization and the people in it. If people conceiving new products receive honest feedback from fellow workers and customers, they can make the changes in those products that will make the products as successful in the market as they can be.
- All these qualities make it easier for organizations to coevolve in their market ecologies. When any one person recognizes a market shift, that information becomes available throughout the organization, allowing people to rally around new ideas and turn them into solutions to customer problems. Because organic structures are less rigid than bureaucratic ones, people and resources can flow more quickly to the places where they will be most valuable to customers. As a result, the organization can grow spontaneously as a response to market shifts.

Beyond these advantages, thinking organically about community structure gives managers a chance to avoid mistakes that other managers, who think mechanically, are making today. For example, managers who think mechanically often confuse growth with increased size. When Disney bought ABC or Aetna merged with U.S. Healthcare, the companies involved talked about "synergies" of operation and continued growth in profits. This might be true if these organizations were merely money-making machines. Managers who think organically, however, see growth the way people at 3M do, as expansion of the business in reaction to changes in the markets a company serves. Many mergers actually end up irritating customers because of difficulties in integrating two different community structures. The acquiring company often acts as conqueror and expects the acquired to begin doing things its way. The friction that occurs in the process and the differences between the markets the two companies serve keep companies such as Disney from achieving their hoped-for synergies. In fact, by fall 1997, both Disney and Aetna were having problems as a result of these mergers.

Managers who see their organizations as mechanical community structures have problems with other techniques—downsizing or reengineering, for example—that could be exposed with an organic point of view. This is not to say that companies should never buy other companies or downsize. An organic model offers managers a perspective on these techniques that helps anticipate difficulties they ignore when they think about them mechanically.

These decisions are mostly in the hands of senior managers. If those managers continue to practice command-and-control, however, they'll be unable to take advantage of any of the benefits we've explored so far. Which brings us to the last design principle, governance. Machines need an operator to govern them; living things govern themselves through their central nervous systems. How does this contrast reflect itself organizationally? What are the differences between senior management as operator of the corporate machine and as central nervous system in the corporate organism? We'll examine those questions in Chapter 8.

CHAPTER 8

The Central (Nervous System) Role of Senior Managers

Every company in America has implemented at least one program intended to empower, one to improve quality, one to embrace customers, and one to "right-size" as a means to flatten its stomach and reduce body fat. . . . What remains untouched is the belief that power and purpose and privilege can reside at the top and the organization can still learn how to serve its stakeholders and therefore survive.

—Peter Block

Question: What should a chief executive do to ensure that everyone in his or her organization is working together for its best interests?

Parable of the Visionary Leader

No people are more respected, even venerated, in U.S. business than visionary leaders. Whether we talk about Henry Ford, Tom Watson, Jr., or Bill Gates, they embody the ideal by which we measure chief executives. I first experienced the mythology that grows up around such visionary leaders in the early 1980s when I was writing the management newsletter for Sun Oil Co., maker of Sunoco gasoline. Sun Oil's visionary leader was J. Howard Pew, the company's dominant figure from the time he became president in 1912 until his death in 1972. The stories I heard about J. Howard, as all who had known him called him, painted the picture of a man who hit the visionary leader trifecta—technological visionary, astute businessman, and good corporate parent.[1]

By the time I heard them, these stories had become legends of a man so much larger than life that he *was* the company. One story, for example, insisted that every day, first thing, when he came to work at 1608 Walnut Street, the Philadelphia headquarters of Sun Oil, J. Howard would check the clock in the lobby and compare it with his pocket watch. Then he'd go up to his office on the nineteenth floor and call maintenance to tell them to reset the lobby clock. For J. Howard, even the accuracy of company time was his responsibility.

J. Howard's attitude, like that of many visionary leaders, was paternalistic in the best sense. For instance, he insisted that every business deal benefit *all* parties involved. During the Great Depression, the stories went, Sun Oil didn't fire a single employee. So committed was J. Howard to each employee that he would become visibly upset when he didn't know one personally.

Most of the stories, however, showed J. Howard as a technological visionary. Wherever Sun Oil made a major contribution to the oil industry, you could expect to find his hand. In the winter of 1901–02, right out of college, J. Howard found a container of crude oil left out in the snow overnight. That discovery inspired him to develop a superior way of refining motor oil, which would set a new industry standard and help make the company's reputation for high-quality products.

Early in 1933, Eugene Houdry was perfecting catalytic cracking, a process that would revolutionize gasoline refining. In the spring, his financial sponsor, Socony-Vacuum, the oil company later known as Mobil Oil, lost interest in his research. So one morning, Houdry showed up at 1608 Walnut Street and asked where the executive offices were. He came out of the elevator on the nineteenth floor and was immediately confronted by a stoop-shouldered six-foot-tall bear of a man, J. Howard, who asked what he wanted. Houdry started explaining his process, and before the morning was over, J. Howard called a rump session of the executive committee, which gave Houdry the go-ahead.

In the mid 1960s, when he was in his 70s, J. Howard decided the company could make money building a factory to synthesize oil from the tar sands in Calgary, Canada. He argued down all the company's skeptical lawyers, accountants, and engineers and built the world's first commercially successful synthetic-oil plant.

Within two years of J. Howard's death in 1972, the stable oil markets in which Sun Oil had prospered vanished, as the Organization of Petroleum Exporting Companies (OPEC) took control of crude oil supplies. Without J. Howard's leadership, senior management lost its way. At first, senior management at Sun Oil diversified the company into new lines of business—from real estate to trucking to computer backup—so it would be less dependent on the oil reserves it could no longer control. By the mid 1980s, however, the company found it couldn't manage those businesses profitably. So it sold them at a loss. It also split into two companies—one for oil exploration and production, the other for refining and marketing—and watched the stock price of both companies fall in the most intense bull market in history. Nothing it did seemed to work. It was only in the summer of 1997 that Sun Oil's performance began to turn around. Still, the company is a remnant of what it had once been.

J. Howard's story is a parable of the trap traditional ideas of leadership set for us. Just knowing these stories was enough to make me wish I could have worked for the man. Yet as attractive as he was, and as attractive a place to work as J. Howard made Sun Oil, the company's success depended entirely on him. As sole keeper of the company's vision and corporate culture, J. Howard was, for 60 years, also its key risk taker and learner. Without him, Sun Oil would lose 60 years of learning and with it both its direction and attractiveness as a place to work.

In this chapter, we explore what thinking organically offers to replace the idea of the chief executive as visionary leader. The key job of the chief executive in a mechanically modeled organization is to manage the vision that keeps the company tied to its market and the corporate culture that can humanize company life. Organic corporations, on the other hand, integrate their corporate vision and culture in an identity and build that identity into every process and structure in their corporate DNA. What, then, do organic principles suggest about the job of a chief executive?

Two Models for the Top

Let's begin with a quick review of the differences between how we govern machines and how living things govern themselves. Because their parts have only limited intelligence, machines need an external intelligence to design and build them, to operate them day to day, to reprogram them when changes must be made, and to repair them when they break down. In short, an external intelligence must control a machine so that it can make the products or services it exists to generate.

In living things, intelligence is distributed, and parts act autonomously. So the job of governing is more complex. We need a central nervous system, but its job isn't to *control* our body's activities. Rather the central nervous system performs several jobs that can't be performed by the parts alone—that is, the jobs that must be done at the highest level of a hierarchy of nested networks:

- *Coordination.* Your central nervous system coordinates the activity of your body's parts. When you reach for a glass of orange juice, your central nervous system doesn't tell each muscle cell how to do its job. It coordinates the messages going out to muscle cells in your arms and fingers and to your eyes; it integrates the messages from nerves in your eyes and fingers; and it enables you to adjust to this information about the process.

- *Decision Making.* Your central nervous system enables you to make decisions for your body as a whole. Sometimes the decisions are automatic, such as pulling your hand back from a hot stove, where the nerve message is relayed directly through the spinal chord and never goes to the brain. In other cases, the decisions require thought, ranging all the way from what clothes to wear on the day of an important meeting to whether you want to earn an MBA before you take your first corporate job.
- *Monitoring.* The central nervous system monitors your body's subsystems to ensure that they're working properly. Your brain's hypothalamus, for example, acts as your body's thermostat, ensuring that your body stays at a healthy temperature. Its vasomotor center monitors the carbon dioxide level of the blood and can change heart rate or constrict blood vessels to adjust that level.

Rather than control the body, as an external intelligence must control a machine, the central nervous system makes sure all its parts can be successful in doing their jobs.

What happens when we apply these two ideas of governing the whole as models for an organization? In both cases, the chief executive must be responsible for making high-level decisions, for ensuring that efforts of all the parts are coordinated, and for monitoring how well those parts are doing their jobs. The key difference is what chief executives control. With a mechanical model, chief executives act as operators of the corporate machine, monitoring markets and controlling how their organizations respond to them. To do that, they must be in control of the formal structure as it directs the informal organization. In maintaining control, managers from the chief executive down assume that their people, as replaceable parts, cannot be trusted to do what's right, whether out of ignorance or lack of concern for the company, without being told to do it.

With an organic model, chief executives act as corporate central nervous systems, monitoring corporate systems to make sure they create environments that enable everyone to act both autonomously *and* in the best interest of the company. Rather than use the formal structure to control, they use it to enhance the natural effectiveness of the informal organization. Here, managers must ensure that their people have both the information, through corporate DNA and nervous system, and concern, through commitment to the corporate identity, to do what is right.

The difference between the mechanical and organic models here is the difference between leadership and what Peter Block (1993) calls *stewardship*. Leadership forges the direction everyone in an organization must take, because the leader, alone, can understand that direction. Stewardship ensures that the system is healthy enough so that all its members, working together, can define the direction the organization must take.

An organic model suggests that, while our organizations may still need leadership from time to time, they will generally do much better when senior executives practice stewardship.

Mechanical Leadership

Even if you'd never heard of bureaucracy, it wouldn't be difficult to figure out the role for a chief executive based on a mechanical model. The chief executive, along with an executive team and corporate staff, is the external intelligence that controls—that is, designs, operates, and repairs—the corporate machine. Chief executives who enhance this control with a powerful vision and a humanizing corporate culture become visionary leaders.

Not all those we think of as visionary leaders have this full range of capabilities. They don't have to, because different capabilities become critical at different stages of development of a business. In the early stages, implementing a corporate vision is the most important function. Henry Ford, for example, was the first to see the potential of mass-produced cars in the early years of the 20th century. He created the production line to make his vision a reality in the Model T, and made Ford, with its focus on a single model, the leading automaker in the world. Almost by accident, Ford also introduced a corporate culture that made his company the envy of industrial workers everywhere. Realizing that it made no sense to put the finest machinery in the hands of indifferent, or angry, workers—turnover ran to 400 percent every year—Ford attracted the best workers and kept them happy with a then-princely wage of five dollars a day. For the first time, industrial workers could look forward to earning enough to buy the products they made (Halberstram 1986).

Unfortunately, by the late 1920s, as his company and its industry matured, Ford's vision of a single model became outdated. As his company lost ground to General Motors, Ford became embittered, and his corporate culture suffered for it. Soon labor problems were worse at Ford than anywhere in the U.S. auto industry. A leader's vision must connect the company with its markets and recognize important shifts, just as your vision enables your car to adjust to changing road conditions. Then the leader must redesign the company to meet shifting market conditions. Henry Ford could not. As a result, Ford became a corporate machine without an operator and squandered automobile industry leadership during the 1920s.

Alfred Sloan, the man who wrested that leadership from Ford, was less a technological visionary than a first-class corporate engineer. Sloan, who became chief executive of GM in 1923, never lost interest in what he called, "the problems of operating a multiple-unit organization with different products made by separate divisions." In fact, the first half of Sloan's reminiscences, *My Years with General Motors* (1990), deals largely with how best to structure and manage GM, including organization charts for 1921, 1937, and 1963. Once a market begins to stabilize, as the automobile industry did in the 1920s, the job as corporate designer and redesigner becomes critical to the chief executive. Because the corporate machine as a whole has little intelligence, the chief executive, as the external intelligence of the corporate machine, must continually examine the market and redesign the company to meet market shifts.

The reputation of some visionary leaders grows from the ability to take advantage of this kind of market shift, the kind Henry Ford ignored. At IBM, for example, Tom Watson, Jr. pushed the company into the new business of making mainframe computers in the early 1950s, a time when the best minds were predicting a market for fewer than 100 of them. Tom Jr.'s bold vision would combine with IBM's customer- and employee-oriented corporate culture to make it the most feared and respected company in the world throughout the 1960s and 1970s.

Today the best example of a visionary leader may be Bill Gates, cofounder of Microsoft. From the founding of the company in 1975, with partner Paul Allen, Gates integrated a vision of the future of personal computers with keen business sense. At the time, he insisted to Allen that the company produce only software. Fifteen years before the market confirmed his judgment, Gates realized that software was where the money would be (Cusumano 1995). With his business-like vision, Gates rode Microsoft's 1982 partnership with IBM to software dominance in the personal computer industry in only eight years, a role predicted in Microsoft's corporate identity—"A computer on every desk and in every home, running Microsoft software" (Manes and Andrews 1994).

Under Gates's leadership, Microsoft is also trying to dominate software in the computer workstation market and on the Internet. To make this happen, Gates designed Microsoft in a team structure in which everything connects back, eventually, to him (Cringley 1996). In this way, Gates remains the central intelligence operating a corporation with annual sales of $6.8 billion. Gates has the flexibility Henry Ford lacked. In 1996, Gates drove Microsoft to compete with Netscape, the leader in Internet browser software, in only six months, after he had ignored this market for years. As of fall 1997, Microsoft continued to gain market share on Netscape. In late spring 1997, Gates reversed field again and pushed Microsoft into the software market for stripped-down, bare-bones network computers, an option he had earlier rejected when announced by companies such as Sun Microsystems, Oracle, and IBM. These two cases suggest Gates operates from a mechanical model. Unlike 3M, where teams would have sprung up to meet these market opportunities, people at Microsoft had to wait for Gates's directive.

To keep the corporate machine in control in complex markets, the chief executive needs support from an executive team and corporate staff. Each member of the executive team is responsible for controlling his or her subsystem of the company and for advising the chief executive on what's happening within it. In some bureaucracies, the demand for control is so strong that chief executives are known to scream at executive team members when they don't know every detail of the operations under them.

Corporate staff provides support in specialized areas of knowledge. The human resources department, for example, helps the chief executive make sure that policies such as compensation and promotion enable the company to get the most from their human resources while observing complex government regulation in these areas. The finance department crunches the numbers that enable the chief executive to demonstrate the success—or failure—of the corporate money-making machine. During a class I conducted on quality improvement at one Baby Bell, a member of the finance department insisted that one requirement of her job was to ensure the profit numbers enabled the company to provide managers with maximum annual bonuses. In this way, she was helping management show the company's performance was predictable and in control.

These senior executives see themselves as the external intelligence operating the corporate machine. As a result, they believe they deserve special treatment. Prime parking places, executive dining rooms, stock options, and six- to seven-figure salaries—these are the rewards for doing a company's thinking. Such "thinking" may consist of dismembering a company and tearing it from the community where it's resided for a century, as "Chainsaw" Al Dunlop did with Scott Paper Co. in the mid 1990s. Nonetheless, by increasing the value of the stock, and making the corporate money machine pay off better for its stockholders, 18 months' work earned Dunlop between $80 million and $100 million.

In recent years, as bureaucracies such as AT&T have tried to become more customer oriented (organic, in the terms we are using), they have taken away the executive dining rooms and parking places and extended stock options to all workers. In spite of these gestures, they continue to insist that the thinking of the chief executive is worth substantially more than the work of any of the people who actually create corporate wealth.

Today chief executives seem to see their jobs more in terms of being a chief executive than of serving a specific company. It wasn't always that way. Before the Whiz Kids took over senior management at Ford in the early 1950s—Robert McNamara would become president in 1960—chief executives at large companies almost always were promoted from within. We've come a long way from this assumption that people long inside an organization know how to run it best. Today the assumption seems to be that once a person learns how to be a chief executive, he or she can do the job anywhere. Sometimes this assumption works, and we get a Lou Gerstner turning around IBM. Other times it fails, and we get Gilbert Amelio riding Apple still farther into the ground. Even AT&T, in fall 1997, named an outsider, C. Michael Armstrong, CEO of Hughes Electronics Corp., as its new CEO. In any case, what's important in mechanically modeled organizations is the proven ability to operate a corporate machine successfully.

Problems of Leadership

The success of Microsoft proves that even in today's rapidly shifting markets, mechanically modeled leadership can work. Still, Microsoft will eventually face the problem of replacing Gates when he steps down. We've already discussed how the inability to replace a visionary leader damaged IBM and Sun Oil. It's worth pointing to one more example.

At Ford, the Whiz Kids, whom Henry Ford II brought in after World War II, focused only on financials and allowed the quality of its cars to deteriorate through the 1970s. That focus blinded them to some fascinating opportunities. At one point in the 1960s, informal conversations indicated that Honda was so desperate for cash it was willing to sell Ford as much as 49 percent of its stock. Ford's Whiz Kids refused even to discuss that deal. They also rejected, over and over, developing the minivan. So Lee Iaccoca and a cast of Ford transplants would use the minivan to help resurrect Chrysler. Largely as a result of the Whiz Kids' finances-only focus, by the second OPEC boycott, the invasion of gas-efficient Japanese cars had so overwhelmed Ford's management that the company would lose about $7 billion between 1979 and 1982 (Halberstam 1986).

At IBM, Sun Oil, and Ford, after their visionary leaders left, chief executives lacked the vision and business sense to understand the epochal changes sweeping through their markets. Focused, instead, on the internal politics for which they repeatedly had been paid and praised and promoted, they abdicated their critical job of enabling their companies to adapt to change. In many cases, these executives did not seem even to *recognize* the enormous opportunities market shifts threw at them.

Cut off from what's happening in their markets, senior managers focus instead on playing the corporate game of advancement and one-upsmanship. Without a vision to help create strategic direction, such senior mangers want to micromanage every decision, slowing down processes throughout the organization and making it increasingly difficult to serve customers' needs. In information-age markets, nothing can be more destructive, as companies ranging from Xerox to AT&T and GM to IBM discovered.

An Organic Alternative

Unlike a machine, your body does not need an external intelligence to operate. All the parts of your body are self-organizing. The job of your central nervous system is not to control the body, although it does make high-level decisions for the body as a whole. The key job of the central nervous system is to make sure that the body as a whole is healthy and that its systems enable the parts to do their jobs successfully. The chief executive in an organic corporation should act as the corporate central nervous system. The job is not to control the organization. It is to ensure that the corporate body is healthy and all the autonomous employee parts are able to do their jobs.

This picture of the chief executive reflects what Block calls *stewardship*. Block (1993) defines stewardship as "the willingness to be accountable for the well-being of a larger organization by operating in service, rather than in control, of those around us." This is not a new idea. It is firmly in the tradition of what Robert Greenleaf called *servant leadership* (Spears 1997). The distinction between traditional leadership and stewardship is critical. Senior executives govern a bureaucracy; ideally they are leaders. In an organic corporation, on the other hand, senior executives are stewards who serve by ensuring their organizations can be self-governing.

In times of crisis, organizations may need a more traditional type of leadership. This is especially true when organizations make the transformation from bureaucracy to organic corporation. Dee Hock at Visa or Georg Bauer at Mercedes-Benz Credit Corporation had to articulate the new idea for their organizations and then begin the transformation process. Once they did that, their roles shifted from leadership to stewardship. If the organization makes the transformation successfully, the company should be able to operate organically, to coevolve with its markets through self-organization. Only in case of major crisis will the role of chief executive revert to leadership.

In many ways, chief executives in bureaucracies and organic corporations have similar jobs. Yet, even in the tasks both perform, the job of an organic chief systems supporter can be subtly different from that of a mechanical systems controller. Consider the founding vision. Henry Ford's vision was of an automobile for the common man. The success that built Ford into the world's leading automaker, and then nearly killed it, all grew from Ford's vision. At 3M, on the other hand, William McKnight's vision was tied less to a specific product than to a unique way of dealing with markets. The company was founded as a mining concern but never got very far as one. But when Francis Oakie wrote to ask for samples of all 3M's abrasives, McKnight's curiosity led to supporting him and 3M's first major success, Wetordry sandpaper (see Chapter 4.) The company developed other products, such as Scotch brand tapes, as 3M employees realized their technology could fill market needs, just as Wetordry sandpaper had.

The difference between Ford and McKnight reflects the models from which they worked. After all, the purpose of a machine is to generate products. Operating from a mechanical model, Ford's vision was of a product. Living things, on the other hand, must nurture relations with their environments to survive. McKnight, operating from an organic model, had a vision based on creating relationships—offering innovative ways to meet customer needs—with 3M's markets.

In both cases, the chief executive is also responsible for developing organizational structure. However, the founder of an organic corporation is less the corporate engineer than the person who enables the organization to evolve its structure. For example, when he encouraged Mercedes-Benz Credit Corporation to transform itself, Georg Bauer intentionally rejected reengineering, unlike Alfred Sloan, who repeatedly reengineered GM over the years he led it. Bauer explained that such an approach would have been too mechanical.[2] He asked a series of employee teams to redesign the company with two purposes in mind. First, Bauer wanted the company to be able to meet the immediate challenges of its changing market. Second, he wanted it to be able to continue to learn and adapt as the market continued to change. Bauer did not want a corporate machine engineered to meet current challenges, with a built-in need for periodic reengineering. He wanted a corporate organism capable of evolving. He knew that would require that the corporate organism evolve its own structures. (For a fuller examination of how Bauer led this transformation, see Chapter 11.)

The distinction between these two ways of restructuring further reveals their models. As operator of the corporate machine, the chief executive must take responsibility for keeping all the parts tuned and for any other repairs that must be made, so that the organization can address market shifts. The stewardship model of chief executive, on the other hand, focuses on encouraging ongoing adaptation. The chief executive at 3M nurtures a corporate environment in which people constantly are developing new products and business units to meet market change. At Mercedes-Benz Credit Corporation, Bauer set out to create a learning organization that could adapt. During the corporate transformation Bauer encouraged people to try things, even when he disagreed. "There are no bad ideas," he told Jan Hopkins of CNN's "Who's in Charge?" (August 28, 1996). His philosophy, he added, was to "step back and let ideas evolve."

The chief executive in an organic corporation can support this kind of experimentation in any number of ways. At Federal Express, for example, every management staff meeting, at all levels, includes the report of a quality improvement team. In this way, managers can get a fuller picture of what is happening in their areas. They also give strokes to the participants, thereby encouraging further efforts. Motorola achieves similar results through an annual competition between quality improvement teams at the company. By signaling this way that the ongoing changes such teams introduce are valued, managers from the chief executive to front-line supervisors encourage every employee to become involved in the coevolution of their companies.

Organic chief executives can take advantage of the rich flow of information from their corporate nervous systems in providing this kind of support. At Federal Express, CEO Fred Smith and his executive team tap the records of package movement provided by bar-code scanners to pinpoint problem areas and provide help where it's needed. Similarly, senior executives at The Ritz-Carlton periodically look over quality improvements made at individual hotels and recommend the best of them to other hotels.

This organic idea that chief executives support rather than control is still new in corporate America. In some cases, it becomes caught up in more mechanical thinking. At Federal Express, for example, management talks about its support in terms of an inverted pyramid. Bureaucracies see the chief executive as the most important person in the organization, at the top of the pyramid, supported by several levels of management, front-line workers, and, ultimately, the customer. At Federal Express, on the other hand, managers explain that the most important people are the customers outside the company and then the employees who serve them directly inside the company. The job of management is to support those customer-service employees with the information and resources they need to do their jobs.

Although the inverted pyramid is appealing and much of the operations at Federal Express grow from it, the managers who use it don't seem to have thought through all its implications. Corporate satirist Scott Adams probably stated this problem best in one of his "Dilbert" cartoons. When Dilbert's boss explains, "We've redesigned the organization chart to show management at the bottom supporting our most important employees," Dilbert responds, "Why do the most important employees get paid the least?" (Adams 1996).

In any case, providing this sort of support demands the chief executive, the executive team, and corporate staff continuously monitor corporate systems to make sure people are supported. Once again, an effective corporate nervous system should be invaluable. At Rosenbluth Travel, CEO Hal Rosenbluth's use of crayon drawings (see Chapter 6) was especially creative. In another case, his office began receiving calls that people at one company location were unhappy. When clients served from that location also called to say their travelers weren't satisfied, Rosenbluth sent a team of human resources associates to get to the root of the problem (Rosenbluth and Peters 1992).

Assisting the chief executive in the role of corporate central nervous system are the senior executive team and corporate staff. Their jobs shift from control to support. An organic approach to this job is especially interesting in industries in which markets are transforming themselves— health care, for example. At Muhlenburg Regional Medical Center, CEO John Kopicki wanted to improve customer satisfaction. If he did, doctors with discretionary patients—patients who could be referred to one of several local hospitals—would be more likely to send them to Muhlenberg. To meet this goal, one of Kopicki's vice-presidents, Mary Anne Keyes, tackled a major irritant for patients and doctors alike—the long, involved procedure for admission. With the old procedure, a doctor with an office full of patients might have to run down to the hospital to admit a patient. The doctor would also have to do time-consuming paperwork. Finally, obtaining all the required tests could take five or six hours. Because the effort was uncoordinated, staff members might have to make repeated visits before a patient was available for a specific test.

Keyes took on the role of corporate central nervous system. Rather than reengineering this process, she assembled a group of doctors and nurses interested in the problem. She gave them one requirement: Make sure all admissions work could be completed within an hour of the patient's arrival at the hospital without compromising quality of care. Their solution was to staff the admissions areas with additional nurses who gave newly admitted patients concentrated attention. The result streamlined the admissions process to an hour. Both patients and doctors loved the new procedure, and it was so successful that Keyes's staff received more than 400 requests for information on how they did it.[3]

The job of corporate staff should also move away from bureaucratic control toward supporting the ability of an organic corporation to self-organize. In a bureaucracy, human resources must make sure company policy conforms to government regulation and ensure the company uses the best personnel systems to coerce people into following orders. In an organic corporation, the key task human resources performs is assisting senior management in nurturing the community structure. Among other things, it should monitor systems to make sure they are aligned with corporate identity. At 3M, for instance, human resources recently developed a set of guidelines for hiring. Human resources made explicit for the first time that the company needed people who were innovative, out-of-the-box thinkers, and provided help to managers who wanted to hire this kind of employee. Similarly, the Rosenbluth human resources team that examined the problem described earlier found that its management was exercising mechanical leadership, treating people as a means to an end. The team talked with associates to find out which managers were causing the problem, and the company had to let some of them go (Rosenbluth 1992).

Ultimately, the chief executive and the executive team, as a corporate central nervous system, are integrated into the organization rather than being its external intelligence. As a result, their compensation should be in line with the rest of the organization, if at a higher level. A variety of organizations have jettisoned perquisites such as executive dining rooms and chauffeured cars. However, there's a world of difference between dropping perquisites as part of a transformation to a more organic state and dropping them as symbols unattached to any reality. Unless the transformation is complete, unless the chief executive is willing to relinquish control and become a corporate steward, selling the corporate Lear jet and closing the executive dining room are meaningless gestures.

Summary

This chapter opened with a look at the differences between the mechanical chief executive, as corporate machine operator, and the organic chief executive, as corporate nervous system. As corporate machine operator, the chief executive must control the formal structure so that it can keep the informal organization moving predictably in the desired direction. This mechanical style for running organizations works as long as the company has a visionary leader to keep it aligned with its markets. Even with a visionary leader, however, a mechanical style can become a problem in today's markets. By focusing on Microsoft's identity, rather than its vision, Bill Gates seems to prove that visionary leadership can still work. Only time will tell whether he can continue to redirect the company, as with the challenge of Java described in Chapter 2.

The alternative is stewardship, the organic chief executive as corporate central nervous system. In an organic corporation, where workers are expected to behave autonomously, no manager can see his or her job as control. The chief executive as steward must support corporate systems so that they continue to create an environment in which the people in the organization push it to coevolve in its markets. This style of chief executive will be most effective in an organization that has incorporated the other design principles of life examined throughout this part of the book.

A chief executive as steward enables an organic corporation to take better advantage of the benefits examined in the chapters on corporate identity, DNA, nervous system, and a hierarchy of nested networks. Those benefits include:

- Developing a stronger awareness of what's happening in today's turbulent markets and what a company must do to coevolve effectively
- Enhancing the flow of information so that people can improve service and continuously learn about customer needs, how to meet them today, and develop new products and services for tomorrow

- Creating trust that enables people to cooperate in pursuit of the identity they share

Companies can't even hope to achieve any of these benefits if their senior management teams don't embrace an organic model. In Chapter 9, we'll see how hanging onto a mechanical model traps senior managers into undermining so many of the programs they introduce to improve corporate performance, from total quality management to teamwork to empowerment. One key obstacle to making this shift is how difficult most managers find giving up mechanical leadership for organic stewardship. What makes this transition so difficult is that managers must exchange control for letting go.

As Keyes put it, "For anyone trained in traditional management science, it's all counterintuitive. It means you have to let go of control and trust that, given information and freedom, the people who work for you can come up with solutions at least as good as the ones you'd develop."[4] For those who've been paid and praised and promoted for 20 years or more for practicing command-and-control, it takes an enormous amount of courage even to try management by letting go.

As difficult as this transformation may be, it's essential for any organization that wants to thrive in the 21st century. Which leads us to a final metaquestion: Can an organic way of thinking help these managers begin to make this transformation? That's what we explore in Part III. Let's turn now to what our organizations may be able to learn by applying the way living things transform themselves.

PART III

Organic Transformation

In the first two parts of this book, we explored what happens when we start thinking about our organizations as living things coevolving in market ecologies. Rather than controlling people, as mechanically modeled organizations do, organic corporations, such as 3M or Federal Express, foster self-control and encourage the informal organization to operate as a living, learning system. Such organizations use life's design principles to provide the information people need to behave autonomously and continuously search for new and better ways to meet the changing needs of their markets. That is, they coevolve through self-organization.

All of which leads us to a final issue. Companies in their early stages of development can build these organic design principles into corporate systems from the beginning. Corporations with 50 or 100 years of operating on a mechanical model, on the other hand, face a more difficult challenge. Their managers have worked from a mechanical model for so long, they often believe it's the only way to operate. Yet, as we shall see, managers who try to make the transformation from bureaucracy to organic corporation with a mechanical model create enormous obstacles to their efforts.

Reengineering demonstrates why. Even Michael Hammer, the consulting guru most identified with it, conceded that reengineering was too mechanical. "I was reflecting my engineering background and was insufficiently appreciative of the human dimension," he told the *Wall Street Journal* (November 26, 1996). At its best, reengineering helps managers design faster, more productive business processes. Unfortunately, business processes are very different from, say, bridges. The result is a series of problems caused by reengineering of business processes:

- Reengineering is a top-down process by which managers impose a new set of procedures on the people who perform them. The result too often is resentment, which can undermine any productivity improvements the new processes offer.
- Reengineering has people go into a room and create a new process from the bottom up, then implement it. This is like trying to write a piece of application software a million lines of code long without testing any pieces of it before running the whole thing on a computer. As a result, small problems aggravate each other, reducing overall effectiveness.
- Reengineering replaces the old mechanical controls of a bureaucracy with new ones. It may build a faster, sleeker corporate machine, but it's still a corporate machine, not the organic learning organization that can thrive in today's markets. Even if the reengineered processes are perfect today, markets will change tomorrow. As Hammer himself noted, reengineered processes would have to be re-reengineered every few years.

So we arrive at our final issue. What can we learn from living things about the way our organizations should transform? To answer that question, we begin by looking at two models of making large-scale alterations—mechanical change and organic transformation. Chapter 9 examines the differences between these two modes of reinventing bureaucracies for today's markets. In Chapters 10 and 11, we study two efforts at reinvention, corporate culture change at Bell Atlantic and transformation at Mercedes-Benz Credit Corporation. Finally, in Chapter 12, we draw on everything we have learned in the course of this book to articulate some general principles of corporate transformation.

CHAPTER 9

You Can't Engineer a Butterfly: Change versus Transformation in Corporate Reinvention

There are only two ways we know of to make extremely complicated things. One is by engineering, and the other is evolution. And of the two, evolution will make the more complex.
—Danny Hillis, coinventor of the first massively parallel-processing computer

Question: How should managers of once-successful bureaucracies go about reinventing their companies so they can thrive in today's market ecologies?

When Georg Bauer took over as chief executive officer of Mercedes-Benz Credit Corporation (MBCC) in 1992, he faced the challenge of the 1990s—how to reinvent a traditional, hierarchical bureaucracy with a history of success for today's turbulent markets. According to just about any measure, Bauer is succeeding. By 1997, only five years after he took over, MBCC's assets more than doubled to more than $10 billion; revenues increased 80 percent; new business was up 84 percent; and productivity jumped 50 percent. In addition, J. D. Powers rated the company number one in dealer satisfaction among luxury automobile import finance companies for three consecutive years.

Not every company that has worked to remake itself for the information age has succeeded so well. Even in companies facing the most competitive markets every day, managers repeatedly stumble in trying to turn their old bureaucracies into the sleek, adaptive organizations that can thrive in today's markets. The sheer number of programs some large corporations have introduced as *the* answer to their problems over the last decade—from total quality management (TQM) to downsizing, from corporate culture change to reengineering, to mention only the best known—suggests how difficult reinventing any company can be.

Consider AT&T. For nearly a century, AT&T's monopoly was the Mother of All Bureaucracies, Mama Bell, a comfortable, successful place to work, with procedures to describe every possible job. Those procedures were so comprehensive that they specified what level manager you had to be to have arms on your office chairs. In the 1970s, however, new technologies introduced competition into the long-distance phone service market. So the company worked with the U.S. Justice Department on divestiture. In 1984, the old monolith split into seven Baby Bells, regional providers of local service, and the new AT&T, which kept its long-distance and computer services businesses.

The new AT&T faced intense competition in long-distance service from MCI and Sprint. Its senior managers knew that *to survive* the company would have to shed its past as a monopoly and become competitive. AT&T's attempts at reinvention included:

- Launching a successful TQM effort and becoming the first company to win two Malcolm Baldrige National Quality Awards in a single year, 1992
- Leveraging its long-distance customer base with a universal service card, which combined calling card and credit card, in 1991
- Trying to strengthen its competitive position in computers by buying another computer maker, NCR, in 1991
- Reengineering its business processes—Michael Hammer and Steven Stanton identify AT&T as a company that used "reengineering to achieve striking improvements in [its] performance" (Hammer and Stanton 1994)
- Downsizing 128,000 employees (*New York Times*, March 3, 1996)

Even these apparently successful efforts at reinventing itself were not enough. AT&T split off what was left of NCR in 1997. Worse, the company that created universal telephone service saw its dominance in the long-distance phone market slipping away, down to 54 percent in March 1997 and likely to continue falling. More recently, the board of directors fired CEO Robert Allen and hired its first outsider CEO in recent history. The price of AT&T stock fell, and many analysts questioned whether the company could prosper in the competitive free-for-all in telecommunications it helped create.

Why have managers at so many companies working to reinvent themselves, like AT&T, had only limited success? The underlying problem seems to be the Einstein Dilemma. Managers who have spent their working lives treating their organizations as if they were machines are going to think mechanically about corporate reinvention. Without re-asking all the fundamental questions about organizations they had long ago answered, they continue to assume corporate reinvention is very much like upgrading an enormous machine. As a result, these managers can only create more efficient corporate machines at a time when their markets demand they refashion them to be more like living things. They can only *re*engineer when they really need to *de*engineer.

Re-asking those old questions and answering them in organic terms yields a different perspective. After all, the processes we use for making large-scale alterations in machines and living things are very different. You *change* a machine to alter it. Living things, on the other hand, must *transform themselves*. What, then, are the differences between these two ways of thinking about corporate reinvention?

Transformation versus Change

When I was a corporate speechwriter, I never met an executive who didn't like the word *change*. One executive who had a reputation for loving to talk was delighted with the line, "The more things change, the more I talk about it!" These managers loved to talk about change because, as often as they explain how difficult change is, it is, at least, familiar.

Think about the number of times you change something in a day. You change your mind, your clothes, your route to work, or your job. All these actions are alike. Change is performed by an active agent on an object. The agent alters a discrete part of reality by means of a tried-and-true mechanical procedure. The rest of the agent's reality doesn't have to change.

Transformation is entirely different. When it becomes a butterfly, a caterpillar consumes and recreates every part of itself except its brain, heart, and guts. Similarly, the information revolution is driving our economy utterly to recreate itself, a transformation we examined in terms of industries like telecommunications and health care, in Chapters 1 and 2. With transformation, you don't have actor and object. A self-organizing system transforms itself. The alteration is systemic, from the inside out. It's a unique organic procedure.

This distinction between change and transformation is at the heart of the troubles organizations like AT&T are having in reinventing them-selves for the information age. You hear the confusion between these two models of large-scale alteration in stories from "change agents" at so many of those organizations. At one, the CEO became notorious for asking, "What can I do to make these people change?" He believed that his job was to make a mechanical change in everyone but himself.

At another company, the executive team asked the leaders of its change effort to build interdepartmental teams. Months later, the change leaders returned to the executive team with a problem. The interdepartmental teams had been superficially successful, they explained. However, the company's reward system was making it impossible for them to achieve full success. The old system rewarded people for their contributions to their home departments. As a result, team members were more committed to the best interests of their departmental bosses than of the interdepartmental teams. Yet when the change leaders asked the executive team to develop a new reward system to give members a reason for shifting their allegiance to their teams, nothing happened.

In both these cases, senior managers trying to reinvent their bureaucracies were thinking *change* when they needed to think *transformation*. For them, the organization was a mechanical system that could be upgraded component by component. It was an object to be changed; they remained outside it. As long as managers think this way, they can only make their organizations better machines.

This is very different from reinventing corporations by means of organic transformation. In organic transformation senior managers see themselves as an integral part of the system. Their job is first to recreate themselves—to replace their command-and-control style with management by letting go—and second to create an environment that will enable the organization to reinvent itself.

The confusion between mechanical change and organic transformation can be seen in the way bureaucratic managers, without meaning to do so, distort organic ideas about management. By thinking of organic behaviors, structures, and strategies through mechanical models, they undermine their intent and create widespread frustration. In Chapter 10, we look specifically at how this happened at Bell Atlantic. Before we get to that story, however, let's take a brief look at what has happened to three such ideas that we've already explored from both the mechanical and organic model—a behavior, how we do our jobs; a structure, one that shifts to meet market shifts; and a strategy, the idea of a corporate purpose.

Mechanical Model	Transitional Model	Organic Model
Job style: Directed	Empowered	Autonomous
Structure: Engineered	Reengineered	Evolved
Purpose: Leader's vision	Vision, mission statement	Identity

According to a mechanical model, we do our jobs by the book and through the direction of the people to whom we report. If employees are equivalent to machine parts, they should be preprogrammed to perform standard operating procedures (SOPs). That's one reason the phrase "Managers think; workers do" is so popular.

An organic model, on the other hand, suggests that people should act autonomously, that they can learn what the organization needs them to do in any situation, just the way every cell and organ in your body "knows" what to do. Managers in an organic corporation can trust this autonomy. For one thing, everyone in the company has access to the procedural information, in its corporate DNA, and the environmental information, from its corporate nervous system, of the whole. For another, corporate systems monitor, recognize, and correct mistakes when they do happen.

Bureaucratic managers trying to get employees to do their jobs organically still think in mechanical terms. For them, employees are powerless mechanical parts. To free them from the tyranny of SOPs, these managers must empower their employees. But the very idea of managers' empowering their people suggests that employees *are* mechanically powerless. In Harrison Owen's (1992) words, "If I empower you, you, to some extent, are in my power." This is why Peter Block wrote that the only person any of us can empower is ourself (Block 1986). Yet bureaucratic managers think in terms of empowering the people who work for them. As a result, bureaucratic efforts at empowerment generally leave employees frustrated, even angry. Although employees are told that they are now empowered to solve their customers' problems, they soon realize that this has become a new method of management control. It would be easy—and meaningless—to blame these bureaucratic managers for the confusion between organic and mechanical ways of doing jobs. Yet as long as they have only a mechanical model of organization, they have little choice but to think this way.

A similar problem has confused the attempt to make organizations' formal structures more organically adaptable to shifting markets. With a mechanical model, senior managers are solely responsible for their companies' structures. Senior managers must monitor the marketplace and, as the corporate machine's repair team, engineer the organizational chart so that the company's structure is able to meet the needs of the market.

With an organic model, on the other hand, structure must evolve. Teams and entire divisions may grow or die to meet the challenges and opportunities posed in the market ecology. Senior managers assume that markets are shifting much too quickly for any small group of people sitting in a room on the top floor to be able to make continuing adjustments and readjustments in the company's structure. Rather they create a structure and a set of corporate systems that enable the company to coevolve with its markets, as 3M does.

In the transition, we talk about reengineering—radically redesigning companies to be lean, responsive, and customer-oriented. Yet the word itself illustrates the mechanical model from which it comes. Managers cannot create mechanical organizations with organic flexibility. Re-engineered organizations have to be re-reengineered every time markets shift. To be organically self-organizing, organizations must evolve.

In a mechanical model, the purpose of an organization is in the corporate vision created and owned by the leader, the external intelligence of the corporate machine. This model assumes that only the leader has the intelligence and understanding of the market to state the company's purpose. When such a leader leaves, the company often loses its sense of purpose, as IBM did when Tom Watson, Jr. left in 1970.

With an organic model, the purpose is the corporate identity that describes how an organization succeeds in its market ecology. Identities such as innovation at 3M or "We are ladies and gentlemen serving ladies and gentlemen" at The Ritz-Carlton hotels, focus everyone in the company on the products they provide, how they deliver them, and how they must act toward each other. Such an identity can be effective in guiding the behavior of a company's employees because every structure and procedure in the corporate DNA is aligned to reflect that identity.

Bureaucratic managers talk about this more organic sense of purpose as the company's vision or mission statement. Like identity, these statements are distributed across the organization so everyone can understand and be guided by them. However, viewed through a mechanical model, these statements often are written by insiders for insiders, to describe the organization as mechanically separate, not to connect it with its market ecology. Moreover, these vision or mission statements are rarely used to align corporate structures and procedures so they can shape employee behavior. People can ignore the statements because the structures and incentives they require aren't integrated systemically into their work lives, as the identity of an organic corporation is.

To illustrate what happens when managers confuse mechanical change and organic transformation—and how they can avoid confusion in their efforts at corporate reinvention—we turn to two case histories. Chapter 10 describes Bell Atlantic's mechanical efforts to reinvent itself around the "Bell Atlantic Way" in the late 1980s and early 1990s. Chapter 11 shows how MBCC transformed itself along more organic lines.

These two are very different organizations, and in many ways, Bell Atlantic's efforts were more courageous than those of MBCC. After all, when Bell Atlantic began its effort, it had more than 80,000 employees; MBCC had only about 600. In addition, Bell Atlantic began its effort six years earlier, in 1986, than MBCC did. In those six years, we learned an enormous amount about what did and did not work in such corporate reinventions. So Bell Atlantic had a more difficult task from the beginning.

Nonetheless, these two companies illustrate clearly and powerfully the results of choosing one model or the other to reinvent themselves.

Once again, the results reflect the Law of Organizational Models: The choice of a model leads managers to think in terms of the specific structures they use in corporate reinvention. Those structures largely determine the way people in the organization behave. In the case of Bell Atlantic, a mechanical model resulted in a mechanical, top-down, managers-know-best approach. Managers *told* employees, who had no part in making the decisions about the change, that they were to behave in an empowered way. Is it any wonder that those employees paid more attention to the command-and-control behavior of their managers than to the more organic words those managers delivered?

At MBCC, on the other hand, an organic model turned the corporate reinvention over to the employee body. People across the organization made the decisions and implemented the actions that reinvented MBCC. In participating in the process, they learned how to act autonomously and work in teams. The transformation became a model for the work style the company wanted to adopt.

With all this in mind, let's turn to the story of the Bell Atlantic Way.

CHAPTER 10

Components of the Bell Atlantic Way: A Tale of Mechanical Change

We are asking people to change their behavior, to accept a new set of conventions for working together. And I try to provide reinforcement in every way I can. For example, I always wear my Quality button to impress colleagues with my rabid dedication. It serves to remind us that we have a very special obligation to support those who support the corporation.

—Ray Smith, Bell Atlantic CEO

Question: What happens when managers rely on a mechanical model to reinvent their organization?

On an otherwise forgettable afternoon some time in 1989, I sat in the auditorium of the Philadelphia headquarters of Bell of Pennsylvania surrounded by the other members of the public relations department. I'd been hired as a speechwriter for the company, one of the state operating subsidiaries of Bell Atlantic, the Baby Bell that provided local telephone service for the mid-Atlantic region. At this meeting, perhaps a year after I had joined the company, we all listened as CEO Ray Smith, who had once been director of this very group, explained why Bell Atlantic needed to change the way it did business.[1]

It was a great message. Bell Atlantic, Smith explained, had grown fat and happy and noncompetitive as a monopoly, first as part of the AT&T Bell System and since the 1984 divestiture, on its own. By the mid 1990s, however, we could expect to see competition in every line of business. Already we were having the best business customers stolen away, and competitors' pay phones were appearing on streets across Bell Atlantic territory. Before long, we would even be challenged for local residential service. The people in the company were entirely unready for this challenge. The company, Smith told us, in what was

165

becoming the standard explanation of the need for the company to change,

> was like a crack football team. We had the best equipment and the best athletes and the finest coaches. The only thing that we didn't have on Saturday morning was someone on the other side of the scrimmage line. We merely rushed up and down the field, catching every pass, recovering every fumble, and stopping at whatever point we scored 100 to nothing (Birchard 1990).

As a result, all the competitive instincts of people in the company were turned inward, group against group and department against department. Management by objectives complicated all that, as each department worked to meet its goals, even if its actions damaged the corporation as a whole.

Smith added that other bureaucratic behaviors—from rules that guided every action people took to shirking of responsibility to rejecting anything not sanctified by tradition—would make it impossible for Bell Atlantic to succeed in the brave new world of competitive telecommunications. "It was clear to us [senior managers] that the conventions we had for dealing with each other as businesses within a monopoly were totally inadequate," he would tell *Chief Executive* magazine in October 1991. "There was internal competition, trickiness, not team building but team competition" (Lacey 1991).

That was the old way, Smith explained, the monopolistic Bell System culture. But with competition developing all around us, we would need a new way to do business, a way that would emphasize teamwork rather than individual action, innovation rather than standard procedures, integrity and personal responsibility rather than loyalty and obedience. Then Smith stopped and asked what we should call that new way. When it was clear no one would guess what to call this new culture, Smith answered his own question: "We'd call it the Bell Atlantic Way."

That was the first time I heard the term Bell Atlantic Way. For much of the next three years, I would throw myself into the company's corporate culture change. I would write occasional speeches for Smith and other executives. I would help redesign the way Bell Atlantic communicated with employees. I would search for the words to help people across the company understand why change was so essential, how other companies were making similar shifts, and what we could do to make it happen. Those three years gave me an invaluable education in bureaucracy, how it needs to reinvent itself, and why it so often has problems in doing that.

Ultimately I learned that Bell Atlantic was trying to do something far more difficult than its managers realized. Because they were so caught up in their old mechanical ways of thinking, the managers tried to engineer a more innovative, customer-oriented Bell Atlantic by changing it as if it were a machine. They were trying to build what we have called an organic corporation, and in many ways they succeeded. Unfortunately, their mechanical approach undercut the effort over and over. In the end, it was far less successful than it could have been.

As one manager with whom I worked on this effort, who continued to work at Bell Atlantic, described the results: "We have a new culture at Bell Atlantic. It's just not the one we envisioned when we started teaching the Bell Atlantic Way."

A Bold Initiative

From the day it became a corporation in 1984, Bell Atlantic was blessed with a worldwide explosion in demand for telecommunications services. In the mid-Atlantic states it served, Bell Atlantic owned the local telephone network. So it would have an enormous competitive advantage in providing a series of exciting new telecommunications services, some existing, some in development, from simple faxes to videos sent to the home over telephone wires to teleconferencing, whereby people hundreds of miles apart could see as well as speak with each other. The demand for all these services was growing exponentially all over the world.

The main limit to growth, the senior management team realized, was the company's noncompetitive culture, as Smith would outline the problem to my colleagues in public relations. Bell Atlantic would be limited by the kinds of mechanical restrictions we explored in Part II— a rule-bound mentality that made loyalty to the boss more important than performance, that ensured no one had to be responsible for anything, and whose mechanical community structure kept all the parts warring with each other. Bell Atlantic's first CEO, Tom Bolger, quickly realized that the company would never perform up to its potential unless it developed a new, more competitive culture. By 1986, senior managers started planning for this corporate culture change. Smith took over as CEO in 1989.

It's easy to overlook how courageous the decision was. For one thing, the task was extremely difficult. Here was a company of more than 80,000 employees with an average length of service of nearly 20 years. Developing a new culture, Smith was fond of saying, was like rebuilding a 747 while it was in flight. Besides, there was no immediate crisis. For its first decade, Bell Atlantic never failed to meet its projected income. In addition, in 1986, the year senior managers began planning the culture change, there was little information on how to manage such an effort. Today, although we know many times more about this process, companies still find it difficult.

Senior managers at Bell Atlantic were the children of Bell, the Mother of All Bureaucracies. They grew up in the organization thinking mechanically. And no one gave them any alternative. In fact, their thinking was so firmly fixed in the old ways that these managers never fully understood the organization they were trying to build. At one conference in the early 1990s, Smith asked his executive team, "What does it [the organization they were trying to build] look like?" Neither Smith nor anyone on the team had an answer. Trapped in their mechanical model, they thought in terms of mechanical change. Their job was to plan the changes for the corporate machine, reach in to make them, and then fine-tune as needed.

Only acts of visionary leadership could have directed their efforts to a more organic approach. In a few cases at Bell Atlantic that happened. Where managers had a gut feeling for what was required, units transformed themselves. But those successes were atypical.

What was typical was an approach to culture change that resembled another major transformation—Bell Atlantic's upgrading the telephone network. To offer many of the new services it envisioned, Bell Atlantic would have to replace its old analog copper wire network, designed to carry only voice communication, with a new digital fiber-optic network, capable of carrying thousands of times more information than copper, to carry computer data and video as well as voice communication. To do that, the company planned first to replace its old analog switching machines in business offices with new digital switches. Next it would replace the copper wire connecting business offices with fiber optics. Finally it would replace the connections between business offices and customers so they could receive enormous amounts of digitized information as voice, computer data, and even video.

The advantage of this approach was control. Bell Atlantic could replace one portion of the network at a time so that only small slivers of service ever had to stop. The company could ensure that the most profitable customers received new services first and that as one part of this project was being completed, another could begin.

That's essentially how Bell Atlantic senior managers planned to introduce the new culture. The effort would begin with the introduction of a vision and set of values to guide employee activity. In Smith's words, "We concluded that before we could replace an imbedded cultural habit with something of a higher nature, we had better explicitly state what that something was" (Birchard 1990). That would be followed by the introduction of a new set of behavioral norms, the Bell Atlantic Way.

At first, senior managers expected to stop there. But they soon realized other components were needed. For one thing, as a regulated monopoly, almost all costs could be written off without affecting financial performance. So employees had no motivation to think about how they spent the company's money. In a newly competitive environment, however, they needed to develop a more cautious ethic for spending. That was called Best Cost. For another thing, a Philadelphia-based vice-president, Regis Filtz, persuaded Smith's senior team that it would also have to introduce a new way for its people to do their jobs, one that was more customer-oriented and focused on continuous improvement, some form of quality improvement.

By 1990, these three concepts—the Bell Atlantic Way behaviors, the Quality Improvement Process (QIP), and the Best Cost spending policy—became the three components—everyone from Smith down called them "components"—of the culture change. Others, such as an employee communications initiative, would be added later. How the components fit together would continue to be a problem. Because all these elements were conceived and introduced as mechanically separate components, most employees had trouble thinking of them as a single culture. Throughout the early 1990s, you could hear employees making comments such as, "If this is Tuesday, I should be practicing quality improvement."

Compliance versus Emergence

Bell Atlantic implemented its culture change just as mechanically as it had planned it. Smith's senior executive team, the Office of the Chairman, developed the company's Vision and Values throughout 1987. They defined a company vision of its future and a set of five values that would enable the company to be more competitive. The final products were circulated, during much of 1988, through seminars attended by 1,400 of Bell Atlantic's 2,200 managers. In these seminars, managers were asked to discuss what they thought the company should be doing and what behaviors would be needed for people to make strong day-to-day decisions. At the end of this process, managers had defined the following five values:

> Integrity—We conduct our business with integrity.
> Respect and trust—We treat each other with respect and, in turn, earn trust by fulfilling our responsibilities.
> Excellence—We strive for excellence in our services, our products and our work.
> Individual fulfillment—We will create an environment in which we can achieve our individual and collective potentials.
> Profitable growth—We pursue long-term profitable growth.

They also reached agreement on a vision statement: "Bell Atlantic's corporate vision is to be a leading international communications and information management company."

Smith repeatedly explained that the process was designed to encourage ownership of and commitment to all the changes reinventing the company would require. Yet this top-down process was mechanical. The Vision and Values were first articulated by senior management, the company's external intelligence. Although other managers were invited to give their input, and real changes were made, those managers also realized that their performance appraisals would be written by the higher-ups whose ideas they were, in effect, being asked to criticize. With a reward system in place that encouraged agreeing with your boss, serious discussion of these issues was extremely difficult. In addition, the Vision and Values were discussed by about two-thirds of company managers but none of the rank and file. This wasn't an attempt to have the Vision and Values of the company emerge as they were explored throughout the company. Rather it was the creation of a management standard with which everyone would be expected to comply.

The end product reflected this mechanical point of view. It stated the sort of view of the inside from the inside that we examined in Chapter 4. Bell Atlantic's vision, for one thing, remained vague. It compared the company with others in its markets rather than clearly specifying *how* it had to be a leader. Would it lead in technology, quality of service, cost, or customer response? No one ever answered these questions. In addition, neither the vision nor values connected the company with its market ecology by mentioning the customer.

Training for the Bell Atlantic Way behaviors and training for the QIP were also mechanically separate. The Bell Atlantic Way was introduced in forums of about 40 to 50 employees each. Those forums were designed during 1988 and 1989 with the assistance of the California-based consulting firm, Senn-Delaney. The behaviors Senn-Delaney developed with Bell Atlantic senior managers emphasized risk taking and empowering employees to take responsibility for problems and finding solutions for them. These concepts were introduced experientially, so most employees who completed the two-and-a-half day Bell Atlantic Way forum were energized and invigorated. Many were so excited about this new way of working together that they were disappointed when they got back to their work teams. Nothing had changed, they complained, and it was impossible to use the skills learned in the forum.

Even before they returned to their workplaces, however, some employees were upset at the way the Bell Atlantic forums were presented. Although the message was about risk taking and personal accountability, the way the sessions were presented emphasized hierarchy and conformity with the new behaviors. Rather than present the information in natural work groups or in a mix of people from across the bureaucracy, the forums were presented according to management level—first the Office of the Chairman early in 1989, then each successive level of the hierarchy within Bell Atlantic. Front-line managers were not offered the forum until 1991. Nonmanagement employees didn't begin it until the middle of 1992.

In addition, facilitators presented the new behaviors as a *fait accompli*, non-negotiable. Once again, the presentation sought compliance with an already chosen set of behaviors. An organic approach might have enabled the behaviors and their definitions to emerge from the interaction of people across the company. Instead, the unspoken message in the forums was that senior management knew best. To many participants already aware of increasingly competitive markets, the new behaviors were self-evident. Yet the company's approach told them that management didn't trust its employees to come to these conclusions on their own. After all, "Managers think; workers do."

While Bell Atlantic developed its new behaviors with Senn-Delaney, it purchased its QIP off the shelf from Philip Crosby Associates. Rege Filtz had already chosen Crosby's approach, rather than those of the other major quality gurus, W. Edwards Deming or Joseph Juran, and boosted performance in his Philadelphia operations. Crosby's approach was the most comfortable to senior managers who grew up in the old Bell System because it was mechanical. For example, Crosby insisted that people use the QIP to "Do It Right the First Time." As Margaret Wheatley and Myron Kellner-Rogers pointed out in *A Simpler Way* (1996), the emphasis on getting things right is mechanical, at odds with the experimentation and error that characterize how living things work.

Whereas every manager in Bell Atlantic was expected to attend a Bell Atlantic Way forum, introduction to the QIP was initially at the discretion of each department. The process was to be taught in a classroom, away from the work environment, as an invariable method with a standard set of tools for solving problems. Because Crosby-style QIP was taught as the one right way, many people at Bell Atlantic couldn't understand how Crosby's (mechanical) doing-it-right-the-first-time could coexist with the (organic) risk taking encouraged in the Bell Atlantic Way forums. Employees who'd been invigorated during the forums at the prospect of finding their own solutions to important problems were often frustrated at the suggestion that the QIP had already found the best way to solve their problems.

By the end of 1990, the contradiction between the two components of the culture change became so obvious that the Office of the Chairman insisted that they be integrated. For about a year, however, nothing happened. While the manager in charge of implementing the new behaviors worked for integration, the manager for quality improvement ran a campaign to delay it, resisting the change as an attack on his personal power. Finally, at the end of 1991, the Office of the Chairman demanded a new program that integrated the QIP with the new behaviors.

Results

The training experience created to integrate the Bell Atlantic Way behaviors with the QIP was one of the great successes of Bell Atlantic's culture change. Called Continuous Learning, it helped employees understand the complementary nature of the new behaviors and quality improvement. Then it gave them a series of tools teams could use to analyze problems and reach consensus on solutions. One of its most important strengths was that people went through Continuous Learning in their natural work teams, learning its tools as they worked through an important problem they'd been trying to solve.

According to several managers in the company, people who worked through Continuous Learning gained an increased appreciation for the new culture. They often learned to work better together in teams to solve a variety of important problems. Perhaps most important, Continuous Learning allowed many employees to internalize the Bell Atlantic Way behaviors and integrate the basic concepts of quality improvement into their daily work lives. One manager added that this new way of doing work in some cases became so strong that it enabled employees to challenge and overcome many of the company's remaining bureaucratic obstacles.

The culture change at Bell Atlantic created some other major successes. For example, the company's employee communications had been typically bureaucratic, senior management explaining only what it believed employees needed to know. The result was that people were cynical and paid little attention to what they learned from the company newspaper or other formal means of communication. Knowing they might not be told the full story, employees paid much more attention to what their immediate supervisors told them or what they learned through the grapevine.

By summer 1991, Smith recognized that this old style of employee communications was making it difficult to implement the culture change. For example, although managers at the company's top levels understood that Bell Atlantic would soon be competing in every business line, the message had been bottlenecked somewhere in middle management. Most people in the company still thought of the company as the old AT&T monopoly, even though competitors' pay phones stood next to Bell Atlantic machines on every other street. Smith recognized that shaking those employees out of their old AT&T mind-set would require a major effort.

To meet the challenge, Smith demanded that the employee communications department redesign itself as "a political campaign," in which each level of the hierarchy would be responsible for getting the message to the one below it. Everyone in employee communications became involved in redesigning the way management got informations to employees. According to the program they developed, managers at every level would become responsible for holding face-to-face work group discussions on important corporate issues every month. The employee communications group worked with Smith to develop a series of about a dozen key messages managers would be responsible, at the very minimum, for ensuring their work groups understood. The main job of the employee communications department would now be to support managers in this effort. Setting up this system and its support took up most of the second half of 1991.

The company tested the redesigned employee communications function in February 1992 with a corporation-wide effort to make sure every employee understood the challenge competition would soon present. The campaign included a teleconference with Smith and other senior managers, a series of publications that highlighted areas in which competitors were challenging, and face-to-face meetings between work groups and their direct supervisors. By the time this effort was completed, employees who'd been blissfully unaware of competition were asking what they could do to help beat it. As of this writing, Bell Atlantic's effort at a corporate nervous system remains one of the major successes of the company's culture change.

Another important change concerned employees' attitudes toward customers. One manager who was deeply involved in quality training, and has since left the company, insisted this was the most important alteration the culture change introduced. He pointed out that when the company first introduced its QIP effort, people had little idea of what a customer was. Like Lily Tomlin's Josephine, the operator for the old AT&T, employees had a monopolist's arrogance about service. They were *the telephone company*. They didn't have to care. The combination of the drive to inform employees about competition and training in quality improvement helped people throughout the company understand. They came to realize that they were doing their jobs for a customer, not always a paying customer, but a customer within the company whose work would eventually reach the paying customers.

The culture change effort also led to enormous improvements in the way work was done. Although most of the company's work processes had made sense when they were introduced, they had built up, layer on layer, over the decades without any thought to changes in the market. As a result, even the most superficial examination of these processes, through the QIP, offered opportunities to improve customer service significantly.

These improvements could be absolutely spectacular when a group's top manager had a gut feeling for the Bell Atlantic Way and QIP. In one group, the gains were so impressive that Michael Hammer and James Champy highlighted them in *Reengineering the Corporation*

(1993). That group was Carrier Access Services, which connected large business customers to long-distance carriers such as AT&T or MCI. Carrier access was led by Regis Filtz, who had championed introducing a QIP. Filtz also ran his operation in the Bell Atlantic Way, encouraging real, empowered risk taking. When Filtz took over this function in 1991, it took an average of 15 days to connect his long-distance provider customers; often it took a month. With competitors taking this business away from Bell Atlantic, it became absolutely necessary to cut cycle time severely. By the end of 1992, Filtz's group was providing new service in an average of three days and was aiming at doing it on demand.

Hammer and Champy cited this accomplishment as a victory of reengineering; they misunderstood it. Although he used the techniques of reengineering, Filtz was, more importantly, one of those managers who seemed instinctively to grasp an organic model. As a champion of the QIP and a leader in the Bell Atlantic Way behaviors, Filtz enabled his group to implement the culture change as completely as any group in Bell Atlantic. Filtz's group was able to redesign the process for connecting to long-distance service so effectively because its day-to-day operations so completely embodied the shift the company stated it wanted to make.

Filtz's accomplishments—and those of managers like him, scattered across the company—were all significant, sometimes even spectacular. Yet they were isolated "islands of excellence," as people in the company called them. They would remain isolated because senior management continued to think of these efforts mechanically. No single fact so thoroughly demonstrated this mechanical outlook as the series of downsizings that began in 1990.

Reducing headcount was unavoidable. As a monopoly, many parts of the old AT&T had become bloated over the years. In the early 1990s, when it faced the possibility of competing for local service, with cable television providers, for example, Bell Atlantic realized its personnel costs were much too high. In addition, technological advances, such as automation of operator services, decreased the number of people needed to operate the telephone system.

However, the *way* these reductions were planned and executed suggests how deeply senior management held its mechanical model of the company. According to Right Associates, a leading career management consultant, such reductions can be made positively. As former Right Associates vice-president John Salveson explained in a presentation introducing his company's report, *Lessons Learned: Dispelling the Myths of Downsizing*, the most effective way to reduce headcount is to form a vision of the company, build a structure that will enable the company to pursue that vision, and then choose the people who can best staff the structure. At one of Salveson's presentations, the Bell Atlantic human resources manager sitting next to me listened to this advice and sighed, "I wish we could do it that way."

Instead Bell Atlantic offered early retirement packages and then a planned series of downsizings throughout the early 1990s. The result was a nosedive in employee morale. At a time when Smith was insisting that people in the company act out of commitment rather than mere compliance, management was taking annual slices from the employee body. Every time people began to become comfortable after one downsizing, another would be announced. As a result, the company experienced a repeated cycle of employee fear and depression, a downward spiral of morale. No one could ever be confident that the layoffs had ended.

These downsizings alone would have limited the success created by the company's culture change. The results eventually became comic just before Thanksgiving 1994, when more than a thousand union members in Philadelphia were disciplined for wearing T-shirts that showed them as "roadkill on the information superhighway." By disciplining its people for a bad joke, growing out of the fear that they, too, might be laid off, management called into question whether it had ever understood the Bell Atlantic Way behaviors in the first place.

The problem with Bell Atlantic's culture change was not that its senior managers weren't smart or didn't care about the company. Rather they were thoroughly fixed in their mechanical model of organization. Without an alternative model, they could only implement a mechanical effort to reinvent the company. As a result, without intending to, they undermined their own efforts to create the kind of company they believed Bell Atlantic would have to be to thrive in the 21st century.

Of course, the final word is far from in. One manager I spoke with insisted that at lower levels he was seeing cross-departmental teamwork in spite of continued bureaucratic structure. And the recently completed merger with NYNEX, the Baby Bell serving New York State and most of New England, offers another opportunity to transform the corporation. People in the company told me that the culture at NYNEX was more bureaucratic than at Bell Atlantic. Whether Bell Atlantic will be able to turbocharge its process of corporate reinvention with the merger or become mired in NYNEX's bureaucracy remains to be seen.

The signs aren't especially promising. For example, at a conference of senior managers in 1994, Smith declared the Bell Atlantic Way a success, and the company eliminated all positions with the terms "Bell Atlantic Way" or "Quality Improvement" in the title. The managers I spoke with felt that this decision devalued the new culture in the eyes of people across the company.

In addition, a report in the *Wall Street Journal* (August 7, 1997) suggested that Smith is backing away from his initial commitment to let NYNEX CEO Ivan Seidenberg take the reins of the merged company a year after completing the merger. It's difficult to draw conclusions, because we can't know why Smith seems to have changed his position. It does, however, hint of the dishonesty woven into many mechanical community structures. Smith's most senior managers were likely to use all their knowledge of the bureaucracy to increase their chances at succeeding him as CEO. The level of uncertainty Smith signaled in backing down from his commitment to Seidenberg could create disruptive tension as the two companies become one.

But who knows? Bell Atlantic's culture change may have recreated the company enough to lead to a full-scale corporate transformation. Similarly, the merger with NYNEX could yield unexpected results and precipitate such a transformation. Moreover, any of the senior managers poised to take over the company when Smith steps down could turn out to be the visionary leader who helps the company evolve to a more organic form. The key is that, until Bell Atlantic can replace its mechanical formal structure with a more organic one, this transformation isn't likely to happen. A few companies have been able to do just that. One of them is Mercedes-Benz Credit Corporation whose CEO asked people throughout the company to tell *him* how to reinvent it for the turbulent markets it faced, to which we now turn.

CHAPTER 11

Evolving a Learning Organization: Organic Transformation at Mercedes-Benz Credit Corporation

Markets will continue to change, and the most successful organizations will continue to adapt. That means we really have to create a learning organization, one where we can be continually learning from each other and from our markets. That's the only way we can develop the new products and divisions that will enable us to remain the market leader.

—Georg Bauer, CEO Mercedes-Benz Credit Corporation

Question: How would managers go about reinventing an organization by means of organic transformation?

In 1992, Mercedes-Benz Credit Corporation (MBCC), the subsidiary that finances Daimler-Benz products in North America, had its most profitable year in company history. Total assets topped $6 billion; the company made $3 billion in acquisitions; and for the first time, revenues topped $1 billion. In spite of these figures, new CEO Georg Bauer wasn't happy. He realized all too clearly that MBCC's competitive advantages would soon be wiped out by shifts in the market. Japanese makers of luxury cars would continue offering attractive lease deals; interest rates were ready to climb; and a sister company, Mercedes-Benz of North America, was about to end its lease subsidies, $500 million worth in 1992.[1] "Leasing and finance were becoming commodities," Bauer noted. "Without the unique advantages we enjoyed, any bank could offer a better rate than we could."

As a result, MBCC's virtual monopoly was about to dissolve in the face of aggressive competition. Yet as a traditional hierarchical bureaucracy—600 people with seven levels of management—the company was unprepared for a competitive battle. Unless MBCC transformed itself in fundamental ways, Bauer was certain the company was headed for trouble.

Equally important, Bauer saw this transformation as a beginning, not an end. "It would be comfortable if we could make a set of changes and stop," he explained. "But it won't be over." The market was going to continue shifting, and Bauer wanted MBCC to be ready to take advantage of those shifts as they occurred. He believed that only by reinventing the company so that it could continually transform *itself* could MBCC remain a leader in its markets.

Bauer also saw how difficult beginning this transformation would be. Because of MBCC's success, contentment pervaded the company. Its people assumed they would continue to be successful by doing what they'd always done. Bauer faced a choice. He could wait until the company was feeling the pain of change and competition, or he could push for a new way while the company was still the undisputed leader in its markets. Bauer decided to lead from a position of strength. He would lead a corporate transformation that would prepare MBCC to maintain and build on its leadership.

The key issue in making such a transformation successful, Bauer decided early on, was universal involvement with the process. As a successful organization set in its ways, MBCC had developed a powerful management structure. So Bauer realized it would be necessary to transcend that structure, shake up the networks of political power, and break up bureaucratic fiefdoms. The only way to do that would be to involve everyone in the organization, to build consensus on what they would have to do, and to strive for commitment from everyone. His experience with the Daimler-Benz organization in Germany convinced Bauer that a mechanical approach—telling people to behave differently— wouldn't work, that it wouldn't get people involved or create the innovation and teamwork he was sure would be essential. Besides, Bauer was certain that people on the front lines would have some of the most powerful ideas, and the best way to spark those ideas was universal involvement.

Bauer rejected reengineering as usually practiced:

> From day one, I wanted this to be different from reengineering. . . . Most business process reengineering tends to take a mechanical approach. It tends to be too technical, too structurally oriented. I felt we also needed to examine the soft, human factors. . . . It would have been a lot easier to plan the changes at an offsite management meeting and drop them on our employees, but I was sure we needed another way to do it.

So Bauer decided to deengineer his company, even if he didn't use that term. He would encourage a self-organizing transformation, one in which employees across the company were invited to help replace MBCC's mechanical formal structure with an organic one. That, Bauer believed, was the only way a sense of ownership could be universal, so that people could embrace rather than resist the needed changes.

Step 1 Communicating the Problem

As Bauer expected, at first people didn't want to change. So Bauer's executive team started explaining the competitive pressures MBCC would soon face. This team then challenged people across the company with a once-in-a-lifetime opportunity. They could take the oncoming change in their own hands and redesign the company for its newly competitive markets. Bauer explained:

> People were shocked that I'd put the future of the organization in their hands. Management was skeptical, too. They tried to read my agenda. I accepted their skepticism as part of the process and reinforced that I had no hidden agenda. Many of my managers admitted that they didn't know what changes to make. So they understood why we had to have everyone help us define our new organization.

Bauer spent his first six months in this effort creating acceptance. "It was a cumbersome process and didn't go nearly fast enough for me," he noted. Among other things, he had to address the issue of fear. Throughout 1992, the business pages were full of stories of downsizing. People at MBCC feared Bauer's transformation would end up in layers of downsizing. That would be fatal. "Once this fear takes hold," Bauer said, "people can't be free to create and innovate enough to build a really new organization."

About five months into the process, Bauer started talking about MBCC becoming a risk-taking, entrepreneurial organization. But he knew how unlikely it was that his people would take risks if they didn't feel safe. So he promised that no one would work themselves out of a job. Then, he showed that the company would deliver on this job guarantee. In one case, a supervisor in administrative services eliminated not only her position but her entire group. All the people in that group went on to new positions in the company.

Step 2 MBCC 2000+: The Structural Study

In March 1992, Bauer asked for a study on how MBCC should change to meet the newly competitive marketplace. One new reality was already clear: The company would have to switch its focus from dealers only, who had been the company's primary customers, to include car buyers. This switch demanded a different way of thinking about and serving customers and a structure that would make it easy to do business with MBCC. "The key question I told people we needed to address," Bauer explained, "was, 'Can you ever do too much for the customer?'"

Bauer's executive team then chose a project team, representing a cross-section of employees. This team would study the company and recommend how it would have to change. The project team would look at all the opportunities, talk to employees, dealers, and end users, and answer two questions: How would MBCC have to restructure itself operationally in order to provide better service? And what cultural shifts would the company have to make to ensure that the restructured company *would* serve customers better?

The final report of the project team, "MBCC 2000+," recommended 19 initiatives to Bauer's leadership team, as Bauer had reconfigured senior management. Among the most important strategic recommendations were creating a customer service strategy for North America; developing a unified Customer Service Center with procedures that would be identical throughout the company; and improving information access throughout the company. Key cultural recommendations included developing a statement of corporate mission and values to guide all the other shifts, and a reward and recognition system to encourage intelligent risk taking.

The project team's approach to implementing these recommendations was designed to involve as much of the employee population as possible. For each initiative, it would first collect and analyze a large body of information, gathered largely from discussions with employees, dealers, and end users. The project team would then develop a recommendation for the leadership team. When the leadership team was satisfied that a recommendation reflected a consensus among employees, dealers, and customers, the initiative would move on to an implementation team, which would work with the employees who performed the processes it was examining. Only when an implementation team was confident it understood what it needed to do would members draw flow charts and pilot the new processes.

By building a piloting stage into the introduction of all new processes, MBCC created an important advantage for itself in its transformation. In an interview with Jan Hopkins of CNN's "Who's in Charge?" (August 28, 1996), Bauer explained that his philosophy was to "step back and let ideas evolve." Hopkins seemed as shocked by this approach as any bureaucratic manager. So she asked, "Were there any bad ideas?" "Certainly not," Bauer replied. "There are no bad ideas. . . . There were ideas where I might have been skeptical. But we tested and tried them. If an idea didn't work, we said, 'Let's skip it.'"

One final note about MBCC's process for implementing its transformation: Bauer encouraged people to celebrate every time they reached a milestone. In his words,

> In hindsight, it was extremely important to bring people together as often as possible to celebrate their successes. Transformation is difficult work. Its purpose is to destroy all the routines that people have spent years developing. So people need to rebuild their connections with each other around the new ways.

This organic, self-organizing approach to corporate reinvention was at the heart of Bauer's success. He and his senior management leadership team enabled the company to evolve, rather than *be* engineered. As with evolution in living things, the company, as evolving system, assessed its (market) environment, tried out new ways to follow those directions (creating "mutations" on old procedures), and incorporated the new ways that worked while rejecting those that didn't.

In reengineering, management often imposes structures meant to empower people, creating a clash between the goal and the method for achieving it. Bauer, on the other hand, enabled his people to transform MBCC, using the very techniques he believed would have to become its behavioral norms. MBCC was becoming a learning organization as its employees took considerable risks through the analysis, testing, and implementation by which all living things learn. In addition, the company implemented a team-based approach through a team-oriented transformation process. Bauer's choice of an organic model for the transformation helped people throughout the company develop the organic structures and, ultimately, behaviors he believed MBCC would need.

Step 3 Implementation

One of the first initiatives MBCC implemented was creating its corporate Mission and Values. By creating consensus around a clear explanation of what it wanted to be, the company would make the rest of the transformation process much, much easier. A quick overview of the organic approach MBCC took with this initiative gives a better idea of how a self-organizing transformation can work. And don't be fooled. At first, MBCC's Mission and Values may sound a lot like the Vision and Values Bell Atlantic created. But the way Bauer's organic transformation developed the Mission and Values was entirely different.

The process at MBCC began with a steering team of about 20 employees. They worked to evolve a mission statement and a list of values. Early on, they held focus groups with nearly half the people in the company, nonmanagement as well as management. With each focus group, the Mission and Values might shift a little until the team was confident it had reached a consensus on what they should be.

MBCC Mission and Values

Mission

To enhance the marketability of Daimler-Benz products through superior financial services and support.

Values

Consistently Superior Customer Service
Outstanding service to customers and dealers must be our hallmark. When we consistently provide superior levels of service, we build lasting relationships that provide the foundation for profitable growth and long-term success.

Entrepreneurial Spirit and Innovation
We value individual and team initiative and the willingness to take sensible risks. We encourage a restless spirit of inquiry in our search for new and creative approaches to meet the needs of customers and dealers with improved products and services.

Flexibility and Responsiveness
The needs of our customers and dealers for financial services continually evolve in response to changes in the marketplace. In order to anticipate and meet customer, dealer and marketplace requirements, we must be adaptable and responsive to change.

Open Communication
Free-flowing communication is the lifeblood of our organization. We are committed to the open and honest exchange of information and opinions throughout the company.

Teamwork
We are dedicated to working in a team environment which recognizes and rewards both individual and team accomplishments. We must all understand the importance of our contribution to the team and the part it plays in the company's overall success.

Integrity and Professionalism
We are professionals first and foremost. We accept nothing less than the highest standards of integrity and ethical conduct, both in our business practices and in our treatment of each other.

MBCC's final mission statement is clear and specific, much more so than Bell Atlantic's vision statement of being a leading company in its industry. Like Ray Smith, Bauer wanted his company to be a leader in its markets. However, MBCC's process enabled it to focus on what the company would have to do to meet that goal. The mission tells employees both what MBCC does, "enhance marketability," and how the company does it, superior "services and support." Although it may not be as concise as 3M's innovation or as snappy as The Ritz-Carlton's "We are ladies and gentlemen serving ladies and gentlemen," MBCC's mission statement is also its identity statement because it clearly states how the company must interact with its market ecology to succeed.

In addition, MBCC's six core values describe an organic connection to the company's markets and an organic idea of how it will function. The first value, superior customer service, states the company's strategy for survival. The second and third explain how the company will deliver on its first value, by encouraging the innovation that will enable employees to respond flexibly to customers' evolving needs. The fourth and fifth values state how people will relate to each other within the organization, communicating openly and working in teams. Finally, the sixth value suggests limits in acceptable practices—integrity and professionalism—that could make any employee proud of working there.

Finally, whereas Bell Atlantic's values never used the word *customer*, the customer is central to MBCC's first three values. This difference grew from the different models on which the two companies based their reinvention. Bell Atlantic's mechanical change focused the company's attention within the company; so there was no need to mention customers. MBCC's organic transformation, on the other hand, makes an immediate connection with its market ecology so that serving its customers becomes its highest value.

The process of developing these statements involved nearly half MBCC's employee body. But that wasn't the end of it. Once the final version was in place, it was introduced throughout the company in local face-to-face meetings. At these meetings, people in every workplace were asked to work out ways they could implement the Mission and Values in their daily activities. Once again, the emphasis fell on having the people who would have to live by these statements decide how they would help make those statements living realities. From the time the project team realized the need for guiding mission and values statements, the employee body evolved it in an extended act of self-organization that eventually included just about everyone.

As workplaces began implementing the mission and value statements, one human resources employee pointed out that merely stating how people in the company needed to act in the new MBCC might not be enough. The company should invest in training its people in the new behaviors. This suggestion was transformed into a two-day training experience—Quality Service Skills—for which every employee in the company was flown to Dallas. Over four months, classes randomly mixed with all levels of managers learned how to acquire information from customers and make sure their understanding was correct; make sure customers understood and accepted their answers; explain what customers had to do; and apologize, if appropriate. For the reinvented MBCC, customer service was no longer solely the job of customer service representatives who answered the telephone all day. It had become the job of everyone in the company.

Anticipating the Customer

Five years after freeing MBCC to reinvent itself through self-organization, Bauer was certain that all 19 initiatives growing out of the "MBCC 2000+" study were successful. As he put it,

> We're clearly a better organization. When Mercedes-Benz did end lease subsidies, and we faced a level playing field for the first time, we were ready. As a result, we continue to lead the market for financing both Mercedes cars and Freightliner trucks in both market share and customer/dealer satisfaction.

One area Bauer pointed to proudly was MBCC's rewriting of its lease agreements. The lease agreements traditionally had been written in legalese, which customers rarely understood. Dealers were frustrated at the amount of paperwork and the addendums needed to write MBCC leases. Early on, Bauer suggested that the procedures could be simplified. The team looking at this issue confirmed customer unhappiness with the lease agreement. To get a fuller picture of the problem, the company surveyed its customers and confirmed that they were infuriated by the complexity of the agreement and its legalese. "Once we had this survey, we began to see, even from the inside, how intimidating our old lease agreement must be to our customers," Bauer explained.

As long as MBCC remained a virtual monopoly, the company didn't have to worry about this complaint. Now, however, customer dissatisfaction with the lease agreement offered the company an important opportunity. "We could add enormous value to our services by working *with* our customers as partners," Bauer noted. So a project team went about demystifying the lease agreement. Their product was a one-page document in clear English that redefined the lease from a consumer point of view. MBCC clarified the key areas that had upset their customers, the exact structure of lease payments, for example, or what the company meant by "excessive wear and tear."

The team working on the lease agreement didn't stop with a clearer, simpler document. The new lease agreement also offered innovative options. Rather than offer a standard 36-month lease, MBCC would allow flexible terms so its customers got what *they* wanted. The new lease also gave customers the option to tailor mileage limits to their own needs. "Our team developed the new lease around the issues our customers believed were important," Bauer noted, "not what we *thought* was important to them. As a result, we enhanced the value of our financing to our customers. The result is the high levels of customer satisfaction we've been receiving."

In 1996, MBCC received confirmation that it had done the right thing. A survey that year sponsored by the Consumer Federation of America and the National Association of Consumer Agency Administrators found that complaints to consumer agencies about automobile leases had more than doubled from 1994 to 1995. The most common problem, the study found, was that consumers did not understand the lease, especially the penalties for early termination or the idea of excess wear and tear. The problem had become so troubling that in the fall of 1996, the Federal Reserve Board introduced rules to standardize lease language and to provide more detailed payment information, both of which MBCC's new lease agreements anticipated.

None of this surprised Bauer. With an organic model of organization, he realized the importance of creating and learning from relationships in today's markets. One focus of MBCC's corporate reinvention, therefore, was to encourage his people to form strong relationships, especially with customers and dealers. "Now that our financing is reduced to a commodity," he said, "relationships are the only thing that will bring our customers back."

Evolution of a Transformational Organization

Many of the qualities of the reinvented MBCC will seem familiar to anyone who has read this far. For example, the company reduced its seven levels of management with a 1:3 manager-to-worker ratio to three levels with a 1:7 ratio. Teams also redesigned every work process in the company to serve customers better and reduce cycle time. As Bauer noted, the key to the success of this effort is not merely to create a faster, more customer-oriented company. Many reengineering efforts are successful as far as that goes. The point of the transformation was to create a transformational organization—what Bauer calls a *learning organization*—continuously evolving to meet the changing demands of its markets. The real challenge, Bauer recognized, was to ensure that his people would not take this one shot at corporate reinvention and then try to get comfortable with the new structure.

Let's look at how people at MBCC used elements of what we've identified as an organic model to create systems that would encourage continuing transformation. For one thing, the teams working on the strategic initiative concerned with upgrading computer information systems ended up building a corporate nervous system for MBCC. This effort began with the new corporate value of open communication. Using this value as a guide, the implementation team working on this initiative chose Lotus Notes to create an open forum where people across the company could discuss all kinds of issues from the computers on their desks.

Lotus Notes, they soon realized, gave them a near-ideal forum for keeping each other updated on the progress of their transformation. People in accounting could learn about what people in marketing were doing. In this way, discussions of the initiatives encouraged a cross-pollination of ideas, because everyone had access to the plans, methods, and experiences of everyone else. Bauer emphasized that at first this ability to make ideas an experience universally available was new and exciting. However, it soon became a convenient way to get timely information embedded in the way people did their jobs.

As people became more and more comfortable doing their jobs this way, discussion databases sent a wave of open communication through the organization. It was now possible for anyone in the company to address a variety of issues instantly. If someone in human resources had an idea for a new product, she could post her idea with a request for comment. Soon, she would have not only the feedback to determine whether her idea would work but also, most likely, a series of suggestions on how to improve and implement it.

One of the most important exchanges early on concerned the veiled hostility between people in the field and corporate staff, a conflict with which many companies struggle. In the past, neither understood what the other did. Use of Lotus Notes gave them the opportunity to learn about each other. We saw, in Chapter 5, how using Lotus Notes to make its changing corporate DNA universally available enabled people in the field and corporate staff at headquarters to understand each other and begin working together. In terms of MBCC's transformation, it's also worth noting how using Lotus Notes to help people across the company share information broke down the bureaucratic impermeability of borders between groups. Once that impermeability broke down, it was possible for people not just to share information, but also to experience themselves as part of a single, organic entity working together for a common purpose.

Another way MBCC addressed the issue of building an organization that would *continue* to transform itself was in its reward and recognition system. "The question," as Bauer put it, "was how to make people feel good about learning from our mistakes." As a result, the teams implementing human resources programs, such as a "gain sharing" program, focused on rewarding people for taking thoughtful risks, learning from their efforts, and readjusting to make those efforts more effective.

Perhaps the most critical such program at any corporation is its process of performance reviews. Performance reviews themselves are a way for employees to learn from both their successes and failures. The form this process takes helps determine what people focus on learning. By the beginning of 1997, the company was still using its older performance management process. However, it was also piloting its Multi-Rater program. To develop that program, an implementation team identified 35 valued behaviors on which each person in the company, up to and including the CEO, would be measured every year. These behaviors, risk taking being one of the most important, are rated by each employee's boss, team, and peers outside the team. As part of this program, when employees receive their rating, they're responsible for writing an action plan based on the feedback and for discussing the plan with a mentor. To support this annual review, leaders are expected to sit down several times a year to discuss skills, needs, and ideas of all team members who report to them.

The result is what people studying complexity theory call *fractal*—that is, the basic patterns at different levels reflect each other. The process for performance reviews has the same relation to people in the company as Bauer wanted people in the company to have to their work. Performance leads to feedback and learning, which, in turn, should lead to adjustment in performance. The cycle then repeats itself. This was also the basic pattern of the transformation.

The final measure of success for this kind of transformation rests with employees. Even if a corporation improves its bottom line, that improvement may be only temporary if its people are becoming increasingly cynical and generally unhappy. At MBCC, the opposite appears to be happening. In 1995, its annual organizational effectiveness survey found that 85 percent of employees rated the Mission and Values favorably; that 90 percent rated the company's commitment to customers favorably; and that 63 percent were now favorable about management's commitment to the new style of operation, up from 45 percent in 1992.

In the end, Bauer said, people at MBCC, himself included, were having

> more fun. It's more rewarding to accept change and take charge of it, rather than feel you're its victim. There's pressure in doing that. But there'd be pressure in any case. We've recognized that taking charge of change is the best way to remain the leader in our market. And we have a lot more fun being the leader.

Bauer emphasized that this was more the beginning than the end of the transformation process. MBCC had only completed the first phase of its transformation. All the fundamentals were now in place. "Once they've become ingrained, we can grow to the level of a true learning organization," he added.

Of course, it's impossible to be certain that MBCC will ultimately succeed in making itself that kind of company. What's clear is that the organic, self-organizing approach Bauer encouraged in MBCC had results very different from those of the more mechanical approach taken at Bell Atlantic. Both companies are unquestionably more effective organizations than before they started their transformations. Yet largely because it used an organic model for its transformation, MBCC was better able to create an environment of innovation and intelligent risk taking that employees seem to enjoy.

Bauer's success was based on his intuitive understanding of an organic model and his ability to translate it into an effective transformation process. He was able to deengineer his company, encouraging his people to replace the mechanical formal structure that restrained their creative energies with an organic formal structure that enabled them to exercise those energies in the company's best interests. Not every manager has Bauer's intuitive understanding. Most of us, still solidly fixed in our old mechanical models, much as managers at Bell Atlantic were, need to develop a better picture of an organic transformation process before we can begin implementing it.

With that in mind, we can turn to the last of our fundamental questions: What have we learned in our exploration of an organic model that we can apply to the *process* of organic transformation?

CHAPTER 12

A Deengineer's Handbook

In a world of emergence, new systems appear out of nowhere. But the forms they assume originate from dynamic processes set in motion by information, relationships, and identity.
—Margaret Wheatley and Myron Kellner-Rogers

Question: What have our explorations of an organic model suggested about how managers should deengineer their bureaucracies?

As we saw in the example of Georg Bauer at Mercedes-Benz Credit Corporation (MBCC), deengineering a bureaucracy is an act of leadership. It requires someone who understands the nature of the shifts to be made, is willing to make the personal transformation needed to practice management by letting go, and is able to involve people throughout the organization. Ideally this is a job for a company's CEO and other senior executives. As a result, this chapter is written specifically for CEOs and their executive teams.

Not all CEOs can take on such a leadership role. Some understand the nature of the shifts their organizations must make but aren't able to make the personal transformation. Others are so fixed in their mechanical models that they don't understand the nature of the needed shifts. In these cases, leadership may come from a member of the senior executive team, the general manager of a manufacturing plant, or the director of a division. These cases are more difficult, because only the CEO has the organizational stature to make the transformation work throughout the company. Still, I believe the principles discussed in this chapter can prove helpful, and even effective, if they're used anywhere in the organization.

The idea that "People will do what they want," which we'll look at shortly, for example, can apply to your boss as easily as to the people in the unit you manage. After all, it's impossible to argue someone with a mechanical model into an organic one. If you insist that you're right and they're wrong, you'll only drive them to defend their positions more aggressively. Like everyone else, they'll do what they want, especially if they're in positions of power. All you can do is demonstrate the power of an organic model, plant its seeds, and wait for such people to make up their own minds. So although this section is written to CEOs, anyone in the organization who is leading an effort in deengineering can use its principles.

Before we get to those principles, I want to emphasize that there is no Frederick W. Taylor–style "one best way," no standard operating procedure, to deengineer *any* organization. Every business is a unique living thing. What works in transforming one business may cause mass confusion in another. The one sure lesson we can take from our examination of organic transformation is that it's best to view every action taken in a deengineering effort as an experiment. Maybe something that worked for MBCC will work for your company. Maybe it won't. The only way to know for sure is to try, then watch what happens.

What we can do is draw a few principles of transformation from what we've learned so far. Remember: If they're going to be effective, these principles must remain flexible guidelines that have to be proved at each step rather than inflexible, invariable mechanical instructions.

Let Go of the Illusion of Control

Organic transformation begins as a decision at the deepest levels of a living thing. Once launched, the transformation emerges according to an internal logic defined by how the living thing interacts with its environment. Top managers of any units, from a company of 80,000 to a work group of 12, must use their *influence* to make sure everyone is moving to fulfill a shared identity. If they try to *control* the way any transformation unfolds, they'll complicate, even undermine, the efforts of everyone in their units. As a result, it's essential that managers let go of the illusion that they can control a transformation.

This distinction between influencing and controlling may be the key difference between the ways Bell Atlantic and MBCC approached their corporate reinventions. Management at Bell Atlantic formulated the company Vision and Values and imposed it on the company; management at MBCC let the company evolve its Mission and Values. Management at Bell Atlantic decided what shifts had to be made and defined the forms they would take; management at MBCC asked representative teams to decide what shifts the company had to make and how to implement them. Bell Atlantic management told employees they would have to live according to new behaviors; MBCC management trusted its employees to make their own decisions.

Practicing management by letting go isn't easy for managers trained in traditional command-and-control. Their mechanical models may remind them that employees are replaceable parts who either don't know how to make solid decisions or are lazy and untrustworthy. To overcome this ingrained thought pattern, it's helpful for managers to start as soon as possible to let go of the things they have always controlled. Bauer did that by making sure everyone in the company had the information traditionally reserved for management. Rather than *tell* employees that markets have shifted and the company must change, managers can show the *full* picture of their market ecologies, including both company strengths and market challenges. Then they can let people make up their own minds about the transformation. Most companies hire intelligent, capable people. As their first act of letting go, managers can trust their people to understand change in their markets and make intelligent decisions.

Rather than telling employees all the details of how markets are changing and what the company needs to do to adapt, managers can invite them to help figure it out and give them the information they ask for to explore the issues that must be addressed: What are the key shifts in the market? What kinds of difficulties have they caused? Will these shifts continue to shake up markets? Will they become more frequent? Is the organization capable of continuing to adapt to these shifts as it operates today? How radically does the company need to alter the way it does things? What will happen if the company does not make radical alterations?

Once people understand the challenge, managers can let go of the process of planning and controlling the transformation itself. Bauer pulled together a team of people from all areas and levels of the company, people excited about doing this work, and let them decide what deengineering the company entailed. This kind of letting go demands a great deal of courage. But remember that this is more than a demonstration of trust. It enables people throughout an organization to learn to make decisions on their own. The sooner they start learning to behave autonomously, the better at it they'll become, and the sooner they'll accept that management means this to be an authentic transformation rather than another "change program" that will blow over if they just keep their heads down.

Support Your People in Their Personal Transformations

In *Complexity and Creativity in Organizations*, Ralph Stacey (1996) pointed out that the kind of creativity organizations need to transform themselves produces a great deal of anxiety. Doing anything differently can cause anxiety. Yet, we're talking about people learning to do almost *everything* differently. Unless the organization helps them to keep that anxiety from overwhelming them, people will find it impossible to be creative. To help contain that anxiety, managers must support their people in changing their workplace behavior.

The people hit hardest in making this personal transformation are often senior managers. They have the most to lose. Most senior managers rely for their sense of personal power on the command-and-control style they've practiced for 20 or 30 years. They can manage that way in their sleep. Now a CEO is asking them to let that control go and practice management in an entirely different way. If the CEO can provide them with a system that will support their efforts and help them learn needed new behaviors and identify mistakes quickly, they'll be more likely to embrace management by letting go, rather than falling back on old habits and working quietly to undermine the new system.

How should you support your managers in this personal transformation? One of the most effective programs for making this kind of far-reaching personal change is the 12-step programs pioneered by Alcoholics Anonymous. Managers leading a transformation don't have to create a "12-Step Program for Recovering Bureaucratic Managers." Rather, they only need to apply the key principles that make such programs successful. These programs recommend three sets of actions to the person making a personal transformation: relying on a wider intelligence, cleaning away the past, and addressing the future. Together these actions can make the personal transformation significantly easier:

- Relying on a wider intelligence. Part of the problem faced by people caught in an old behavior, such as bureaucratic management, is that they've learned to rely solely on personal judgment. Yet, that judgment is fixed in a mechanical model. So most managers need to find a new basis for judging. That can be the wider intelligence of the employee body. By drawing on the information in a corporate nervous system and gathering feedback on significant decisions from a variety of people affected by those decisions, managers can free themselves of the self-imposed limitation of relying solely on their own mechanical judgment.
- Cleaning away the past. Like anyone who practices any behavior for 20 or 30 years, managers who practice command-and-control develop habits that become automatic and difficult to break. In many cases, such habits are so ingrained that we forget we once *chose* to behave this way. As a result, new habits are difficult to form. No matter how much we want to change, in crisis we find ourselves falling back on the old habits. Unless as managers we become aware of our command-and-control habits, we'll find ourselves falling back into them, no matter how much we know we need to develop new behaviors. For this reason, managers must examine their old management style and how it keeps them from managing effectively in today's turbulent markets.

Managers also can profit from talking about their old behaviors with others to obtain a more objective view. One of the participants in a VHA task force (see Chapter 2), Debbie Zastocki, senior vice president for Patient Care, Chilton Memorial Hospital, made just this point:

When [members of the task force] were in the early stages of learning about managing groups to be self-organizing, we'd ask questions like, "How have you made your group different to encourage self-organization?" In these discussions, I learned I hadn't really changed, that I was verbalizing the new behavior, talking the talk, but I wasn't walking the walk.[1]

- Addressing the future. In helping one another to understand their old command-and-control habits, managers can free themselves to choose new ways of managing. It takes time to form new habits. At first, this choice may seem uncomfortable. Such a choice must also be made in every situation. Effective programs offer people techniques for figuring out what those choices are.

Too many change efforts jump right to developing this new way of managing. Without understanding that their old sense of judgment was based on a mechanical model and that this model limited their ability to manage effectively, managers can't understand the nature of the choices they must make during this transition period. At Bell Atlantic, managers were never asked either to recognize the limitations of their judgment or to analyze and discuss the results of their old management style. As a result, when crises occurred, most managers fell back into their command-and-control habits.

In addition to using these three sets of actions, the most effective programs that encourage personal transformation support people in several ways. For example, they recognize that "People will do what they want." To avoid exciting resentment, no one tells participants they *must* do anything. Recommended new behaviors are presented as suggestions. Similarly, managers who insist people in their groups begin practicing new ways of doing things may find that even when these new ways are obviously sensible, their people will resent being *told* what to do. At Bell Atlantic, CEO Ray Smith insisted that employees make a commitment to the company. The result was grudging compliance. On the other hand, managers who present the new ways as a club people are free to join let their people *choose* the new ways, giving them the option to decide for themselves.

Successful programs also give members a chance to talk about what is happening to them as a result of the changes they're trying to make. One way is regular meetings. These meetings are safe places where anonymity is the rule. People generally feel free to say almost anything. In such a safe place, people can admit old behaviors, such as a slip into command-and-control behavior, without having to worry about being attacked or ridiculed. These programs also suggest members find sponsors, people with more experience who can help them examine and understand new feelings, in addition to working privately to master new behaviors.

As with most of what we have examined throughout this book, I present the idea of a change program for managers (and other interested employees) as a suggestion. The specifics of such a program or even the main principles on which it is built aren't critical. The important thing is that the leading manager of a unit undergoing transformation make sure that people receive the support they need, in the form that's most appropriate for that organization, in making this shift in behavior.

Incidentally, some of the best forms of support are the most familiar. Story telling, for example, is one of the very best ways to help people contain their anxiety during major shifts, as well as in doing their jobs day to day. Some of the most effective stories expose the leading manager's vulnerability or discomfort with transformation. For example, the CEO of a company that introduced a 12-step quality improvement process during the mid 1980s accelerated acceptance by telling the following story over and over:

> In a meeting, a senior manager was describing how his team gathered information to solve a problem. (The first six steps of the process focused on gathering information; analysis of the problem began with the seventh step. The process was a departure from old ways, because managers had most often made gut decisions without gathering and analyzing all available information.) In the middle of the presentation, the CEO said, "Get to the point! Everyone knows the cause of that problem."
>
> The presenting manager turned to the CEO and replied, "You're jumping to the seventh step."
>
> At first the CEO was ready to explode in anger at this challenge, but as he thought it over, he realized he was jumping to the seventh step, assuming he knew the cause of the problem without analyzing the available information. So he let the manager continue.

Telling this story did several things. First, it allowed the CEO to emphasize that the quality improvement process was important enough to override his personal judgment. If he'd insisted he was right, no one in the room would ever have taken the process seriously. Second, by telling this story over and over, including on a corporate television show that went to locations throughout the company, the CEO admitted that it was all right both to feel uncomfortable with the new process and to challenge your superiors if they indicated their judgment overrode the process. Pretty soon, people across the company used the statement "You're jumping to the seventh step" almost as a mantra to reinforce the importance of the quality improvement process.

Creating a support program and telling stories are only two of many ways to provide the support people need to feel comfortable reinventing your organization. The best thing you can do is work with people throughout the organization to determine which support systems will work best for you.

Involve People as Fully as They Want to Be Involved

In Chapter 7, we contrasted the mechanical image of the employee as a replaceable part with the organic image of a valued contributor to the health of the whole. To deengineer a bureaucracy, the leading manager must help people move from the passive experience of being a replaceable part to the active experience of being a valued contributor.

We've already mentioned some of the ways managers can involve people in the transformation process. Like Bauer, they can turn over the planning and implementation of the transformation to people throughout the organization. Bauer enhanced this involvement by not rejecting any ideas before trying them out. Rejection would have offered a chance for the person who suggested the idea to pull back.

Developing a picture of a company's market ecology is an excellent additional opportunity to involve everyone. In fact, why not give people extra reasons to involve *themselves* by making this exercise fun? Management can publish an information book on market shifts and then announce a contest in which interdepartmental teams compete to develop ecographs of the market ecologies. Give prizes to the teams that create the most evocative images of where markets are leading the company.

By encouraging everyone to involve themselves—giving them reasons to join the transformation rather than insisting they commit themselves to it—you avoid the resistance that created such obstacles at Bell Atlantic. Another way to reduce resistance is to give people many chances to participate in making changes in their job functions. For instance, when it held meetings to announce the Mission and Values, MBCC involved people by asking them to examine how they could incorporate them into their daily work lives.

By involving people from the beginning of your deengineering effort, you build an environment where people can feel like the valued contributors an organic model calls for, rather than the replaceable parts of a mechanical model. Not everyone will want to make this personal transformation. Some will continue to want only to put in their 40 hours and get their paychecks. How you handle this is a question only you and your coworkers, fully immersed in the day-to-day details of your organization, can answer.

Guide the Process from a Perspective That Takes in the Whole Enterprise

Although it shouldn't control this effort, senior management does need to guide any transformation. That guidance can start with senior managers' encouraging active participants in the deengineering to learn about living things and how they can apply life's design principles to the organization (see Further Reading).

In Part II, we looked at several key organic principles. Each organization must decide which principles it needs and in which order the company should incorporate them. The job of the manager leading a company through the process of deengineering is to ask the questions that will enable participants to be thorough and appropriate in designing and testing them. The principles managers focus on should probably include:

• A *corporate identity* so that everyone knows what the organization must do to succeed in its market ecologies. Before defining that identity, the organization must understand its market ecologies. Among the questions people must ask about their markets are:

  • Who are the key players in any market ecology? Customers? Suppliers? Competitors? Government agencies? Unions? What are their relationships?
  • Can the markets be broken into feeding levels? If so, on which level or levels should the organization focus?
  • How turbulent are these markets? Has a dominant player begun to lock in? Is the level of turbulence high enough to make challenging that dominant player viable? What are the key forces driving turbulence? Are they likely to stop driving it soon?
  • Where are the organization's closest allies in any market ecology? What new allies can it cultivate? Is it in the dominant alliance? If not, how many other alliances are there, and what is its position in those alliances?
  • Given all this information, what strategy makes most sense for the organization? What opportunities within the market is the company most prepared to exploit? Should it seek dominance or cultivate a niche? Is it ready to move from a strong position on one feeding level to challenge on another? Does it want to be a technology or service leader? What can it do to most create value for and success in other members of the market ecology?

For a fuller examination of these issues see Chapter 3.

As a company's position in its market ecologies becomes clear, people can define its corporate identity. A manager leading this effort may want to ask such questions as:

- What is the critical contribution the company makes in its market ecology? What qualities do customers and partners most value?
- How should people in the company interact with each other and with customers and partners?
- What values or behaviors are most important if the company is to take advantage of opportunities in its markets?
- How can you communicate this identity so that everyone in the company will understand and become excited about it?

Chapter 4 explores corporate identity in more detail.

- A way of making the organization's structures and procedures flexible and universally available as *corporate DNA*. The manager leading the effort can ask the following questions:

  - What kind of process does the company want to develop to test suggestions for improvements in products and the way it does business? Does it have a quality improvement process? Is the process effective? How might it be improved? Are there ways to make suggestions and the company's responses more accessible?
  - Will it be easier for people in the organization to find procedures and structures about which they are curious if the information is on paper or a computer program? Do people want some of this information in both paper and electronic form? What is the best way to make large amounts of information quickly available?
  - How can the organization be sure its corporate DNA remains easy to update?
  - What kind of review procedure should the company develop to assure that all procedures and structures in its corporate DNA remain aligned with the corporate identity?

These issues, and others connected to corporate DNA, are examined in Chapter 5.

- A *corporate nervous system* so that people anywhere in the company can access information about events inside or outside the company. Questions for guiding development of this system may include:

  - What types of information are essential for people in the company to know? How much of this information has to be made available at people's workstations? How much can be located more centrally?
  - What media already exist? To what extent can existing media form this system? To what extent are additional media required? Can the organization make use of more informal means of communication?

Does a corporate computer network or intranet make sense financially and functionally?
- If additional media are needed, can the organization form a partnership with a vendor or consultant in a way that will strengthen its
position in its market ecologies?

More information on corporate nervous systems is available in Chapter
6.

- An *organic structure* that will connect people, rather than isolate them,
enabling them to self-organize and innovate more easily. In this case, the
manager leading the effort may want to ask the following questions:

- Are the organization's current boundaries impermeable or semipermeable? If the former, how can they be made more permeable?
- To what extent are people cross-trained? Will introducing cross-
training universally make boundaries more permeable?
- What can the organization do to make responsibility a shared matter
so that sales, marketing, engineering, and manufacturing, for example, are working together?
- What shifts have to be made in compensation, reward, and promotion policies to provide incentives that encourage more permeable
boundaries?
- What can the company do to make its boundaries with customers
and suppliers more permeable?

More on the issue of organic structure appears in Chapter 7.
If the teams that implement an organization's transformation omit
any of these systems, the senior management team will want to discuss
that omission. Perhaps there are excellent reasons; perhaps team members overlooked a vital piece of the process. Such guidance can help
people developing these systems to identify gaps or mistakes before they
create problems down the line.

Encourage Evolution, Rather than Redesign, of Structures
and Procedures

In Chapter 9 we saw that one of the key weaknesses of reengineering
is that it designs entire processes without testing the parts in the
field separately. When there are problems with such fully designed
processes, it's difficult to know where to begin examining them. The
organic alternative is to let processes evolve. Birds, for example, evolved
from dinosaurs over millions of years, as one mutation after another,

each building on those before it, enabled them to develop significant differences.

In *Out of Control*, Kevin Kelly (1994) calls this process *chunking*. The idea is to locate an area everyone agrees can be improved and to develop a new approach. Try that approach, keep what works, and discard the rest. Then build on this chunk, repeating the process of trial and error. This, for example, was how Mary Ann Keyes at Muhlenberg Regional Hospital reduced the admission process to one hour (see Chapter 8).

There are two major advantages to chunking. First, the process being reinvented can continue much as it always has while it's being redesigned. Only the chunked part of the process must be altered. Second, each shift in the way people work or in corporate structure can be piloted before it becomes part of the new, evolving corporate DNA.

To guide this process, senior managers can state the task to be completed as minimum specifications (Morgan 1986), allowing people full freedom within these few key specifications. That's also how Keyes charged the team that redesigned admissions at her hospital. Similarly, senior managers can ask the team developing a corporate identity to articulate as briefly as possible what is special about the way the organization succeeds in its market ecologies, develop a consensus around it, and involve as many people as possible. Then the senior management team needs to monitor its progress, alerting the identity team if it starts moving in the wrong direction and suggesting alternatives when needed.

Senior managers play a critical role monitoring this process because they have the most comprehensive view of what's happening in the organization. They're likely to know about connections or relationships that people on implementation teams may overlook. For example, Bauer suggested simplifying the MBCC lease agreement so it would be easier for customers to understand. Conversations with customers showed this was a critical problem. Yet no one else had noticed how important it was.

Perhaps the most important thing for managers to keep in mind throughout deengineering is that we all make mistakes, even senior managers. Many of us learned somewhere along the line that we shouldn't make mistakes and that others shouldn't either. That's mechanical thinking. At best, mistakes lower the efficiency of a machine; at worst, they can wreck it. But in organizations that are continually coevolving in their market ecologies, this isn't a very helpful attitude. After all, the only way to *not* make mistakes is to do nothing new. So value your people's mistakes—and your own mistakes—because all mistakes give us a chance to learn. You may even want to celebrate intelligent mistakes.

Be Prepared to Let Go, Again and Again

For many managers leading deengineering efforts, the most difficult shift in behavior will be to continue letting go. Especially if the company hits a crisis, the temptation to revert to command-and-control will be powerful. This is one reason a support system can be so valuable. If a company institutionalizes a safe space in which managers can discuss operations, managers can learn to alert each other as they revert to command-and-control tactics.

A system for monitoring events throughout the company can provide an additional measure of comfort. As senior managers see through repeated experience that the monitoring system can help them recognize problems and that people in the organization respond to such systems, they'll find it easier to overlook their automatic reaction—to move in and solve the problem themselves. This monitoring system is a part of the idea discussed in Chapter 8 of senior manager as a corporate central nervous system. After all, when your blood pressure gets too high, your brain recognizes it and signals for action to lower it. Similarly, senior managers need a way to recognize when "corporate blood pressure" gets too high so that they can signal to have others in the company correct the situation. Each company will develop the kind of senior management monitoring system appropriate to that specific company to capture the information it finds most important.

Now it's almost time for me to let go. As we noted repeatedly, an organic model is extremely rich. Each of us will find different ways to implement it, depending on the nature of our organizations and the specific functions we find interesting. Up to this point, I've tried to present the central insights I gained in thinking organically about organizations. Now it's your turn to take the methods defined in these pages and apply them to your organization. Although I've finished examining the organizational implications of an organic model, there is one last issue with which I'd like to conclude—the cultural implications of this model.

CONCLUSION

The New American Century

Dr. Margaret King and Jamie O'Boyle, partners of Culture Analysis & Studies, a Philadelphia-based consulting firm, seem an unlikely pair. King looks like, and is, the archetypal academic. With a doctorate in American Studies and the first graduate degree awarded in Popular Culture, she did cross-cultural research at the prestigious East-West Center in Honolulu. In contrast, O'Boyle, with his black eye patch and straight-for-the-jugular style, brings the tools of military intelligence analysis. He accumulated his hands-on cross-cultural experience in places like Northern Ireland, the former Soviet Union, East Africa, and the Middle East.[1]

Despite widely different backgrounds, King and O'Boyle reached the same conclusion: Culture is not about *what* people think; it's about *why* they think it. For them, culture is a complex adaptive system that cannot be understood by studying the parts. In fact, they like to compare culture with quantum mechanics. "In physics, field theory focuses on the unseen forces that shape the behavior between subatomic particles," O'Boyle explains. "Our quantum view of culture focuses on the space between individuals, which is filled by unseen cultural forces that shape group behavior."

In talking with King and O'Boyle, I made a surprising realization: Americans hate bureaucracy because it violates all the values our culture celebrates. Organic corporations, on the other hand, demand exactly those values. As a result, if an organic model is on the way to becoming the standard for world business, the fit between this model and our culture will give U.S. businesses an enormous competitive advantage. That advantage could easily lead to an economic boom in the first 20 years of the 21st century that could put the boom of the 1960s to shame. We may be on the verge of a New American Century.

A Culture Primer

For King and O'Boyle, cultural forces enable individuals to form groups to meet shared needs—from food, shelter, and reproduction to entertainment and high art. Cultures articulate these forces in everything from consumer goods to housing, story telling to attitudes toward personal space, which both reflect and reinforce the culture system. To identify the major forces that shape U.S. culture, King and O'Boyle study patterns that define how Americans have met these shared needs for our 200-plus years of history. To do so, they compiled a database of popular culture— the products we buy; the stories we prefer in our books, television, and film; the fashions we select; and other ways we "vote" in the most meaningful way, with our wallets.

For King and O'Boyle, the major factors that shaped U.S. culture include:

- We are an immigrant nation; the vast majority of our ancestors came here for a second chance. As a result, our values encourage us to give almost anyone a second chance and to protect the disadvantaged.
- For our first century and a half, the United States seemed to be a nation of unlimited resources and spaces to be settled, so we have a culture of plenitude, not scarcity.
- Our national character was forged in a revolutionary war against a colonial "parent," so we value freedom over order and authority.

The United States is unique, King and O'Boyle explain, because our revolution occurred when the nation was still young. Unlike most other formerly colonial nations, we had no older culture to fall back on. So we institutionalized postadolescent values—independence, self-assertion, self-expression—usually associated with coming of age and breaking away from parents. O'Boyle likes to illustrate what they discovered about the basic nature of U.S. culture by translating the first four Amendments in the Bill of Rights:

First Amendment—Freedoms of religion, speech, press, and assembly
> Translation—Don't tell me what to think, say, read, or how to pick my friends!

Second Amendment—Right to keep and bear arms
> Translation—You can't make me!

Third Amendment—No quartering of troops in homes

Translation—Stay out of my room!

Fourth Amendment—No search and seizure without due process

Translation—Don't mess with my stuff!

These adolescent attitudes, O'Boyle will tell you, are typical of our culture and reflect our history.

From this point of view, King and O'Boyle note, our culture encourages several key attitudes:

1. We Americans are individuals who should be free to make up our own minds. Our emphasis on individual freedom comes across in everything from the popularity of movie character Dirty Harry Callahan to the interstate highway. This emphasis on the individual makes us value rebels, so much so that even Lee Iacocca and Ronald Reagan sought public support by identifying themselves as rebels.

2. Americans respect achievement, not the authority of position. Our cultural heroes are people who have achieved something important, whether Ralph Nader or Oprah Winfrey, Michael Jordan or Bill Gates. In more traditional societies, no position of authority is more revered than father. Yet the title of the popular 1950s television series "Father Knows Best" is ironic; father didn't have a clue. For U.S. culture, this revered authority figure becomes a bumbler for whom everyone else has to cover.

3. Americans believe nothing and nobody is perfect. This attitude stands out in the Declaration of Independence, which tells us the United States was founded "to achieve a *more perfect* union." In one American myth in which we do find perfection, George Washington, who *never* told a lie, is the exception that proves the rule. Only the man who led the effort that made the United States independent could be perfect. Because we believe nothing is perfect, we're world-class tinkerers. Thomas Edison became a cultural hero because he was willing to try 1,000 different materials before he found one that could light a bulb effectively.

4. Americans are future-oriented; we respect leaders for their visions. The great American heroes of history—Presidents Lincoln or Franklin Delano Roosevelt, for example—are those whose vision of a better future enabled the nation to pull through crises that many people believed would destroy it. Americans love science fiction for the same reason—nothing captures our attention like visions of the future. Similarly, in the 1996 presidential campaign Bill Clinton's bridge to the next millennium, even though it was only four years away, beat out Bob Dole's attempt to build a bridge to the past.

Bureaucracy and American Values

Across the board, the behaviors and values appreciated in U.S. culture are devalued by bureaucracies. Rather than championing individual judgment, bureaucracy tells us we have to follow the boss's orders or standard operating procedures. This is the origin of the American myth that we're supposed to hate our bosses. Contrary to the value Americans put on achievement, bureaucratic bosses often have power *only* because of their position. Rather than trying to perfect their systems, bureaucracies institutionalize old ways in standard operating procedures. As in the story about Bell Atlantic CEO Ray Smith (see Chapter 5), the statement, "That's not the way we do things around here," is typical of bureaucracy. Yet no statement could be more un-American. The visionary leaders who built major companies—Henry Ford, Tom Watson, or Bill Gates—often become cultural heroes because of their future orientation. However, organizations become bureaucracies after losing these leaders.

Corporate cultures working against the larger culture of which they're part create high levels of stress, producing real emotional damage that undercuts corporate performance. For this reason, in bureaucracies:

- People feel devalued, manipulated, and isolated, because, from our culture's viewpoint, they *are*
- Service deteriorates as employees treat customers as badly as management treats them
- People are punished for risk taking, so innovation dies off and organizations lose the ability to adapt to market shifts
- Senior managers, especially, become twisted distortions of themselves as the struggle for position forces them to work against all the lessons our culture taught them as children

You may be wondering why, if bureaucracy clashes this way with American culture, the most bureaucratic companies, GM, AT&T, and IBM, for example, were the most successful for so long. Actually, these companies were started by visionary leaders who had the qualities to be heroes of the culture. The organizations developed during a time when the Newtonian world view convinced people that the world itself was a machine. So why should businesses not be run like machines? When those leaders left, the organizations moved toward becoming bureaucracies. However, they were large and powerful enough to prosper, even in the face of these contradictions.

American Values in the Organic Corporation

The autonomy and self-organization an organic model requires are exactly the behaviors American culture encourages. Organic corporations demand that people have the freedom to trust their judgment. Self-organization, after all, *starts* with the assumption that people can behave on their own, autonomously, in an organization's best interest. As a result, we get stories about exceptional service at FedEx because people are encouraged to operate from their own judgment. An organic model makes achievement far more important than position. As we saw in Chapter 4, 3M encourages its people to challenge the hierarchy if they can deliver. That's the point of all the company stories that seem to celebrate insubordination.

Organic corporations survive by coevolving in constantly changing market ecologies. As a result, nothing can be viewed as perfect. Self-organization unleashes the innovative tinkering energies of people throughout the company so it can meet its customers' needs as quickly as those needs emerge. Organic corporations encourage their people to be the visionaries American culture teaches us to respect. It is because the company encourages its people to be visionaries that 3M's people continue to create products like Post-it Notes.

Ultimately, self-organizing corporations promote the same values as the culture in which we grew up. As a result, their people should be able to work more comfortably, and the organizations should be more effective than bureaucracies. In organic corporations:

- People feel that they're valuable contributors to an important enterprise because their thoughts are continually sought, acted on, and rewarded
- Service is superior because, first, no one says, "That's not in my job description," and, second, free-flowing information lets people all over the organization address problems
- The organization is continually adapting to changes in its markets as its people act as its eyes and ears
- The sense of common ownership creates a universal feeling that everyone is in the enterprise together as a community of shared concerns and values

As this way of doing business becomes more widespread early in the next century, organic corporations will unleash the full innovative spirit that American culture has already cultivated in us. As a result, we may see an unparalleled outpouring of new products and ways of providing service. That will give U.S. companies a powerful competitive advantage over companies in cultures less hospitable to the individualism and innovation so central to our culture.

Moreover, what happens in U.S. business will spill over to the rest of society. Today's public schools were designed on the mechanical model of industrial mass production. The shift to an organic model in business will recreate the way we think about education, exponentially improving our ability to prepare young people for today's complex world. Similarly, as businesses recognize how much they will profit from the kind of community-building we saw in the Camden Health Improvement Learning Collaborative (see Chapter 2), we're likely to see the regeneration of communities throughout the country and their ability to address a wide variety of problems—drug addiction, domestic abuse, gang violence—that now seem unsolvable.

Perhaps I'm being unreasonably optimistic. But in writing this book, I've become convinced that the shift to an organic model of organization in the early years of the 21st century can do more than generate an economic boom greater than any our nation has ever known. Beyond that, it has the potential to transform our society, eliminating many of its dysfunctions and precipitating a New American Century.

Notes

Introduction

1. Although I came to the term *deengineering* independently, I discovered that it first appeared in print as a significant concept in a cover-story interview with Margaret Wheatley in the April 18, 1994, issue of *Industry Week*. I wasn't able to find any major published uses of the term after that. However, I am told several people have used it in unpublished papers on applying complexity theory to organizations. I agree with Wheatley's use of the term almost entirely. The main difference is that I draw on an organic model for corporate systems to replace the mechanical controls of bureaucracy, whereas Wheatley draws on complexity theory. My approach is less abstract, but not significantly different.

Chapter 1

1. In the year during which I finished this book, a great deal of literature appeared that links complexity theory with organizations. In Further Reading, I have listed a few works with which readers interested in pursuing this link may want to begin. For those of us who believe an organic model of organization can become the standard for business that will replace bureaucracy, this link is critical, because all living things are complex adaptive systems and can survive only as parts of larger complex adaptive systems—our cultures and ecologies.

2. One of the biggest surprises in writing this book was discovering that there is no comprehensive history of the personal computer market ecology. As a result, the story of what happened after Intel introduced the 386, as well as the larger history in the next chapter, draws on several sources, primarily Carroll (1994), Cringley (1996), Cusumano and Selby (1995), Ferguson and Morris (1993), Ichbiah (1993), and Kaplan (1995).

Chapter 2

1. These principles are taken primarily from the following sources: Bakker (1986), Gould (1991), Leakey and Lewin (1995), Ward (1994), Weiner (1994) and Wilson (1992).
2. The sources for this account of the history of personal computers are listed in note 2 of Chapter 1.
3. This speculative history of the future of health care is largely shaped by feedback from several health care administrators to whom I was introduced through Curt Lindberg at VHA, Inc.: Linda Dewolf, Jim Roberts, and Kelley Breazeale at VHA; Jim Dwyer of Memorial Hospital of Burlington Co., N.J.; and Mark Levine of the Hamot Health Foundation in Erie, Pa. All were interviewed during October 1997. Linda Rusch of Hunterdon Medical Center, N.J., was interviewed in September 1997.

Chapter 3

1. The numbers used to construct these ecographs are simplified to keep these diagrams clear. Unfortunately, market statistics on personal computers weren't collected systematically until about 1990. So much of the information for 1989 and, especially, 1982 represents best guesses derived from sources that were available.

Part II

1. Most studies of the life cycles of organizations agree that this introduction of a formal structure is critical in development. Land and Jarman (1992) define it as one of the two breakpoints in the organizational pattern of change, the transition from the forming to the norming stage of growth. Adizes (1988) identifies it as the transition from the go-go to the adolescence stage, "a transformation in the consciousness of the organization, a change that is relatively difficult for some organizations to make."

Chapter 4

1. The key sources for information about IBM are Ferguson and Morris (1993) and Carroll (1994).
2. My sources for 3M include *Our Story so Far: Notes from the First 75 Years of 3M Company* (1977); a speech by William Coyne (1996); and interviews with Geoff Nicholson, staff vice-president for Corporate Technical Planning and International Technical Operations, in April 1997, and Dominic Tallarico, Integrated Solutions, in July 1997.
3. The information on Federal Express is taken largely from a trip to the company's Memphis headquarters on August 27 and 28, 1992. Among those interviewed at the time were Kenneth Masterson, vice-president for Legal,

Regulatory, and Government Affairs and Security, and Jeff Rodeck, vice-president for Operations, Americas and the Caribbean. I was largely limited to the information during the 1992 trip because the company wouldn't subsequently provide a spokesperson for a formal interview. As a result, I've written this section on Federal Express's corporate systems as if the information I got several years ago were current. By the time this book is published, some of its systems are likely to have changed. What's important, however, is not so much the specifics of those systems as the way they're aligned, as parts of Federal Express's corporate DNA, to meet its identity.

Chapter 5

1. Information about The Ritz-Carlton is taken from a 1993 speech by Horst Schulze, president; interviews with Lauren Kline, quality advisor at the Philadelphia Ritz-Carlton, in September and October 1993; and an interview with Pat Mene, vice-president for quality, in May 1996.
2. I worked for Bell Atlantic from 1988 to 1993 and heard Smith tell this story several times.
3. For a discussion of DNA fuller than mine but still brief, see Rothschild's introduction (1990). Whitfield (1995) also presents a good discussion in his chapter on reproduction and growth.
4. Interview with Mercedes-Benz Credit Corporation CEO Georg Bauer, August 1996.

Chapter 6

1. Gouillart and Kelly, in *Transforming the Organization* (1995), used the idea of a corporate nervous system in a different way from the way I do here. "Technology," they wrote, "is to corporate life what the *nervous system* is to human life" (italics in original). Their focus, however, is on making business processes more efficient and coordinated—what I call a corporate endocrine system—than on making information universally available. The ninth chapter of their book, in which they discuss this issue, is therefore a valuable complement to what we're exploring in this chapter.
2. Readers interested in how we perceive and learn may enjoy Maturana and Varela's *Tree of Knowledge* (1992). It presents, for example, an excellent description of the process our bodies and minds go through as we build the mental models, such as models of organization, that to a large extent shape what we allow ourselves to perceive and how we therefore act.

Chapter 7

1. The story of John Cocke is reconstructed from comments in Ferguson and Morris (1993) and Carroll (1993).
2. For sources on the structure of 3M, see Chapter 4, note 2.

Chapter 8

1. I heard the stories about J. Howard Pew when I was at Sun Oil Co. between 1979 and 1983. The family had always been very protective of its privacy, and I've never seen any of the mythic versions of the stories retold here in print anywhere else.
2. Interview with Mercedes-Benz Credit Corporation CEO Georg Bauer, August 1996.
3. From an interview with Keyes in July 1997.
4. Ibid.

Chapter 10

1. Most of the information in this chapter is taken from personal experience, my own and that of others. I worked for Bell Atlantic between September 1988 and February 1993, when I left in one of its downsizings. Starting in spring 1991, I became deeply involved in the company's culture change effort. That involvement included teaching quality improvement, writing occasional speeches for CEO Ray Smith, and providing staff assistance to the executive team setting corporate quality breakthrough goals for 1993. I've also drawn on interviews with several people at Bell Atlantic, most of whom asked not to be identified. When I asked a media relations representative for people involved in the culture change to interview for Bell Atlantic's point of view, she was unable to find anyone willing to speak on the record.

Chapter 11

1. The information on the transformation of Mercedes-Benz Credit Corporation came largely from an interview with CEO Georg Bauer in August 1996 and subsequent conversations with his representatives.

Chapter 12

1. From an interview with Debbie Zastocki in September 1997.

Conclusion

1. The culture analysis of King and O'Boyle is taken from conversations since July 1994.

Further Reading

This book is a beginning. An organic model will work best, I'm convinced, when each of us has formed that model for ourselves. So I wanted, explicitly, to invite interested readers to push their explorations in the directions that will satisfy them most. To make that exploration easier, here's a brief annotated bibliography of books I found most helpful.

Background

The first topic you may want to examine is the shift from the mechanical world view of the industrial age to the more organic view of the present age. Two books stand out. Kevin Kelly's *Out of Control* (1994) explains the age now dawning—Kelly calls it "neo-biological civilization"—as completely and compellingly as it's likely to be explained. Kelly's discussions of complexity theory and how it affects us provide a strong foundation on which to build. *The Web of Life* (1996) by Fritjof Capra offers an equally accessible description of complexity theory. Capra also examines mechanical thought in some detail. Capra's discussion of the principles we now believe critical to life offers a powerful beginning for an examination of how life works.

You can complement these two books with two by Alvin Toffler. *The Third Wave* (1980) offers a full picture of the social world created by the mechanical view of the Second Wave and the world likely to be created by the neobiologic view of the Third Wave. In *Powershift* (1990), Toffler examines the inevitable clash between champions of these waves. *Powershift* is especially recommended to agents of change working to introduce an organic model into a bureaucracy.

Complexity Theory

Because living things and their environments, organizations and their markets, are all complex adaptive systems, you might next want to look into the literature on complexity theory. This literature examines the patterns that seem to underlie all systems in which the interaction of many autonomous parts produces emergent behavior in a larger system. The capital of complexity studies is the Santa Fe Institute in New Mexico. You can check its Internet Web site at www.santafe.edu.

Both Capra and Kelly can give you a good start in complexity theory. Another general introduction is Roger Lewin's *Complexity* (1992). Lewin provides an engaging overview of work being done in this field as well as a feeling for many of the people involved. One of those people is Stuart Kauffman, whose *At Home in the Universe* (1995) examines his belief that evolution is much less random than generally believed. In clear, forceful language, Kauffman argues that much of the work in complexity theory suggests certain limits within which natural selection must work. For those who can follow the advanced mathematics he uses, Kauffman's *The Origins of Order* (1993) also will be helpful.

If you're interested in a powerful demonstration of the ideas developed in complexity theory, without the theory, you may want to check out James Lovelock's *Gaia* (1979). Lovelock explores why the earth seems to function as a single living thing continuously creating the conditions that enable life to survive.

More and more books have appeared recently applying complexity theory to organizations. A good place to start is Gareth Morgan's *Images of Organization*, second edition (1997), which was published too late for me to refer to in this book. Morgan examines the function played by metaphor in the way we think about our organizations. The new edition specifically examines the application of self-organization and biological metaphors. Margaret Wheatley and Myron Kellner-Rogers present many of these ideas more poetically in *A Simpler Way* (1996). Combined with Wheatley's *Leadership and the New Science* (1992), it provides a basic grounding for those who are qualitatively rather than quantitatively oriented. For another book with a qualitative approach coupled with a rigorous theoretical and research-oriented underpinning, try Ralph Stacey's *Complexity and Creativity in Organizations* (1996). If you'd like to learn more about the type of structure 3M uses, you'll find Stacey's description of the environment that generates creativity—a space that is both structured and freeing—especially interesting. Finally, those readers who'd like a better understanding of deengineering can consult Jeffery Goldstein's *The Unshackled Organization* (1994). I didn't discover Goldstein's book until after I'd finished this one. That was unfortunate, because his explanation of how you can use complexity theory to transform your organization provides a much-needed balance between theory and his practical experience.

In addition to complexity-oriented studies of organizations, I wanted to recommend one other book, Peter Block's *Stewardship* (1993). Block's examination of what it means to choose "service over self-interest" in leading an organization is illuminating and provocative, in the best sense of the word.

Living Systems

If you decide to use the human body as the model for an organic corporation, as I did, a good place to start your reading is with Isaac Asimov's *The Human Brain*, revised edition (1994). Asimov provides a strong grounding in clear, no-nonsense language. While you are developing a basic understanding, you may want to supplement the type of reading Asimov offers with some of the lavishly illustrated books on the subject. *The Way Life Works* (1995), for example, by Mahlon Hoagland and Bert Dodson, was written for children. I found its clarity and simplicity very helpful in the early going. *The Human Body Explained* (1995), edited by Philip Whitfield, is much more sophisticated. Nonetheless, the extensive illustrations complement the text and advanced my understanding. If you're more adventurous, you may also want to look at *The Tree of Knowledge* (1992) by Humberto Maturana and Francisco Varela. Their view of how we learn from the viewpoint of how the nervous system functions changed what I thought about the way I think. Combined with *The Web of Life* (Capra 1996), these books will give you the framework from which you can develop the understanding you need to apply life's design principles to any element of your business.

When you switch your study to evolution, you might want to begin with *The Dinosaur Heresies* by Robert Bakker, Jr. (1986). Even though much of what Bakker wrote is now considered incorrect, his passion and conviction make the reading a pleasure as well as generally illuminating. Next, you can read just about anything by Stephen Jay Gould. *Wonderful Life* (1989) is one of his best; it focuses on the endless variety of which life is capable. From there, you may also want to check out Peter Ward's *The End of Evolution* (1994) or *The Sixth Extinction* (1995) by Richard Leakey and Roger Lewin. Both books give a sense of the vast sweep of life's history and the importance of creative destruction to evolution. If you want to develop a fuller appreciation for the creativity with which life inhabits the planet, you may want to look at Edmund O. Wilson's *The Diversity of Life* (1993), an overview from a man whose life is dedicated to its study.

There's an enormous amount of information available on all these subjects. Much of it has appeared since I had to stop reading seriously so I could finish this book. As a result, this reading list, like the book as a whole, is only a beginning.

Bibliography

Adams, Scott. 1996. *Fugitive from the Cubicle Police.* Kansas City: Andrews and McMeel.

Adizes, Ichak. 1989. *Corporate Lifecycles: How and Why Corporations Grow and Die and What to Do About It.* Englewood Cliffs, N.J.: Prentice Hall.

Armstrong, Arthur, and John Hagel III. 1996. "Real Value of On-Line Communities." *Harvard Business Review*, 74, no. 3 (May/June): 134–141.

Asimov, Isaac. 1994. *The Human Brain: Its Capacities and Functions.* rev. and exp. New York: Mentor.

Bakker, Robert T. 1986. *The Dinosaur Heresies: New Theories Unlocking the Mystery of the Dinosaurs and Their Extinction.* New York: William Morrow.

Birchard, Bill. 1990. "Leading Culture Change." *Enterprise* (Fall): 10–14.

Block, Peter. 1986. *The Empowered Manager: Positive Political Skills at Work.* San Francisco: Jossey-Bass.

———. 1993. *Stewardship: Choosing Service Over Self-Interest.* San Francisco: Barrett-Koehler Publishers.

Bridges, William. 1991. *Managing Transitions: Making the Most of Change.* Reading, Mass.: Addison-Wesley.

Burns, Tom, and G. M. Stalker. 1961. *The Management of Innovation.* London: Tavistock Publications.

Capra, Fritjof. 1996. *The Web of Life: A New Scientific Understanding of Living Systems.* New York: Anchor Books.

Carroll, Paul. 1994. *Big Blue: The Unmaking of IBM.* New York: Crown Publishers.

Case, John. 1997. "Opening the Books." *Harvard Business Review*, 75, no. 2 (March/April): 118–127.

Collins, James C., and Jerry I. Porras. 1994. *Built to Last: Successful Habits of Visionary Companies.* New York: Harper Business.

Coyne, William E. 1996. "Building a Tradition of Innovation." The UK Innovation Lecture, March 5.

Cringely, Robert X. 1996. *Accidental Empires: How the Boys of Silicon Valley Make their Millions, Battle Foreign Competition, and Still Can't Get a Date.* rev. ed. New York: Harper Business.

Cusumano, Michael A., and Richard W. Selby. 1995. *Microsoft Secrets: How the World's Most Powerful Software Company Creates Technology, Shapes Markets, and Manages People.* New York: Free Press.

Deal, Terrence E., and Allan A. Kennedy. 1982. *Corporate Cultures: The Rites and Rituals of Corporate Life.* Reading, Mass.: Addison-Wesley.

Deming, W. Edwards. 1982. *Out of the Crisis.* Cambridge, Mass.: Massachusetts Institute of Technology, Center for Advanced Engineering Study.

Ferguson, Charles H., and Charles R. Morris. 1993. *Computer Wars: How the West Can Win in a Post-IBM World.* New York: Times Books.

Goldstein, Jeffrey. 1994. *The Unshackled Organization: Facing the Challenge of Unpredictability through Spontaneous Reorganization.* Portland, Ore.: Productivity Press.

Gould, Stephen Jay. 1991. *Bully for Brontosaurus: Reflections in Natural History.* New York: W. W. Norton & Co.

———. 1989. *Wonderful Life: The Burgess Shale and the Nature of History.* New York: W. W. Norton & Co.

Gouillart, Francis J., and James N. Kelly. 1995. *Transforming the Organization.* New York: McGraw-Hill.

Grant, Susan. 1984. *Beauty and the Beast: The Coevolution of Plants and Animals.* New York: Scribners.

Halberstam, David. 1986. *The Reckoning.* New York: Avon Books.

Hammer, Michael, and James Champy. 1993. *Reengineering the Corporation: A Manifesto for Business Revolution.* New York: Harper Business.

Hammer, Michael, and Steven A. Stanton. 1994. *The Reengineering Revolution: A Handbook.* New York: Harper Business.

Hoagland, Mahlon, and Bert Dodson. 1995. *The Way Life Works.* New York: Times Books.

Ichbiah, Daniel, with Susan L. Knepper. 1993. *The Making of Microsoft: How Bill Gates and His Team Created the World's Most Successful Software Company.* Rocklin, Calif.: Prima Publishing.

Jones, Peter, and Thomas Levenson (co-writers/co-producers). "Einstein Revealed." *Nova* (Co-produced by Green Umbrella, London, England, and WGBH-TV, Boston, Mass.) First aired October, 1996.

Kaplan, Jerry. 1995. *Start Up: A Silicon Valley Adventure.* Boston: Houghton Mifflin.

Kauffman, Stuart. 1993. *The Origins of Order: Self-organization and Selection in Evolution.* New York: Oxford University Press.

———. 1995. *At Home in the Universe: The Search for the Law of Self-Organization and Complexity.* New York: Oxford University Press.

Kelly, Kevin. 1994. *Out of Control: The Rise of Neo-Biological Civilization.* Reading, Mass.; Addison-Wesley.

Lacey, Peter. 1991. "Dial 911 for Teamwork." *Chief Executive,* 71 (October): 39–42.

Land, George, and Beth Jarman. 1992. *Breakpoint and Beyond: Mastering the Future—Today.* New York: Harper Business.

Leakey, Richard, and Roger Lewin. 1995. *The Sixth Extinction: Patterns of Life and the Future of Humankind.* New York: Doubleday.

Lewin, Roger. 1992. *Complexity: Life at the Edge of Chaos.* New York: Collier Books.

Lovelock, James E. 1979. *Gaia: A New Look at Life on Earth.* New York: Oxford University Press.

Manes, Stephen, and Paul Andrews. 1994. *Gates: How Microsoft's Mogul Reinvented an Industry—and Made Himself the Richest Man in America.* New York: Simon & Schuster.

Maturana, Humberto R., and Francisco J. Varela. 1992. *The Tree of Knowledge: The Biological Roots of Human Understanding.* rev. ed. Boston: Shambhala Publications.

Moore, James F. 1996. *The Death of Competition: Leadership and Strategy in the Age of Business Ecosystems.* New York: Harper Business.

Moore-Duncan, Dorothy L. Letter from Region 4 Director, National Labor Relations Board, to Robert F. O'Brien, January 8, 1998.

Morgan, Gareth. 1986. *Images of Organization.* Newbury Park, Calif.: Sage Publications.

———. 1997. *Images of Organization.* 2nd ed. San Francisco: Berrett-Koehler Publishers.

Olins, Wally. 1990. *Corporate Identity: Making Business Strategy Visible Through Design.* Boston: Harvard Business School Press.

Our Story so Far: Notes from the First 75 years of 3M Company. 1977. St. Paul, Minn.: Minnesota Mining and Manufacturing Co.

Owen, Harrison. 1992. *Open Space Technology: A User's Guide.* Potomac, Md.: Abbott Publishing.

Peters, Thomas J., and Robert H. Waterman, Jr. 1982. *In Search of Excellence: Lessons from America's Best-Run Companies.* New York: Harper & Row.

Rosenbluth, Hal F., and Diane McFerrin Peters. 1992. *The Customer Comes Second: And Other Secrets of Exceptional Service.* New York: William Morrow.

Rothschild, Michael. 1990. *Bionomics: The Inevitability of Capitalism.* New York: Henry Holt.

Schaef, Anne Wilson, and Diane Fassel. 1988. *The Addictive Organization.* New York: HarperCollins.

Schein, Edgar H. 1991. *Organizational Culture and Leadership: A Dynamic View.* San Francisco: Jossey-Bass.

Schulze, Horst. 1993. "Total Quality Management at The Ritz-Carlton." Presented at the Philadelphia Area Council on Excellence Annual Quality Conference, June 18.

Sculley, John, with John A. Bryne. 1988. *Odyssey: Pepsi to Apple . . . The Journey of a Marketing Impresario.* New York: Harper & Row.

Senge, Peter M. 1990. *The Fifth Discipline: The Art and Practice of the Learning Organization.* New York: Doubleday.

Sloan, Alfred P., Jr. 1990. *My Years with General Motors.* New York: Doubleday.

Spears, Larry C., ed. 1997. *Insights in Leadership: Service, Stewardship, Spirit, and Servant Leadership.* New York: John Wiley & Sons.

Stacey, Ralph D. 1996. *Complexity and Creativity in Organizations.* San Francisco: Berrett-Koehler Publishers.

Stack, Jack, with Bo Burlingham. 1992. *The Great Game of Business.* New York: Doubleday.

Stalk, George, Jr., and Thomas M. Hout. 1990. *Competing Against Time: How Time-Based Competition Is Reshaping Global Markets.* New York: Free Press.

Stewart, Thomas A. 1996. "3M Fights Back." *Fortune,* 133, no. 2 (February 5): 94–99.

Toffler, Alvin. 1980. *The Third Wave.* New York: Bantam Books.

———. 1990. *Powershift: Knowledge, Wealth, and Violence at the Edge of the 21st Century.* New York: Bantam Books.

Tucker, Bruce. 1993. "Tommy Boy Can CD the Future." *Fast Company* (November): 51–60.

Walton, Mary. 1986. *The Deming Management Method.* New York: Dodd, Mead.

Ward, Peter. 1994. *The End of Evolution: A Journey in Search of Clues to the Third Mass Extinction Facing Planet Earth.* New York: Bantam Books.

Weiner, Jonathan. 1994. *The Beak of the Finch.* New York: Vintage Books.

Wheatley, Margaret J. 1992. *Leadership and the New Science: Learning about Organization from an Orderly Universe.* San Francisco: Berrett-Koehler Publishers.

Wheatley, Margaret J., and Myron Kellner-Rogers. 1996. *A Simpler Way.* San Francisco: Berrett-Koehler Publishers.

Whitfield, Philip, ed. 1995. *The Human Body Explained: A Guide to Understanding the Incredible Living Machine.* New York: Henry Holt.

Wilson, Edward O. 1993. *The Diversity of Life.* New York: W. W. Norton.

Index

For Product Safety Concerns and Information please contact
our EU representative GPSR@taylorandfrancis.com
Taylor & Francis
Verlag GmbH, Kaufingerstraße 24, 80331 München, Germany.

*For Product Safety Concerns and Information please contact
our EU representative GPSR@taylorandfrancis.com Taylor & Francis
Verlag GmbH, Kaufingerstraße 24, 80331 München, Germany*

T - #0082 - 230425 - C0 - 229/152/12 - PB - 9780750698443 - Gloss Lamination